Data Management Systems

Evolution and Interoperation

Bhavani M. Thuraisingham, Ph.D.
Lexington, Massachusetts

CRC Press
Boca Raton   New York

Library of Congress Cataloging-in-Publication Data

Thuraisingham, Bhavani M.
    Data management systems : evolution and interoperation / Bhavani
Thuraisingham.
       p. cm.
    Includes bibliographical references and index.
    ISBN 0-8493-9493-7 (alk. paper)
    1. Database management. I. Title.
QA76.9.D3T455   1997
005.74—dc21

97-5938
CIP

No claim to original U.S. Government works
International Standard Book Number 0-8493-9493-7
Library of Congress Card Number 97-5938
Printed in the United States of America 1 2 3 4 5 6 7 8 9 0
Printed on acid-free paper

PREFACE

Recent developments in information systems technologies have resulted in computerizing many applications in various business areas. Data has become a critical resource in many organizations and therefore efficient access to data, sharing the data, extracting information from the data, and making use of the information has become an urgent need. As a result, there have been many efforts on integrating the various data sources scattered across several sites. These data sources may be databases managed by database management systems or they could simply be files. To provide the interoperability between the multiple data sources and systems, various tools are being developed. These tools enable users of one system to access other systems in an efficient and transparent manner.

We define data management systems to be systems that manage the data as well as extract meaningful information from the data. Therefore, data management systems include database systems, data warehouses, and data mining systems. Data could be structured data such as those found in relational databases or it could be unstructured such as text, voice, imagery, and video. There have been numerous discussions in the past to distinguish between data, information, and knowledge. For example, some consider data to be just raw bits and bytes while information is something more meaningful, and knowledge is intelligence. We do not attempt to clarify these terms. For our purposes, data could be just bits and bytes or it could convey some meaningful information to the user. We will however distinguish between database systems and database management systems. A database management system is that component which manages the database which consists of persistent data. A database system consists of both the database and the database management system. We have also distinguished between information systems and data management systems. In our terminology, information systems include data management systems. Furthermore, information systems may be constructed from data management systems. Some of these points will be clarified in this book.

A key component to the evolution and interoperation of data management systems is the interoperability of heterogeneous database systems. Efforts on the interoperability between different database systems were reported since the late 1970s. However, it is only recently that we are seeing commercial developments in heterogeneous database systems. Major database system vendors are now providing interoperability between their products and other systems. Furthermore, many of the database system vendors are migrating towards an architecture called the client-server architecture which facilitates distributed data management capabilities. In addition to efforts on the interoperability between different database systems and client-server environments, work is also directed towards handling autonomous and federated environments.

This book describes the evolution and interoperation of data management systems with a special emphasis on the evolution of database systems, interoperability of heterogeneous database systems, as well as some of the emerging technologies such as multimedia databases, data warehousing, data mining, Internet databases, and database support for collaborative applications. Chapter 1, which is the introduction to this book, provides an overview of data management systems, the current status, and future vision, as well as describes a framework, which can be regarded as a reference model, for data management. This framework will play a major role in defining the contents of this book. The core of this book, consisting of ten chapters, is divided into three parts. Part I, which consists of two chapters, describes concepts in database systems and distributed database systems technologies. Much of the discussion in this book is built on the information presented in part I. Chapter 2 provides an overview of database systems. In particular, the evolution of database systems, architectures, data models, and functions is discussed. Chapter 3 describes concepts in distributed database systems.

Part II, which consists of four chapters, describes concepts on the interoperability of heterogeneous database systems as well as migrating legacy databases. Heterogeneity and autonomy as well as federated database system concepts are discussed in chapter 4. Chapter 5 describes database system interoperability based on client-server architectures. In addition to architectural and functional aspects, various standards for interoperability including a discussion of Object Management Group's (OMG) Common Object Request Broker Architecture (CORBA) are also provided. Chapter 6 addresses heterogeneity with respect to data types. That is, database systems which manage multimedia data types, such as text, audio, video, and imagery, are described. Such database systems are called multimedia database systems. While chapters 4, 5, and 6 address some aspect of interoperability, Chapter 7 describes issues on migrating legacy databases and systems to newer architectures and infrastructures.

Part III, which consists of four chapters, describes current trends in data management systems such as information extraction from the databases. Chapter 8 describes issues on building data warehouses, where a data warehouse may be regarded as a repository of data that is assembled from possibly multiple heterogeneous databases. Data mining technology, for extracting meaningful information from the data in the databases that are possibly heterogeneous in nature, is described in chapter 9. Digital library technology and Internet database management, which deal with the management of and access to large amounts of multimedia data possibly stored in the world wide web (WWW) servers, is discussed in chapter 10. Finally, in chapter 11, database management for collaborative applications is discussed. Note that while collaborative applications are part of the applications layer and not part of the data management framework, these applications require database support. It is the database support that is addressed in chapter 11.

Each part begins with an introduction and ends with a conclusion. Introduction to a part describes the contents of the corresponding chapters. The conclusion relates the contents of the part to the framework. Directions for data management systems evolution and interoperation as well as some guidelines to build information systems is the subject of chapter 12, the last chapter of this book.

Commercial status is given in the appendix. In particular, the appendix provides an overview of commercial data management system products. We have briefly discussed the current status of various groups of products and then selected one or two products from each group and described them in more detail. The groups include relational database systems, object-oriented database systems, object-relational database systems, replication servers, interoperability servers, component-based database systems, data warehouses, and data mining systems.

Throughout the text various important topics are addressed. For example, multilevel security for database systems, distributed database systems, as well as heterogeneous database systems integration is addressed as part of chapters 2, 3, and 4. Note that none of the previous texts in distributed and heterogeneous database systems have given sufficient consideration to this topic and concepts in multilevel security can be applied not only to defense type applications, but also to commercial applications. Aspects of security are also discussed in chapters 6, 8, and 9 with respect to multimedia database systems, data warehousing, and data mining. Integrity, database design, and database administration are also given some consideration in this book. Other features such as data administration, data quality, the cost of evolving data management systems, and different types of database systems such as real-time database systems and deductive database systems are briefly discussed. Various standards for data management are described as needed throughout this book. The role of metadata is discussed in practically every chapter. Since data management systems is such a broad area, a detailed discussion of all aspects of this technology is beyond the scope of this book. For example, topics such as benchmarking and performance analysis are beyond the scope of this book.

It should be noted that this book is organized with respect to the Data Management Systems Framework described in chapter 1. The three major layers of this framework are: Layer I: Database Management and Distribution layer, Layer II: Interoperability and Migration layer, and Layer III: Information Extraction and Sharing layer. Parts I, II, and III focus on the layers I, II, and III, respectively. In building data management systems, one may utilize supporting technologies such as distributed object management, agents, and more lower-level technologies such as mass storage, networking, distributed processing, and operating systems. Furthermore, data management systems technologies discussed in this book are utilized by application-oriented systems such as collaborative systems, knowledge-based systems, visualization systems, and mobile computing systems. The relationships between data management systems technologies, supporting technologies, and application technologies are also illustrated in our framework.

Many of the previous texts on distributed and heterogeneous database systems have focused on the principles and theoretical aspects such as correctness of the concurrency control and commit protocols as well as query optimization algorithms. This text focuses on presenting the complicated ideas in a simplified manner, but at the same time describes the essential concepts required to understand the developments. Furthermore, it also provides the complete vision of data management and describes how the existing technologies and the emerging technologies fit together to provide for the efficient access and sharing of data as well as extracting meaningful information from the data. It is written for a reader who has some basic knowledge in database systems with an interest in covering a wide range of topics in interoperability and evolution of data management systems. It is an ideal source for technical managers who need a broad perspective on heterogeneous database integration and related technologies. References to various texts and papers are cited throughout the book and included in the list of references toward the end of this book. We recommend many of these references should a reader need in-depth coverage of a particular topic. Some of the references given here are on white papers posted on the WWW. It should be noted that this information is continually changing.

It should be noted that our discussion of commercial products is not comprehensive and is somewhat arbitrary. We have discussed products only to illustrate the essential points of a particular technology and not to market any specific product or prototype. A discussion of the numerous data management products that are emerging is beyond the scope of this book. We have also avoided the elaborate discussion of prototypes and products because due to the rapid advances, the information that is current today will be outdated tomorrow. Therefore, even the little that we have discussed in this book could soon be outdated. This is one of the main reasons we included the discussion of the products in the appendix. Vendors periodically put out material on their products and we encourage the reader to take advantage of the various material available. This is the only way to keep up with the latest developments with the commercial technology. Much of the information that We have given on commercial products has been checked with the respective vendors.

As stated earlier, the focus of this book is the data management systems framework. The various data management systems topics have been described with respect to this framework. The views and conclusions expressed in this book are those of the author and do not reflect the views, policies, or procedures of the author's institution or sponsors. I thank my husband Thevendra, my late parents, my professors and teachers, my management, sponsors, and colleagues, all others who have supported my education and my work, and especially those who have reviewed various portions of this book. I dedicate this book to my son Breman who has been a source of inspiration to me.

Bhavani Thuraisingham, Ph.D.
Lexington, Massachusetts

About the Author

Bhavani Thuraisingham, Ph.D., Senior Principal Engineer with the MITRE Corporation, Bedford, Massachusetts, heads the Data and Information Management Department in the Advanced Information Systems Center and is a Director of MITRE's Database Specialty Group. She also heads the Corporate Initiative on Evolvable Interoperable Information Systems and, in this position, is responsible for the initiatives on data management, real-time systems, object technology and architectures, software reengineering, and economics analysis as they relate to information systems evolution and interoperation. Her current work focuses on data mining/knowledge discovery as it relates to text databases, as well as database security, real-time database management, massive multimedia database management, distributed object management technology, and data warehousing. Her interests also include heterogeneous database integration and Internet database management.

Prior to joining MITRE in January 1989, Dr. Thuraisingham was a Principal Research Scientist with Honeywell Inc. and, before that, was a Senior Programmer/Analyst with Control Data Corporation. She was also an adjunct professor of computer science and a member of the graduate faculty at the University of Minnesota.

Dr. Thuraisingham earned an M.Sc. from the University of Bristol and Ph.D. from the University of Wales, Swansea, both in the United Kingdom. She is a member of the ACM, IEEE Computer Society, the British Computer Society, and AFCEA.

Dr. Thuraisingham has published over three hundred technical papers and reports, including over forty journal articles, and is the holder of two U.S. patents for MITRE on database inference control. She also serves on the editorial boards of various journals, including *IEEE Transactions on Knowledge and Data Engineering*. She gives tutorials in data management, including object-oriented databases, distributed/heterogeneous databases, data warehousing and mining, and Internet databases and has chaired conferences and workshops, served on numerous panels, and is a member of OMG's real-time special interest group. She has edited several books as well as special journal issues in data management and object technology, along with being the guest editor of the *Data Management Handbook* series (WGL) by Auerbach. She gives invited presentations at conferences, including featured talks at Object World East and West '96, IFIP Database Security Conference '96, IEEE Engineering Solutions Conference '96, the Data Warehousing and Year 2000 Conference '96, and has also delivered the featured addresses at AFCEA's DoD Database Colloquiums from 1994 through 1996. Her presentations are worldwide, including the United States, United Kingdom, Canada, Germany, Italy, Spain, India, Hong Kong, Japan, Switzerland, France, Singapore, and, Australia.

TABLE OF CONTENTS

CHAPTER 1

INTRODUCTION

1.1 TRENDS

Recent developments in information systems technologies have resulted in computerizing many applications in various business areas. Data has become a critical resource in many organizations and therefore efficient access to data, sharing the data, extracting information from the data, and making use of the information has become an urgent need. As a result, there have been several efforts on integrating the various data sources scattered across several sites. These data sources may be databases managed by database management systems or they could simply be files. To provide the interoperability between the multiple data sources and systems, various tools are being developed. These tools enable users of one system to access other systems in an efficient and transparent manner.

We define data management systems to be systems that manage the data, extract meaningful information from the data, and make use of the information extracted. Therefore, data management systems include database systems, data warehouses, and data mining systems. Data could be structured data such as those found in relational databases or it could be unstructured such as text, voice, imagery, and video. There have been numerous discussions in the past to distinguish between data, information, and knowledge. We do not attempt to clarify these terms. For our purposes, data could be just bits and bytes or it could convey some meaningful information to the user. We will, however, distinguish between database systems and database management systems. A database management system is that component which manages the database containing persistent data. A database system consists of both the database and the database management system.

A key component to the evolution and interoperation of data management systems is the interoperability of heterogeneous database systems. Efforts on the interoperability between database systems were reported since the late 1970s. However, it is only recently that we are seeing commercial developments in heterogeneous database systems. Major database system vendors are now providing interoperability between their products and other systems. Furthermore, many of the database system vendors are migrating towards an architecture called the client-server architecture which facilitates distributed data management capabilities. In addition to efforts on the interoperability between different database systems and client-server environments, work is also directed towards handling autonomous and federated environments.

This book describes the evolution and interoperation of data management systems with a special emphasis on the evolution of database systems, interoperability of heterogeneous database systems, as well as some of the emerging technologies such as multimedia databases, data warehousing, data mining, Internet databases, and database support for collaboration.

The organization of this chapter is as follows. Since database systems is a key component of data management systems, in this chapter we first provide an overview of the developments in database systems. These developments are discussed in section 1.2. Then we provide a vision for data management systems in section 1.3. Since a major focus of this book is on heterogeneous database integration, section 1.4 briefly discusses this concept. Our framework for data management systems is discussed in section 1.5. The contents of this book are based on this framework. Building information systems from our framework with special instantiations is discussed in section 1.6. Finally, the organization of this book is given in section 1.7.

1.2 DEVELOPMENTS IN DATABASE SYSTEMS

Figure 1-1 provides an overview of the developments in database systems technology. While the early work in the 1960s focused on developing products based on the network and hierarchical data models, much of the developments in database systems took place after the seminal paper by Codd describing the relational model [CODD70]. Research and development work on relational database systems was carried out during the early 1970s and several prototypes were developed throughout the 1970s. Notable efforts include IBM's (International Business Machine Corporation's) System R and University of California at Berkeley's Ingres. During the 1980s many relational database system products were being marketed (notable among these products are those of Oracle Corporation, Sybase Inc., Informix Corporation, Ingres Corporation, IBM, Digital Equipment Corporation, and Hewlett Packard Company). During the 1990s products from other vendors have emerged (e.g., Microsoft Corporation). In fact, to date numerous relational database system products have been marketed. However, Codd has stated that many of the systems that are being marketed as relational systems are not really relational (see, for example, the discussion in [DATE90]). He then discussed various criteria that a system must satisfy to be qualified as a relational database system. While the early work focused on issues such as data model, normalization theory, query processing and optimization strategies, query languages, and access strategies and indexes, a little later the focus was shifted toward supporting a multi-user environment. In particular, concurrency control and recovery techniques were developed. Support for transaction processing was also provided.

Research on relational database systems as well as on transaction management was followed by research on distributed database systems around the mid 1970s. Several distributed database system prototype development efforts also began around the late 1970s. Notable among these efforts include IBM's System R*, DDTS (Distributed Database Testbed System) by Honeywell Inc., SDD-I and Multibase by CCA (Computer Corporation of America), and Mermaid by SDC (System Development Corporation). Furthermore, many of these systems (e.g., DDTS, Multibase, Mermaid) function in a heterogeneous environment. During the early 1990s several database system vendors (such as Oracle Corporation, Sybase Inc., Informix Corporation) have provided data distribution capabilities for their systems. Most of the distributed relational database system products are based on client-sever architectures. The idea is to have the client of vendor A communicate with the server database system of vendor B. In other words, the client-sever computing paradigm facilitates a heterogeneous computing environment. Interoperability between relational and non-relational commercial database systems is also possible. The database systems community is also involved in standardization efforts. Notable among the standardization efforts are the ANSI/SPARC 3-level schema architecture,[1] IRDS (Information Resource Dictionary System) standard for Data Dictionary Systems, the relational query language SQL (Structured Query Language), and RDA (Remote Database Access) protocol for remote database access.

Another significant development in database technology is the advent of object-oriented database management systems. Active work on developing such systems began in the mid-1980s and they are now commercially available (notable among them include the products of Object Design Inc., Ontos Inc., Gemstone Systems Inc., Versant Object Technology). It was felt that new generation applications such as multimedia, office information systems, CAD/CAM,[2] process control, and software engineering have different requirements. Such applications utilize complex data structures. Tighter

---

[1] ANSI stands for American National Standards Institute. SPARC stands for Systems Planning and Requirements Committee.
[2] CAD/CAM stands for Computer Aided Design/Computer Aided Manufacturing.

integration between the programming language and the data model is also desired. Object-oriented database systems satisfy most of the requirements of these new generation applications [CATT91].

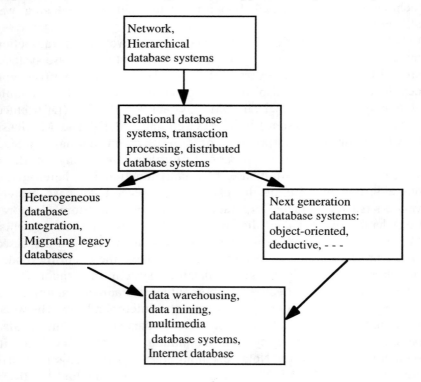

Figure 1-1. Developments in Database Systems Technology

According to the Lagunita report published as a result of a National Science Foundation (NSF) workshop in 1990 [NSF90], relational database systems, transaction processing, and distributed (relational) database systems are stated as mature technologies. Furthermore vendors are marketing object-oriented database systems and demonstrating the interoperability between different database systems. The report goes on to state that as applications are getting more and more complex, more sophisticated database systems are needed. Furthermore, since many organizations now use database systems, in many cases of different types, the database systems need to be integrated. Although work has begun to address these issues and commercial products are available, several issues still need to be resolved. Therefore, challenges faced by the database systems researchers in the early 1990s were in two areas. One is next genera-tion database systems and the other is heterogeneous database systems.

Next generation database systems include object-oriented database systems, functional database systems, special parallel architectures to enhance the performance of database system functions, high performance database systems, real-time database systems, scientific database systems, temporal database systems, database systems that handle incomplete and uncertain information, and intelligent database systems (also sometimes called logic or deductive database systems).[3] Ideally, a database system should provide the support for high performance transaction processing, model complex applications, represent new kinds of data, and make intelligent deductions. While significant progress has been made during the late 1980s and early 1990s, there is much to be done before such a database system can be developed.

Heterogeneous database systems have been receiving much attention during the past decade. The major issues include handling different data models, different query processing strategies, different transaction processing algorithms, and different query languages. Should a uniform view be provided to the entire system or should the users of the individual systems maintain their own views of the entire system? These are questions that have yet to be answered satisfactorily. It is also envisaged that a complete solution to heterogeneous database management systems is a generation away. While research should be directed towards finding such a solution, work should also be carried out to handle limited forms of heterogeneity to satisfy the customer needs. Another type of database system that has received some attention lately is a federated database system. Note that some have used the term heterogeneous database system and federated database system interchangeably. While heterogeneous database systems can be part of a federation, a federation can also include homogeneous database systems.

The explosion of users on the Internet as well as developments in interface technologies has resulted in even more challenges for data management researchers. A second workshop was sponsored by NSF in 1995 and several emerging technologies have been identified to be important as we go into the twenty-first century [NSF95]. These include digital libraries, managing very large databases, data administration issues, multimedia databases, data warehousing, data mining, data management for collaborative computing environments, and security and privacy. Another significant development in the 1990s is the development of object-relational systems. Such systems combine the advantages of both object-oriented database

---

[3] For a discussion of the next generation database systems, we refer to [SIGM90].

systems and relational database systems. Also, many corporations are now focusing on integrating their data management products with Internet technologies. Finally, for many organizations there is an increasing need to migrate some of the legacy databases and applications to newer architectures and systems such as client-server architectures and relational database systems. We believe that there is no end to data management systems. As new technologies are developed, there are new opportunities for data management research and development.

A comprehensive view of all data management technologies is illustrated in figure 1-2. As shown, traditional technologies include database design, transaction processing, and benchmarking. Then there are database systems based on data models such as relational and object-oriented. Database systems may depend on features they provide such as security and real-time. These database systems may be relational or object-oriented. There are also database systems based on multiple sites or processors such as distributed and heterogeneous database systems, parallel systems, and systems being migrated. Finally, there are the emerging technologies such as data warehousing and mining, collaboration, and the Internet. Any comprehensive text on data management systems should address all of these technologies. However, our focus is on the evolution and interoperation of data management systems and, furthermore, a description of all of the technologies is beyond the scope of this book. Therefore, we have selected some of the relevant technologies and put them in a framework. The contents of this book are based on the technologies that constitute the framework. This framework is described in section 1.5. The organization of this book is the subject of section 1.7.

1.3 DATA MANAGEMENT SYSTEMS: STATUS, VISION, AND ISSUES

Data management systems have evolved over the past four decades and today we have various types of such systems. These include database systems, distributed database systems, heterogeneous database systems, multimedia database systems, data warehousing systems, data mining systems, and Internet-based database systems. As illustrated in figure 1-3, there is limited integration between these various types of systems. For example, there is little integration between heterogeneous database systems and data mining systems.

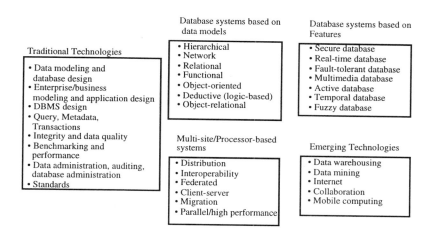

Figure 1-2. Comprehensive View of Data Management Systems

This integration is necessary to extract information from multiple heterogeneous data sources. That is, to provide the efficient access and sharing of data as well as the extraction of information from data to develop useful data management systems, integration of these various types of systems is essential.[4]

A vision for the use of data management systems is illustrated in figure 1-4.[5] As stated in [THUR95b], the ultimate goal is to provide for the seamless access and fusion of massive amounts of data in a heterogeneous and real-time environment to carry out the functions of an enterprise with diminishing resources. To achieve this vision, massive, multimedia, and heterogeneous database systems have to be integrated so that analysts and decision makers can effectively query and obtain relevant information as well as update the information in a timely manner.

---

[4] Note that our definition of data management systems is not standard terminology. Furthermore, one could also include database systems such as real-time database systems, secure database systems, deductive database systems, and active database systems. While such systems have been discussed in this book, our main focus is on distributed/heterogeneous database systems, migrating legacy databases, multimedia database systems, data warehousing, data mining, and Internet databases.

[5] This figure is taken from presentations given on the Massive Data and Information Systems Initiative at the MITRE Corporation. For an example, see [THUR95a].

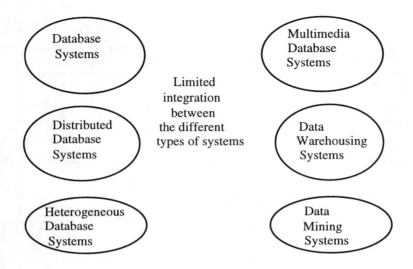

Figure 1-3. Current Status of Data Management Systems Technology

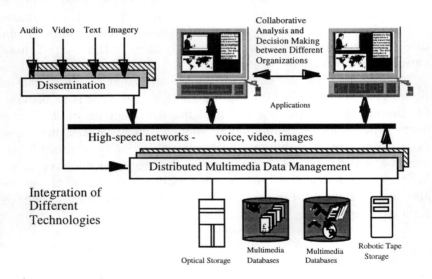

Figure 1-4. Vision for Data Management Systems

In addition to integration problems, there are still several outstanding problems in each technology area. Figure 1-5 illustrates the issues that need further investigation in various data management systems technologies. For example, in the case of heterogeneous database systems integration, handling semantic heterogeneity is a difficult problem. Appropriate transaction models as well as security policies are also needed to handle heterogeneity. For multimedia database systems, the problems include synchronizing different data types such as voice, video, and text. For real-time database systems the issues are on developing appropriate transaction management and concurrency control techniques, integrating with active databases, and specifying quality of service primitives.

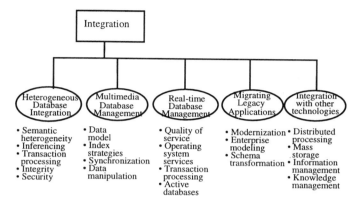

Figure 1-5. Outstanding Problems

While there are numerous issues that need to be resolved, this book focuses on the developments and challenges for specific data management system technologies such as heterogeneous database systems integration, migrating legacy databases, multimedia database systems, data warehousing, data mining, digital libraries, and Internet databases.

1.4   INTEROPERABILITY OF HETEROGENEOUS DATABASE SYSTEMS

Since heterogeneous database systems integration is a key component of data management systems, we briefly discuss some of the issues here. Figure 1-6 illustrates an example of interoperability between heterogeneous database systems. In this example, a relational database system, a legacy database system such as a hierarchical database system, and an object-oriented database system are connected through a network. The goal is to provide transparent access, both for users and application programs, for querying and executing transactions (see, for example, [THUR95b]).

There are several technical issues that need to be resolved for the successful interoperability between these diverse database systems. Heterogeneity could be with respect to different data models, schemas, query processing techniques, query languages, transaction

management techniques, semantics, integrity, and security. Furthermore, there are two approaches to interoperability. One is the
federated database management approach where a collection of
cooperating, autonomous, and possibly heterogeneous component
database systems, each belonging to one or more federations, communicates with each other. The other is the client-server approach
where the goal is for multiple clients to communicate with multiple
servers in a transparent manner. This book addresses both aspects to
interoperability: federated database systems approach as well as
client-server-based interoperability. In addition, various aspects of
heterogeneity are also discussed in detail.

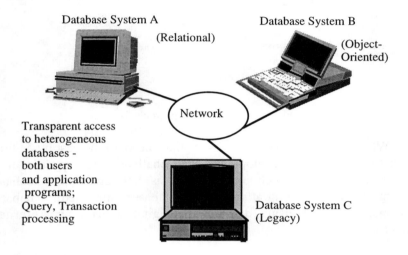

Figure 1-6. Interoperability of Heterogeneous Database Systems.

1.5 DATA MANAGEMENT SYSTEMS FRAMEWORK

For the successful development of evolvable interoperable data
management systems, heterogeneous database systems integration is
a major component. However, there are other technologies that
have to be successfully integrated with each other to develop techniques for efficient access and sharing of data as well as for the
extraction of information from the data. To facilitate the development of data management systems to meet the requirements of
various applications in fields such as medical, financial, manufacturing, and military, we have proposed a framework, which can be
regarded as a reference model, for data management systems. Various
components from this framework have to be integrated to develop
data management systems to support the various applications.

Figure 1-7 illustrates our framework, which can be regarded as a model, for data management systems.[6] This framework consists of three layers. One can think of the component technologies, which we will also refer to as components, belonging to a particular layer to be more or less built upon the technologies provided by the lower layer. Layer I is the Database Technology and Distribution layer. This layer consists of database systems and distributed database systems technologies. Layer II is the Interoperability and Migration layer. This layer consists of technologies such as heterogeneous database integration, client-sever databases, multimedia database systems to handle heterogeneous data types, and migrating legacy databases.[7] Layer III is the Information Extraction and Sharing layer. This layer essentially consists of technologies for some of the newer services supported by data management systems. These include data warehousing, data mining, Internet databases, and database support for collaborative applications.[8,9] Data management systems may utilize lower level technologies such as networking, distributed processing, and mass storage. We have grouped these technologies into a layer called supporting technologies layer. This supporting layer does not belong to the data management systems framework. This supporting layer also consists of some higher-level technologies such as distributed object management and agents.[10] Also, shown in figure 1-7 is the application technologies layer. Systems such as

---

[6] Note that this three-layer model is subjective and is not a standard model. This model has helped us in organizing the contents of this book.

[7] We have placed multimedia database systems in Layer II as we consider it to be a special type of a heterogeneous database system. A multimedia database system handles heterogeneous data types such as text, audio, and video.

[8] Note that one could also argue whether database support for collaborative applications should be discussed here. This is because collaborative computing is not part of the data management framework. However, such applications do need database support and our focus will be on this support.

[9] Although Internet database management is an integration of various technologies, we have placed it in Layer III as it still deals with information extraction. Note that the data management framework consists of technologies for managing data as well as for extracting information from the data. However, what one does with the information, such as collaborative computing, sophisticated human computer interaction, natural language processing, and knowledge-based processing, does not belong to this framework. As we will see, they belong to the application technologies layer.

[10] Note that technologies such as distributed object management enable interoperation and migration.

collaborative computing systems and knowledge-based systems which belong to the application technologies layer may utilize data management systems. Note that the application technologies layer is also outside of the data management systems framework.

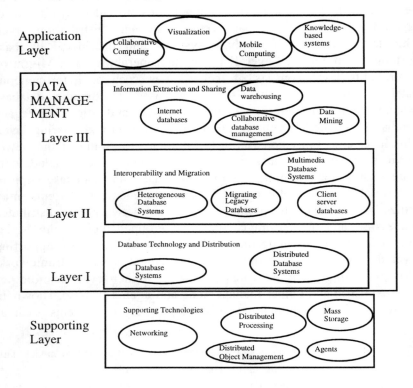

Figure 1-7. Data Management Systems Framework

The technologies that constitute the data management systems framework can be regarded to be some of the core technologies in data management. However, features like security, integrity, real-time processing, fault tolerance, and high performance computing are needed for many applications utilizing data management technologies. We have discussed some of these features in this book. Applications utilizing data management technologies may be medical, financial, or military, among others. We illustrate this in figure 1-8, where a 3-dimensional view relating data management technologies with features and applications is given. For example, one could develop a secure distributed database management system for medical applications or a fault tolerant multimedia database management system for financial applications. [11]

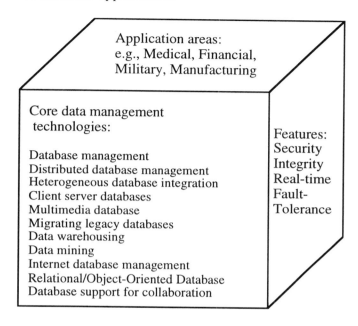

Figure 1-8. A Three-dimensional View of Data Management

The contents of this book are based on the framework that we have proposed. Details of the organization are given in section 1.7. As stated in section 1.3, integrating the components belonging to these various layers is important to develop efficient data management systems. In addition, data management technologies have to be integrated with the application technologies to develop successful information systems. However, at present there is limited integration between these various components. This book focuses mainly on the concepts, developments, and trends belonging to each of the components shown in the framework.

---

[11] In some cases one could also consider multimedia data processing and reengineering which is an essential part of system migration to be at the same level as features like security and integrity. One could also regard them to be emerging technologies. However in this book we have treated multimedia database management and system migration as part of the core data management technologies.

1.6   BUILDING   INFORMATION   SYSTEMS   FROM   THE FRAMEWORK

Figure 1-7 illustrated a framework for data management systems. As shown in that figure, the technologies for data management include database systems, distributed database systems, heterogeneous database systems, migrating legacy databases, multimedia database systems, data warehousing, data mining, Internet databases, and database support for collaboration. Furthermore, data management systems take advantage of supporting technologies such as distributed processing and agents. Similarly, application technologies such as collaborative computing, visualization, expert systems, and mobile computing take advantage of data management systems.[12]

Many of us have heard of the term information systems on numerous occasions. These systems have sometimes been used interchangeably with data management systems. In our terminology, information systems are much broader than data management systems, but they do include data management systems. In fact, a framework for information systems will include not only the data management system layers, but also the supporting technologies layer as well as the application technologies layer. That is, information systems encompass all kinds of computing systems. It can be regarded as the finished product that can be used for various applications. That is, while hardware is at the lowest end of the spectrum, applications are at the highest end.

The vision and the interoperability diagrams illustrated in figures 1-3 and 1-4 can be put together from the technologies illustrated in the framework diagram of figure 1-7. For example, for the vision diagram in figure 1-3, one needs collaboration and visualization technologies at the application technology level so that analysts can collaboratively carry out some tasks. At the data management level, one needs both multimedia and distributed database technologies. At the supporting level, one needs mass storage as well as some distributed processing capability. This special framework for the vision diagram in figure 1-3, which is extracted from the generic framework in figure 1-7, is illustrated in figure 1-9. Another example is a special framework for the interoperability diagram in figure 1-4. One may need some visualization technology to display the integrated information from the heterogeneous databases. At the data management level, we have heterogeneous database systems technology. At the

---

[12] Note that databases could also support expert systems as in the case of collaborative applications. A discussion of all the ways in which application technologies utilize data management systems is beyond the scope of this book.

supporting technology level, one may use distributed object management technology to encapsulate the heterogeneous databases. This special framework is illustrated in figure 1-10.

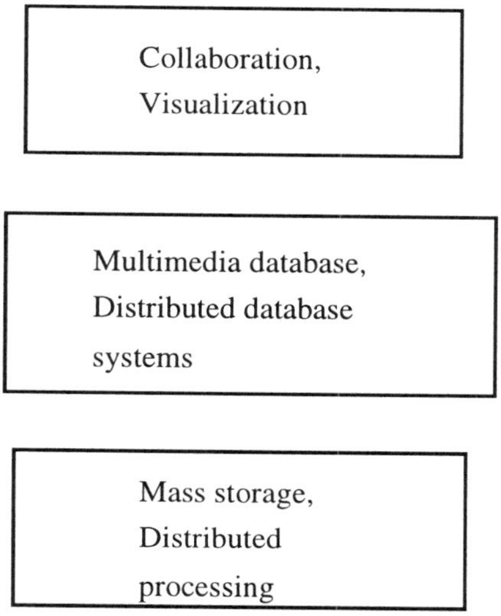

```
┌─────────────────────────────┐
│                             │
│      Collaboration,         │
│      Visualization          │
│                             │
└─────────────────────────────┘

  ┌─────────────────────────────┐
  │                             │
  │    Multimedia database,     │
  │    Distributed database     │
  │    systems                  │
  └─────────────────────────────┘

  ┌─────────────────────────────┐
  │                             │
  │      Mass storage,          │
  │      Distributed            │
  │      processing             │
  └─────────────────────────────┘
```

Figure 1-9. Framework for Data Management Vision

Finally, let us illustrate the concepts that we have described above by using a specific example. Suppose, a group of physicians/surgeons want a system where they can collaborate and make decisions about various patients. This could be a medical video teleconferencing application. That is, at the highest level, the application is a medical application and more specifically a medical video teleconferencing application. At the application technology level, one needs a variety of technologies including collaboration and teleconferencing. These application technologies will make use of data management technologies such as distributed database systems and multimedia database systems. That is, one may need to support multimedia data such as voice and video. The data management technologies in turn draw upon lower level technologies such as distributed processing and networking. We illustrate this in figure 1-11.

In summary, information systems include data management systems as well as application-layer systems such as collaborative computing systems and supporting-layer systems such as distributed object management systems. Note that this book focuses only on data management systems. Aspects of application-layer technologies and supporting-layer technologies are discussed only if they are relevant to explain a particular concept. For example, distributed object management is described in some detail as it is becoming important for client-server interoperability.

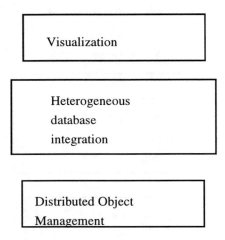

Figure 1-10. Framework for Heterogeneous Database Interoperability

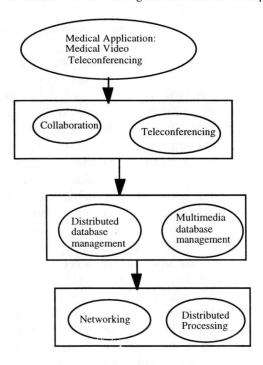

Figure 1-11. Specific Example

While application technologies make use of data management technologies and data management technologies make use of supporting technologies, the ultimate user of the information system is the application itself. Today numerous applications make use of information systems. These applications are from multiple domains such as medical, financial, manufacturing, telecommunications, and defense. Specific applications include signal processing, electronic commerce, patient monitoring, and situation assessment. Figure 1-12 illustrates the relationship between the application and the information system.

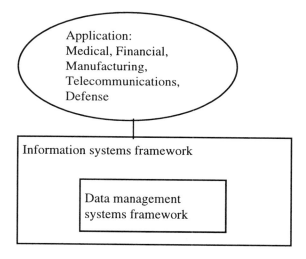

Figure 1-12. Application-Framework Relationship

1.7 ORGANIZATION OF THIS BOOK

This book consists of three parts. Parts I, II, and III consist of chapters describing the components in the layers I, II, and III, respectively, of the framework. Figure 1-13 illustrates the framework indicating the chapter number which addresses the topic related to the component.

Part I, which consists of two chapters, describes concepts in database systems and distributed database systems technologies. Much of the discussion in this book is built on the information presented in part I. Chapter 2 provides an overview of database systems. In particular, the evolution of database systems, architectures, data models, and functions are discussed. Chapter 3 describes concepts in distributed database systems. A discussion of distributed databases for mobile computing applications is also given.

Part II, which consists of four chapters, describes concepts on the interoperability of heterogeneous database systems as well as migrating legacy databases. Heterogeneity and autonomy as well as federated database system concepts are discussed in chapter 4. It also includes a discussion of some of the heterogeneous database system prototypes. Chapter 5 describes database system interoperability based on client-server architectures. A discussion of Object Management Group's (OMG) Common Object Request Broker Architecture (CORBA) for interoperability is also provided. Multimedia database systems for handling heterogeneous data types is described in Chapter 6. Chapter 7 describes issues on migrating legacy databases and systems to newer architectures and infrastructures.

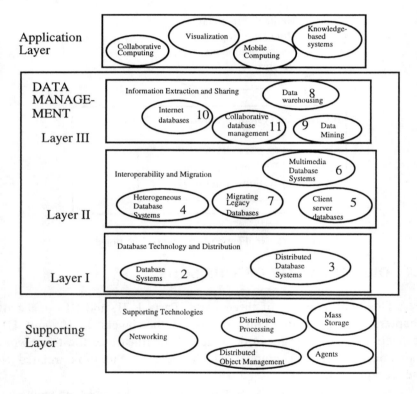

Figure 1-13. Organization of this Book with Respect to the Framework

Part III, which consists of four chapters, describes current trends in data management systems. Chapter 8 describes issues on building data warehouses, where a data warehouse may be regarded as a repository of data that is assembled from possibly multiple heterogeneous databases. Data mining technology, for extracting information from the data in the databases that are possibly heterogeneous in nature, is described in chapter 9. Digital library technology and Internet databases, which deal with the management of and access to large amounts of multimedia data possibly stored in the world wide web (WWW) servers, are discussed in chapter 10. Finally, in chapter 11, database management for collaborative applications is discussed. Note that while collaborative applications are part of the applications layer and not part of the data management framework, these applications require database support. It is the database support that is addressed in chapter 11.

Each part begins with an introduction and ends with a conclusion. Introduction to a part describes the contents of the corresponding chapters. The conclusion relates the contents to the framework. Directions for data management systems evolution and interoperation are the subject of the last chapter, chapter 12. The contents of the book are also summarized in this chapter. In addition, some guidelines for building information systems are also given.

Commercial status is given in the appendix. That is, the appendix provides an overview of commercial data management system products. We have discussed briefly the current status of various groups of products and then selected one or two products from each group and described them in more detail. The groups include relational database systems, object-oriented database systems, object-relational database systems, replication servers, interoperability servers, multidatabase servers, component-based integration servers, data warehouses, and data mining systems.[13]

Various features such as security, integrity, the role of metadata, and standards are discussed throughout this book. For example, security is addressed for database systems, distributed database systems, heterogeneous database integration, multimedia database systems, data warehousing, and data mining. The role of metadata is discussed for database systems, distributed database systems, heterogeneous database integration, client-server database management, multimedia database management, migrating legacy databases, data warehousing, data mining, Internet database management, and database support for collaboration. Other topics such as real-time

---

[13] Note that we have selected the products to be discussed in the appendix entirely based on our experience and/or knowledge of the products. This does not mean that these products are superior to other products. We are also not endorsing any product. There are several products and many more emerging for the various groups discussed here. A discussion of all of these products is beyond the scope of this book. Our discussion is intended to give the reader some idea of some of the features that are being offered in the products.

database management, deductive database management, database design, fault tolerance issues, and database systems survivability are briefly discussed. Topics such as benchmarking, performance analysis, modeling and simulation for data management, and other database systems such as scientific databases and high performance database management are beyond the scope of this book.

While technologies for data management systems evolution and interoperation are the main focus of this book, these technologies also provide support for the emerging topic of data dissemination. This deals with getting the right data/information at the right time to the analyst/user (directly to the desktop if possible) to assist in carrying out various functions. The complete range of technologies for data dissemination is also beyond the scope of this book.

Concepts and Developments in Database and Distributed Database Systems

Part I

INTRODUCTION TO PART I

The goal of the two chapters in part I is to give a broad over-view of the concepts and developments in database and distributed database system technologies. With respect to the framework for data management systems illustrated in figure 1-7, the two chapters in part I describe the Database Systems and Distribution Layer. Several references are cited in part I should a reader need in-depth coverage of a particular topic.

Chapter 2 provides an overview of database systems technology. In particular, data models, architectures, database design, database management system functions, multilevel security, and deductive database management are discussed. Database management system functions include query processing, transaction management, storage management, metadata management, and maintaining integrity and security. Some special types of database systems as well as issues on database systems survivability are also described.

Heterogeneous database integration issues have been influenced by the early developments in distributed database management. Therefore, chapter 3 will discuss some of the essential concepts in distributed database systems. In particular, an architecture for a distributed database system, data distribution issues, query processing, transaction management, security, integrity, and distributed database administration issues are discussed. While much of the focus is on distributed relational database management, a brief overview of the issues in distributed object-oriented database systems is also provided. In addition, distributed database systems technology for mobile computing applications as well as networking issues are described.

CHAPTER 2

DEVELOPMENTS IN DATABASE SYSTEMS TECHNOLOGY

2.1 OVERVIEW

Database systems play a key role in data management systems evolution and interoperation. Database systems technology has advanced a great deal during the past four decades from the legacy systems based on network and hierarchical models to relational and object-oriented database systems based on client-server architectures. This chapter provides an overview of the important developments in database systems relevant to the contents of this book: data management systems evolution and interoperation in general and heterogeneous database systems integration in particular. The discussion in the remainder of this book builds on the information presented in this chapter.

As stated in chapter 1, we consider a database system to include both the database management system (DBMS) and the database (see also the discussion in [DATE90]). The DBMS component of the database system manages the database. The database contains persistent data. That is, the data is permanent even if the application programs go away.

The organization of this chapter is as follows. In section 2.2 data models are described. In particular, relational, entity-relationship, object-oriented, object-relational, and logic-based data models are discussed. In section 2.3 various types of architectures for database systems are described. These include an architecture for a centralized database system, schema architecture, as well as functional architecture. Database design issues are discussed in section 2.4. Database system functions are discussed in section 2.5. These functions include query processing, transaction management, metadata management, storage management, maintaining integrity and security, and fault tolerance. Database administration issues are discussed in section 2.6. Some other types of database management systems are the subject of section 2.7. In particular, multilevel secure database management systems, deductive database systems, real-time database systems, parallel database systems, and an overview of other types of database systems are provided. Some recent trends in using component integration technology to develop database systems are provided in section 2.8. While sections 2.2 to 2.8 discuss technological aspects of data management, in section 2.9 steps to data management, from concept to implementation, are discussed. In particular, section 2.9 focuses on how an organization goes about getting an operational database system to manage its data. Finally, in section 2.10 we describe issues on database system survivability. That is, while much of the focus of this book is on designing systems to manage the explosion of data and information, survivability of this information in crisis situations is also a critical aspect of information technology. Therefore, section 2.10 briefly addresses the role of database systems in information survivability.

2.2 DATA MODELS

2.2.1 Overview

It is widely accepted among the data modeling community that the purpose of a data model is to capture the universe that it is representing as accurately, completely, and naturally as possible [TSCI81]. While philosophers have been interested in various types of universes for centuries, recently, it has interested the data model, logic, and database researchers a great deal. In particular, the work of Gallaire, Minker, Kowalski, Nicolas, Reiter, and Clark among others have described the differences between the actual and perceived universes and they have developed approaches for modeling the perceived universe (see, for example, [GALL78, MINK88, FROS86, BROD84]).

The actual universe has the truth about all of the entities in the universe. The perceived universe is the people's view of the universe. This view is usually determined by someone or a group of people in authority. One can regard the perceived universe to be an interpretation of the actual universe. Whether the perceived universe is a model of the actual universe depends on how accurately the perceived universe fits the actual universe. For data modeling purposes, it is the perceived view of the universe that is of interest. This is because the views of the users of the database must be correctly reflected. Figure 2-1 illustrates what has been discussed here.

Research in data modeling has concentrated mainly in two areas from which two types of data models were developed: traditional and semantic models. Traditional models include the network, hierarchical, and relational models (see, for example, [DATE90]). Semantic models include the entity-relationship [CHEN76] (also referred to as the ER model), functional [BUNE82], logic-based [ULLM88], and object-oriented models [BANE87]. Models such as the relational model are being extended to support complex objects. For example relational and object-oriented models have been integrated to produce object-relational data models [ACM91a]. Recently, another type of model has been included in the classification of data models. This is the hyper-semantic data model [TRUE89]. Such a model not only includes the constructs provided by semantic data models, but provides inference capabilities necessary to model knowledge-based applications. That is, hypersemantic data models integrate the constructs of semantic and logic-based models. Although semantic data models also provide powerful constructs (e.g., inheritance, generalization, aggregation, and composition) by themselves, these are insufficient to model knowledge-based applications, which require inferencing capabilities. [14]

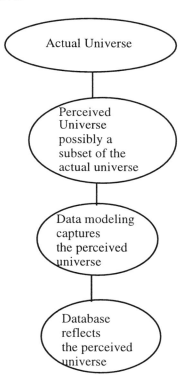

Figure 2-1. Data Modeling

In this section we discuss the essential points of relational, entity-relationship (ER), object-oriented, object-relational, and

---

[14] Note that many of the legacy systems which still dominate the business world are based on network and hierarchical models. However, many of the new initiatives are choosing the relational approach. Object-based approaches are being used for some applications. Logic-based approaches have not really taken on. But they are of much interest to the research community. In a functional model, the database is a collection of functions and query processing amounts to function execution. This is also an approach that has not taken on. Semantic models evolved from ER as well as some of the artificial intelligence models.

logic-based data models. We have chosen these five models because at present these models are of much interest to the database community. It should be noted that we do not discuss information modeling in this book. Various views of information modeling have been proposed. Some early ideas were reported in [THUR92a]. A more accepted view, where information modeling includes data modeling as well as process modeling, is given in [BENY90]. Object-oriented design and analysis approaches are becoming popular for information systems application design. A discussion of the various object-oriented modeling, design, and analysis approaches is also beyond the scope of this book.[15] For a brief overview comparing the various approaches we refer to [FOWL95].

2.2 Relational Data Model

With the relational model [CODD70], the database is viewed as a collection of relations. Each relation has attributes and rows. For example, figure 2-2 illustrates a database with two relations EMP and DEPT. EMP has four attributes, SS#, Ename, Salary, and D#. DEPT has three attributes D#, Dname, and Mgr. EMP has three rows also called tuples, and DEPT has two rows. Each row is uniquely identified by its primary key. For example SS# could be the primary key for EMP and D# for DEPT. Another key feature of the relational model is that each element in the relation is an atomic value such as an integer or a string. That is, complex values such as lists are not supported.

EMP

SS#	Ename	Salary	D#
1	John	20K	10
2	Paul	30K	20
3	Mary	40K	20

DEPT

D#	Dname	Mgr
10	Math	Smith
20	Physics	Jones

Figure 2-2. Relational Database

---

[15] We have utilized Rumbaugh et al.'s Object Modeling Technique (OMIT) in our work on database support for collaboration. This work is discussed in chapter 11. For a discussion of OMT, an example object-oriented design and analysis methodology, we refer to [RUMB91].

Various operations are performed on relations. The SELECT operation selects a subset of rows satisfying certain conditions. For example, in the relation EMP, one may select tuples where the salary is more than 20K. The PROJECT operation projects the relation onto some attributes. For example, in the relation EMP one may project onto the attributes Ename and Salary. The JOIN operation joins two relations over some common attributes. For example, in the case of the relations EMP and DEPT, they can be joined over D# to obtain correlations between employees and the departments they work in. The JOIN operation between EMP and DEPT is illustrated in figure 2-3. There are various properties that a relation must satisfy. A detailed discussion of these properties is given in [DATE90, ULLM88]. We have briefly discussed some of these properties in the section on database integrity (i.e., 2.5.6).

EMP JOIN DEPT

SS#	Ename	Salary	D#	Dname	Mgr
1	John	20K	10	Math	Smith
2	Paul	30K	20	Physics	Jones
3	Mary	40K	20	Physics	Jones

Figure 2-3. Join Operation

Various languages to manipulate the relations have been proposed. Notable among these languages is the ANSI Standard SQL (Structured Query Language). This language is used to access and manipulate data in relational databases [SQL3]. There is wide acceptance of this standard among database management system vendors and users. It supports schema definition, retrieval, data manipulation, schema manipulation, transaction management, integrity, and security. Other languages include the relational calculus first proposed in the Ingres project at University of California at Berkeley [DATE90].

Note also that the notion of a view is now part of many commercial database systems. A view is a virtual relation. For example, in the case of the employee relation, for certain applications, users may only need the employee name and salary attributes. Therefore, a view EMP1 could be formed from EMP which projects EMP onto the attributes Ename and Salary. That is, the EMP1 view relation will have two attributes, Ename and Salary. Usually the data is not physically stored in the view. Users' queries on the view are transformed into those on the relation, and responses are given. The advantage of the view mechanism is that not all of the attributes need to be known to the user. This means that views can be used to protect the data in the database. A problem with the view concept is with update. That is, when the view is updated, what actually happens is that the relations from which the view is formed have to be updated. Some anomalies with view updates have been identified and these are discussed in [DATE90].

2.2.3   Entity-Relationship Data Model

One of the major drawbacks of the relational data model is its lack of support for capturing the semantics of an application. This resulted in the development of semantic data models. The entity-relationship (ER) data model developed by Chen [CHEN76] can be regarded to be the earliest semantic data model. In this model, the world is viewed as a collection of entities and relationships between entities. Figure 2-4 illustrates two entities, EMP and DEPT. The relationship between them is WORKS.

Relationships can be either one-one, many-one, or many-many. If it is assumed that each employee works in one department and each department has one employee, then WORKS is a one-one relationship. If it is assumed that an employee works in one department and each department can have many employees, then WORKS is a many-one relationship. If it is assumed that an employee works in many departments, and each department has many employees, then WORKS is a many-many relationship.

Figure 2-4. Entity-Relationship Representation

Several extensions to the entity-relationship model have been proposed. One is the entity-relationship-attribute model where attributes are associated with entities as well as relationships, and another has introduced the notion of categories into the model (see for example the discussions in [ELMA85, YANG88]). It should be noted that ER models are used mainly to design databases. That is, most database CASE tools are based on the ER model, where the application is represented using such a model and subsequently the database (possibly relational) is generated.[16] Current database management systems are not based on the ER model. That is, unlike the relational model, ER models did not take off in the development of database management systems.

2.2.4   Object-Oriented Data Model

While ER models are semantic data models, they do not support features like inheritance and aggregation (to be discussed in this section) which facilitate complex data representation. Object-oriented data models were developed for this purpose. Although several object-oriented data models have been proposed, there is no standard object model. Various groups are proposing standards. Notable among these is the object model proposed by the Object Database Management Group (ODMG) [ODMG93].[17] Furthermore, languages such as SQL are being extended to support objects. Much of our discussion on object-oriented data models is influenced by the work on the ORION project [BANE87].

With an object-oriented data model, the database is viewed as a collection of objects. Each object has a unique identifier called the object-ID. Objects with similar properties are grouped into a class. For example, employee objects are grouped into EMP class while department objects are grouped into DEPT class as shown in figure 2-5. A class has instance variables describing the properties. Instance variables of EMP are SS#, Ename, Salary, and D# while the instance variables of DEPT are D#, Dname, and Mgr. Objects in a class are its instances. As illustrated in the figure, EMP has three instances and DEPT has two instances.

A key concept in object-oriented data modeling is encapsulation. That is, an object has well defined interfaces. The state of an object can only be accessed through interface procedures called methods. For example, EMP may have a method called Increase-Salary. The code for Increase-Salary is illustrated in the figure. A message, say Increase-Salary(1, 10K), may be sent to the object with object ID of 1. The object's current salary is read and updated by 10K.

Two other key concepts are inheritance and aggregation.[18] A class may have subclasses. A subclass inherits all the properties (i.e.,

---

[16]   CASE stands for Computer Aided Software Engineering.

[17]   ODMG is a consortium of about a dozen corporations specifying standards for object database management.

[18]   Inheritance is also known as the IS-A hierarchy. Aggregation is also known as the IS-PART-OF hierarchy.

instance variables and methods) from its superclass. This feature is illustrated in figure 2-6. Document class has two subclasses, books and journals. In addition to properties inherited, the subclasses may have additional properties. In the case of book, it may have the property ISBN number and in the case of journal, it may have the property volume number. It could also be the case that a class may be the subclass of two superclasses. In this case, it may inherit the properties of both the superclasses. This feature is called multiple inheritance. There are several issues related to multiple inheritance such as inheriting conflicting properties. For a discussion we refer to [BANE87].

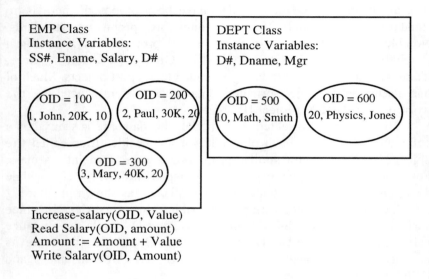

Figure 2-5. Objects and Classes

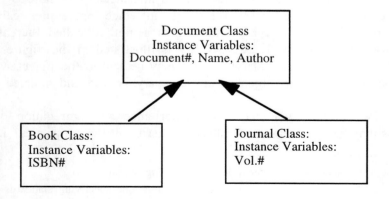

Figure 2-6. Inheritance

Certain objects are aggregate objects. For example, a book may consist of introduction, sections, conclusion, and references. This feature called aggregation is illustrated in figure 2-7. An aggregate object is also sometimes called a composite object.

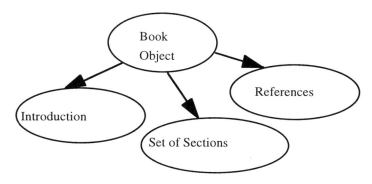

Figure 2-7. Aggregate Object

A special feature of object-oriented database systems is the tight integration with programming languages. For example, in some cases, the persistent database can be created with a programming language such as C++. Therefore, there is little difference between application programming in C++ and database programming in C++ (see, for example, [LOOM95]). However, in relational systems, there is impedance mismatch. The database understands only languages such as SQL. So, an application program written in a language such as C has to have special calls to SQL. Some argue that by having imped-ance mismatch the database system is not tied to a particular pro-gramming language and so it will be easier to support multiple languages. Some argue that having impedance mismatch is difficult for programming intensive applications.

2.2.5 Object-Relational Data Model

Object-relational database systems were developed to overcome some of the problems with relational and object-oriented database systems. Relational data model is based on well defined principles. Furthermore, a notable feature of relational database systems is the query language. The SQL language developed initially for relational databases is an ANSI standard. However relational data models cannot support complex objects which are needed for new generation applications such as CAD/CAM and multimedia. On the other hand, object-oriented data models can support complex structures. How-ever, in general, object-oriented database systems do not have good support for querying.

To overcome these problems, relational database vendors are building some sort of support for objects. Object-oriented database vendors are developing better query interfaces as well as better support to represent relationships. In addition, a third kind of system, object-relational database system, has been developed. These systems provide support both for relations and objects. Note that there is no standard object-relational model. With one approach, the relations are extended so that the data elements are no longer atomic. That is, the data elements could be complex objects. Figure 2-8 illustrates this concept where the book relation has an attribute called components. This attribute describes the components of the book. Object-relational systems are still young and we can expect them to mature over the next few years. Several object-oriented database system products as well as a few object-relational database system prototypes are discussed in [ACM91a].

Book Extended Relation

ISBN#	Components
1	-
2	- -
3	- - -

Figure 2-8. Object-Relational Model

2.2.7 Logic-based Data Model

The last model we describe here is the Logic-based data model. Such a model received prominence in the late 1970s after the logic and database workshop in France. It was at this time that logic programming languages like Prolog were becoming popular. However, much of the developments with the logic model took place after the start of the Japanese Fifth Generation Project in the early 1980s when it was declared that logic programming was the desired language for the project.

Essentially a logic model views the database as a collection of logic clauses. Note that logic clauses could be based on first order logic or higher order logic. However, due to the tight integration with relational databases and logic programming, the clauses are generally based on a restricted first order logic called Horn clause logic. Figure 2-9 illustrates a database which uses Horn logic for data representation. It essentially describes the parent-grandparent database. It consists of three clauses describing the parent relationship and one clause describing a rule for grand-parent relationship. This way one does not have to store all the data for the grand-parent relation. From the parent relation and the rule, one could deduce the grand-parent relation. Further details on DBMSs based on logic as a data model are given in section 2.7. For a discussion of logic programming we refer to [LLOY87].

```
Parent(John, Mary) <-
Parent(Mary, Jane) <-
Parent(Mary, Jim) <-
Grand-parent(X,Z) <- Parent (X,Y) and Parent (Y,Z)
```

Figure 2-9. Logic for Representation

2.3 ARCHITECTURAL ISSUES

This section describes various types of architectures for a database system. First we illustrate a very high-level centralized architecture for a database system. Then we describe a functional architecture for a database system. In particular, the functions of the DBMS component of the database system are illustrated in this architecture. Then we discuss the ANSI/SPARC's three schema architecture which has been more or less accepted by the database community [DATE90]. Finally, we describe extensible architectures.

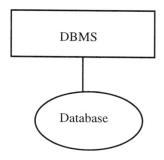

Figure 2-10. Centralized Architecture

Figure 2-10 is an example of a centralized architecture. Here, the DBMS is a monolithic entity and manages a database which is centralized. Functional architecture illustrates the functional modules of a DBMS. The major modules of a DBMS include the query processor, transaction manager, metadata manager, storage manager, integrity manager, and security manager. The functional architecture of the DBMS component of the centralized database system architecture (of figure 2-10) is illustrated in figure 2-11.

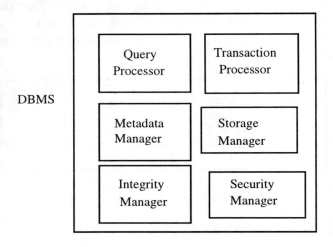

Figure 2-11. Functional Architecture for a DBMS

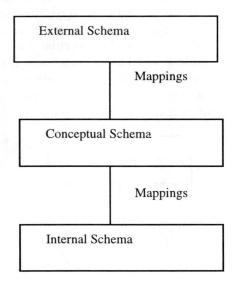

Figure 2-12. Three-Schema Architecture

Schema describes the data in the database. It has also been referred to as the data dictionary or contents of the metadatabase. Three-schema architecture was proposed for a centralized database system in the 1960s. This is illustrated in figure 2-12. The levels are the external schema which provides an external view, the conceptual schema which provides a conceptual view, and the internal schema which provides an internal view. Mappings between the different schemas must be provided to transform one representation into another. For example, at the external level one could use ER representation. At the logical or conceptual level one could use relational representation. At the physical level, one could use a representation based on B-Trees.[19]

There is also another aspect to architectures and that is extensible database architectures. For example, for many applications, a DBMS may have to be extended with a layer to support objects or to process rules or even to handle multimedia data types. Such an extensible architecture is illustrated in figure 2-13. We will discuss this architecture in various chapters.

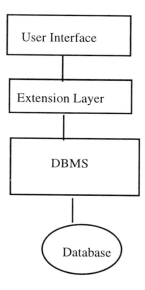

Figure 2-13. Extensible DBMS

2.4 DATABASE DESIGN

Designing a database is a complex process. Much of the work has been on designing relational databases. There are three steps. These steps are illustrated in figure 2-14. The first step is to capture the entities of the application and the relationships between the

---

[19] Note that a B-Tree is a representation scheme used to physically represent the data. However, it is at a higher level than the bits and bytes level. For a discussion on physical structures and models we refer to [DATE90].

entities. One could use a model such as the entity-relationship model for this purpose. More recently, object-oriented data models, which are part of object-oriented design and analysis methodologies, are becoming popular to represent the application.

The second step is to generate the relations from the representations. For example, from the entity-relationship diagram of figure 2-4, one could generate the relations EMP, DEPT, and WORKS. The relation WORKS will capture the relationship between employees and departments.

The third step is to design good relations. This is the normalization process. Various normal forms have been defined in the literature [MAIE83, DATE90]. For many applications, relations in third normal form would suffice. With this normal form, redundancies, complex values, and other situations that could cause potential anomalies are eliminated.

Figure 2-14. Database Design Process

2.5 DATABASE MANAGEMENT SYSTEM FUNCTIONS

2.5.1   Overview

Functional architecture of a DBMS was illustrated in figure 2-11. The functions of a DBMS carry out its operations. A DBMS essentially manages a database and it provides support to the user by enabling him to query and update the database. Therefore, the basic functions of a DBMS are query processing and update processing. In some applications such as banking, queries and updates are issued as part of transactions. Therefore transaction management is also another function of a DBMS. To carry out these functions, information about the database has to be maintained. This information is called metadata. The function that is associated with managing the metadata is metadata management. Special techniques are needed to manage the data stores that actually store the data. The function that is associated with managing these techniques is storage management. To ensure that the above functions are carried out properly and that the user gets accurate data, there are some additional functions. These include security management, integrity management, and fault management (i.e., fault tolerance).

The above are some of the essential functions of a DBMS. However, more recently there is much emphasis on extracting information from the data. Therefore, other functions of a DBMS may include providing support for data mining, data warehousing, and collaboration.

This section focuses only on the essential functions of a DBMS. These are: query processing, transaction management, metadata management, storage management, maintaining integrity, security control, and fault tolerance. Note that we do not have a special section for update processing as we can handle it as part of transaction management. We discuss each of the essential functions in sections 2.5.2 to 2.5.7.

2.5.2 Query Processing

Query operation is the most commonly used function in a DBMS. It should be possible for users to query the database and obtain answers to their queries. There are several aspects to query processing. First of all, a good query language is needed. Languages such as SQL are popular for relational databases. Such languages are being extended for other types of databases. The second aspect is techniques for query processing. Numerous algorithms have been proposed for query processing in general and for the JOIN operation in particular (see, also [KIM85]). Also different strategies are possible to execute a particular query. The costs for the various strategies are computed and one with the least cost is usually selected for processing. This process is called query optimization. Cost is generally determined by the disk access. The goal is to minimize disk access in processing a query.

As stated earlier, users pose a query using a language. The constructs of the language have to be transformed into the constructs understood by the database system. This process is called query transformation. Query transformation is carried out in stages based on the various schemas. For example, a query based on the external schema is transformed into a query on the conceptual schema. This is then transformed into a query on the physical schema. In general, rules used in the transformation process include the factoring of common subexpressions and pushing selections and projections down in the query tree as much as possible. If selections and projections are performed before the joins, then the cost of the joins can be reduced by a considerable amount.

Figure 2-15 illustrates the modules in query processing. User interface manager accepts queries, parses the queries, then gives it to the query transformer. Query transformer and query optimizer communicate with each other to produce an execution strategy. The database is accessed through the storage manager. Responses are given to the user by the response manager.

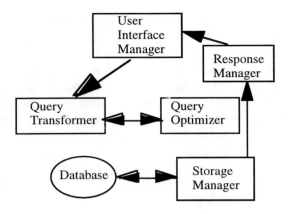

Figure 2-15. Query Processor

2.5.3   Transaction Management

A transaction is a program unit that must be executed in its entirety or not executed at all. If transactions are executed serially, then there is a performance bottleneck. Therefore, transactions are executed concurrently. Appropriate techniques must ensure that the database is consistent when multiple transactions update the database. That is, transactions must satisfy the ACID (Atomicity, Consistency, Isolation, and Durability) properties. Major aspects of transaction management are serializability, concurrency control, and recovery. We discuss them briefly in this section. For a detailed discussion of transaction management we refer to [DATE90, ULLM88, KORT86]. A good theoretical treatment of this topic is given in [BERN87].

Serializability: A schedule is a sequence of operations performed by multiple transactions. Two schedules are equivalent if their outcomes are the same. A serial schedule is a schedule where no two transactions execute concurrently. An objective in transaction management is to ensure that any schedule is equivalent to a serial schedule. Such a schedule is called a serializable schedule. Various conditions for testing the serializability of a schedule have been formulated for a DBMS.

Concurrency Control: Concurrency control techniques ensure that the database is in a consistent state when multiple transactions update the database. Three popular concurrency control techniques which ensure the serializability of schedules are locking, time-stamping, and validation.

Locking: Two-phase locking is used to provide concurrency control (i.e., a transaction acquires all necessary locks first before releasing any). Two types of locks may be obtained. They are shared locks and exclusive locks. A shared lock for a data item is requested by a transaction for the read operation. The request is granted if no other transaction has a write lock for the same data item. An exclusive lock is requested by a transaction for the write operation. The request is granted when no other transaction has either a shared lock or an exclusive lock for the same data item. Note that the locking technique can cause deadlocks. For example, consider the situation where a transaction T1 has a lock on object O1 and requests a lock on O2 while a transaction T2 has a lock on O2 and requests a lock on O1. This will cause a deadlock. Various approaches have been proposed to handle deadlocks. In one approach, a deadlock detection graph is used to detect deadlocks, and solutions may include aborting certain transactions. For details we refer to [ULLM88].

Time-stamp: In the time-stamp technique, each transaction is assigned a time-stamp when it begins execution. Similarly a data item is also assigned a read stamp and a write stamp which are the time-stamps of the most recent transaction which read or updated that data item. When a transaction requests to read or write a data item, certain checks are made between the time-stamp of the transaction and the read/write stamps of the data item. If the checks are satisfied, then a transaction continues; otherwise the transaction aborts and restarts with a new time-stamp.

Validation: In the validation technique (also called optimistic concurrency control) a transaction goes through three phases. A read phase, a validation phase, and a write phase. During the validation phase, it is checked whether by committing the transaction there may be some conflicts with other transactions. If there are, then the transaction is not committed.

Recovery: If a transaction aborts due to some failure, then the database must be brought to a consistent state. This is transaction recovery. One solution to handling transaction failure is to maintain log files. The transaction's actions are recorded in the log file. So, if a transaction aborts, then the database is brought back to a consistent state by undoing the actions of the transaction. The information for the undo operation is found in the log file. Another solution is to record the actions of a transaction, but not make any changes to the database. Only if a transaction commits should the database be updated. There are some issues. For example, the log files have to be kept in stable storage. Various modifications to the above techniques have been proposed to handle the different situations.

2.5.4   Storage Management

The storage manager is responsible for accessing the database. To improve the efficiency of query and update algorithms, appropriate access methods and index strategies have to be enforced. That is, in generating strategies for executing query and update requests, the access methods and index strategies that are used need to be taken into consideration. The access methods used to access the database would depend on the indexing methods. Therefore, creating and maintaining appropriate index files is a major issue in database management systems. By using an appropriate indexing mechanism, the query processing algorithms may not have to search the entire database. Instead, the data to be retrieved could be accessed directly. Consequently, the retrieval algorithms are more efficient.

Much research has been carried out on developing appropriate access methods and index strategies for relational database systems. Some examples of index strategies are B-Trees and Hashing [DATE90]. Current research is focusing on developing such mechanisms for object-oriented database systems with support for multimedia data.

2.5.5   Metadata Management

Metadata describes the data in the database. For example, in the case of the relational database illustrated in figure 2-2, metadata would include the following information. The database has two relations, EMP and DEPT. EMP has four attributes and DEPT has three attributes, etc. One of the main issues is developing a data model for metadata. In our example, one could use a relational model to model the metadata also. The metadata relation REL shown in figure 2-16 consists of information about relations and attributes.

In addition to information about the data in the database, metadata also includes information on access methods, index strategies, security constraints, and integrity constraints. In addition, one could also include policies and procedures as part of the metadata. In other words, there is no standard definition for metadata. There are however efforts to standardize metadata [META96]. Metadata becomes a major issue with some of the recent developments in data management such as digital libraries. Some of the issues are discussed in Chapter 10.

Once the metadata is defined, the issues include managing the metadata. What are the techniques for querying and updating the metadata? Since all of the other DBMS components need to access the metadata for processing, what are the interfaces between the metadata manager and the other components? Metadata management is fairly well understood for relational database systems. The current challenge is in managing the metadata for more complex systems such as digital libraries and Internet-based database systems.

Relation REL

Relation	Attribute
EMP	SS#
EMP	Ename
EMP	Salary
EMP	D#
DEPT	D#
DEPT	Dname
DEPT	Mgr

Figure 2-16. Metadata Relation

2.5.6 Database Integrity

Concurrency control and recovery techniques maintain the integrity of the database. In addition, there is another type of database integrity and that is enforcing integrity constraints. There are two types of integrity constraints enforced in database systems. These are application independent integrity constraints and application specific integrity constraints. Integrity mechanisms also include techniques for determining the quality of the data. For example, what is the accuracy of the data and that of the source? What are the mechanisms for maintaining the quality of the data? How accurate is the data on output? In this section we only discuss the enforcement of application independent and application specific integrity constraints. Our focus will be on the relational data model. For a discussion on integrity based on data quality, we refer to [MIT].

Application independent integrity constraints include the primary key constraint, the entity integrity rule, referential integrity constraint, and the various functional dependencies involved in the normalization process (see the discussion in [DATE90]). We discuss some of the integrity rules and associated definitions below as given in [DATE90].

Primary Key: A primary key uniquely identifies a tuple in a relation. For example, in an employee relation, either the social security number or the employee number may be the primary key. Since it is possible to have more than one unique identifier, each such unique identifier is called the candidate key. One of the candidate keys is designated as the primary key. The others are alternate keys.

Uniqueness: Candidate key is unique in the sense that at any given time, no two tuples of a relation have the same value for the candidate key.

Minimality: If candidate key K is composite (consists of two or more attributes), then if any component of K is eliminated, the result cannot be a candidate key. For example, let K consist of K1, K2, and K3. Then if we delete say K3, then K1 and K2 cannot form the candidate key.

Entity integrity: A component of a primary key cannot have any null values

Foreign key: Foreign key in the relational model is defined as follows [DATE90]. Consider an attribute FK (possibly composite) of relation R1. This attribute is a foreign key if and only if the following properties are satisfied. (i) There is a relation R1 with primary key PK and the components of PK match with those of FK. (ii) Each value of FK either has all of its components null or all of its components nonnull. (iii) If the components of FK are nonnull for a tuple in R2, then the values of these components must match identically with the values for the corresponding components of PK for some tuple in R1. For example consider the relations employee and department. Department number may be the primary key in the department relation. However, department number may be an attribute in the employee relation to indicate the department that an employee works in. In this case, the department number in the employee relation could be a foreign key provided the conditions described above are satisfied.

Referential Integrity: The referential integrity rule states that there must be a matching primary key value for every foreign key value in the database.

We illustrate the essential points with the example relational database of figure 2-2. As stated earlier, the relation EMP has attributes SS#, Ename, Salary, and D#. DEPT has attributes D#, Dname, and Mgr. SS# is the primary key of EMP and D# is the primary key of DEPT. D# is a foreign key in DEPT. The integrity rules must ensure that each SS# in EMP and D# in DEPT is unique. Any D# value in EMP must be referenced in DEPT.

Application specific integrity constraints are those constraints that are specific to an application. Examples include "an employee's salary cannot decrease" and "no manager can manage more than two departments". Various techniques have been proposed to enforce application specific integrity constraints. For example, when the database is updated, these constraints are checked and the data is validated.

2.5.7   Database Security

In this section we focus on discretionary security. In section 2.6, we provide an overview of multilevel secure database management systems.

The major issues in security are authentication, identification, and enforcing appropriate access controls. For example, what are the mechanisms for identifying and authenticating the user? Will simple password mechanisms suffice? With respect to access control rules, languages such as SQL have incorporated GRANT and REVOKE statements to grant and revoke access to users. For many applications simple GRANT and REVOKE statements are not sufficient. There may be more complex authorizations based on database content. Negative authorizations may also be needed. Access to data based on the roles of the user is also being investigated.

Numerous papers have been published on discretionary security in databases. These can be found in various security related journals and conference proceedings (see, for example, [TING92, IFIP]).

2.5.8   Fault Tolerance

The previous two sections discussed database integrity and security. A closely related feature is fault tolerance. It is almost impossible to guarantee that the database will function as planned. In reality, various faults could occur. These could be hardware faults or software faults. As mentioned earlier, one of the major issues in transaction management is to ensure that the database is brought back to a consistent state in the presence of faults. The solutions proposed include maintaining appropriate log files to record the actions of a transaction in case its actions have to be retraced.

Another approach to handling faults is checkpointing. Various checkpoints are placed during the course of database processing. At each checkpoint it is ensured that the database is in a consistent state. Therefore, if a fault occurs during processing, then the database must be brought back to the last checkpoint. This way it can be guaranteed that the database is consistent. Closely associated with checkpointing is acceptance tests. After various processing steps, the acceptance tests are checked. If the techniques pass the tests, then they can proceed further.

Fault tolerance is becoming increasingly important for information survivability. This aspect will be discussed in section 2.10.

2.6 DATABASE ADMINISTRATION

A database has a database administrator (DBA). It is the responsibility of the DBA to define the various schemas and mappings. In addition, the functions of the administrator include auditing the database as well as implementing appropriate backup and recovery procedures.

The DBA could also be responsible for maintaining the security of the system. In some cases, security is maintained by the system security officer (SSO). The administrator should determine the granularity of the data for auditing. For example, in some cases there is tuple (or row) level auditing while in some other cases there is table (or relation) level auditing. It is also the administrator's responsibility to analyze the audit data.

Note that there is a difference between database administration and data administration. Database administration assumes that there is an installed database system. The DBA manages this system. Data administration functions include conducting data analysis, determining how a corporation handles its data, and enforcing appropriate policies and procedures for managing the data of a corporation. Data administration functions are carried out by the data administrator. For a discussion of data administration, we refer to [DOD94, DOD95, DOD96].

2.7 SOME OTHER TYPES OF DATABASE SYSTEMS

2.7.1 Overview

In section 2.1 we discussed five of the popular data models for both database management and database design. These are relational, object-oriented, object-relational, entity-relationship, and logic-based models. However, while some issues for object-oriented database systems were addressed, much of the discussion in this chapter has focused on relational database systems. In this section we first provide an overview of some of the other types of database systems. Then we select some of these systems and describe them in more detail.

Other database systems include multilevel secure database systems where the system manages a database in which the data are assigned different sensitivity levels. Real-time database systems are systems where the queries and transactions meet timing constraints. Parallel database systems are systems that exploit parallel architectures to process queries and transactions. Deductive databases systems are those based on logic as a data model. We discuss these four types of database systems in sections 2.7.2 to 2.7.5.

In addition to these systems, other database systems include high performance database systems, fault tolerance database systems, active database systems, temporal database systems, and multimedia database systems. Research is also being carried out on integrating two or more of these systems. For example, real-time database systems and active database systems are being integrated to produce active real-time database systems. We briefly describe some of these different kinds of database systems.

While real-time database systems are concerned with predictable execution, high performance database systems are concerned about fast processing. The goal is to execute as many transactions as possible within a certain period. Fault tolerant database systems must be resilient to faults and other errors in processing. Active database systems are systems which enforce triggers and certain actions are taken under certain conditions when certain events occur. An example rule is the following. If temperature of the water in the tank exceeds 100 degrees, then pour 5 gallons of water into the tank. This rule is triggered when the temperature of the water in the tank exceeds 100 degrees. The action to be taken is pour 5 gallons of water into the tank. Temporal database systems associate temporal information with the data. For example, these systems provide answers to queries such as "when did John work at company X"? They provide techniques to manage historical information. Multimedia database systems provide techniques for managing multimedia data such as voice, video, and text.[20] As mentioned in the previous paragraph, work is also being carried out on integrating different types of database systems. For example, active database systems are being integrated with real-time database systems. In this case, a possible rule is the following. When the temperature in the tank exceeds 100 degrees, then pour 5 gallons of water into the tank within 20 seconds.

Much research is being carried out on various types of database systems (see for example [SIGM90]). A discussion of all these systems is beyond the scope of this text. We provide an overview of multimedia database systems in chapter 6 as it relates more closely with the theme of this book and the framework we have provided.

In general, one integrates DBMS technology with a technology X and obtains X-DBMS. For example, technology X may be security technology, real time technology, high performance computing technology, or fault tolerant technology. This concept is illustrated in figure 2-17.

---

[20] Multimedia DBMSs is the subject of chapter 6.

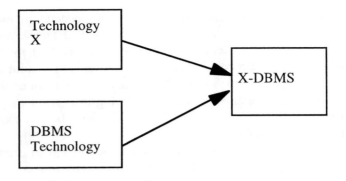

Figure 2-17. Integrating Technology X with DBMS

In sections 2.7.2-2.7.5 we discuss four types of database systems. One is multilevel secure database systems, the second is deductive database systems, the third is real-time database systems, and the fourth is parallel database systems. We chose these four systems as they are somewhat relevant to some of the discussions in this book. However, there are many other database systems that are equally important as the systems discussed here. Devoting a special section to each of these systems is beyond the scope of this book.

2.7.2   Multilevel Secure Database Systems

This section provides a brief overview of Multilevel Secure Database Management Systems (MLS/DBMSs). These systems have also been referred to as Trusted Database Management Systems. A summary of the developments in MLS/DBMSs is given in [THUR92b].

In an MLS/DBMS, users cleared at different security levels access and share a database with data at different security levels (also called sensitivity levels) without violating security. It is generally assumed that the security levels form a lattice where Unclassified < Confidential < Secret < TopSecret. An MLS/DBMS may also support users and data at different compartments or categories.[21]

The security policy of MLS/DBMSs include a policy for mandatory access control (MAC) and discretionary access control (DAC). Mandatory security controls restrict access to data depending on the

---

[21] Note that we have used the term MLS/DBMSs instead of multilevel secure database systems to be consistent with the terminology used in the literature. As in the case of database systems, a multilevel secure database system includes both an MLS/DBMS and a multilevel database. MLS/DBMS manages the multilevel database. Multilevel database is a database in which the data are assigned different security levels (or sensitivity levels).

sensitivity levels of the data and the clearance level of the user. In general, most MLS/DBMSs enforce a MAC policy where a subject reads an object (such as row or relation) if the subject's security level dominates the security level of the object and a subject updates an object if the subject's security level is that of the object. In other words a restricted form of the *-property of the Bell and LaPadula policy [BELL75] is enforced.[22] As mentioned in section 2.5.7, discretionary security measures are usually in the form of rules which specify the type of access that users or groups of users may have to different kinds of data. Other components of the security policy include policies for integrity, identification and authentication, auditing, and accounting. In general, security critical functions are performed by trusted processes. These processes must be verified to operate correctly.[23]

Research in MLS/DBMSs began with the work of Thomas Hinke and Marvin Schaefer in 1975 [HINK75]. Some early work was also done at The MITRE Corporation. For example, the Naval Surveillance System Model was developed [GRAU82]. Much of the work in MLS/DBMSs resulted as a consequence of the Air Force Summer Study in 1982 [AFSB83]. Since then, some early MLS/DBMS prototypes were developed at MITRE. Advanced research and development efforts such as SeaView [LUNT90] and Lock Data Views [STAC90] efforts began around 1986. Work on Trusted Database Interpretation was initiated around 1987. The first commercial products were available around 1988.

The Trusted Database Interpretation (TDI) [TDI91], which interprets the Trusted Computer Systems Evaluation Criteria (TCSEC) [TCSE85] for database systems, was published in 1991. The TCSEC defines a set of criteria for the classes C1, C2, B1, B2, B3, and A1 such that a system to be evaluated at a class should satisfy the criteria for that class. The TDI addresses issues on evaluating systems built by parts (or components). The TDI is now being used to evaluate commercial MLS/DBMS products.

MLS/DBMSs are less mature than operating systems. Different approaches have been proposed to develop an MLS/DBMS, and there is no one correct approach. For example, in one approach the operating system provides mandatory security and the DBMS runs at a single security level as an untrusted application, while in another

---

[22] The *-property states that a subject can write into an object if the level of the object is at or above the level of the subject.

[23] Note that the verification methods used will depend on the assurance expected from the system. For high assurance systems, formal verification techniques may be needed.

approach parts of the DBMS are trusted to provide mandatory security. Some prototypes and commercial products have been developed based on the various approaches. Various multilevel relational data models have been proposed (see, for example, [JAJO90]). While the majority of the MLS/DBMSs employ variations of the relational data model, there is also work on securing object-oriented database systems [THUR90a]. Some of the research challenges in MLS/DBMSs include the inference and aggregation problem. For example, the inference problem occurs when users pose sets of queries and deduce unauthorized information from the legitimate responses that they receive [THUR93a]. While the inference problem is in general unsolvable, solutions have been proposed to handle limited aspects of this problem.

Some of the major issues in multilevel database management include the following. In MLS/DBMSs, there is a finer level of granularity than in multilevel operating systems. For example, while the entities of classification for an operating system are in general files, in DBMSs they could be entire databases, relations, attributes, tuples, or even data elements. DBMSs are concerned with relationships between data. For example, data could be classified based on content, context, and time. DBMS integrity constraints often conflict with security. Concurrency control techniques, such as locking, designed for DBMSs cause covert channels for MLS/DBMSs.[24] Various concurrency control algorithms are being adapted for MLS/DBMSs [THUR93b].

Developments in MLS/DBMSs are following the developments in DBMSs fairly closely. There have been many developments in this field during the past two decades. Major database system vendors are now marketing MLS/DBMS products.

2.7.3   Deductive Database Systems

Deductive database systems have also been referred to as logic database systems. These are systems where the data model is based on the logic described in section 2.2.6. Deduction rules are used to make new inferences. This way all of the data need not be stored in the database. That is, with the deduction rules, one could infer additional data. Deductive database systems was a very popular topic in the 1980s [ULLM88]. Work in this area resulted mainly from developments in databases, artificial intelligence, and logic programming research [GALL78. LLOY87]. Although it seems that these systems

---

[24] Note that covert channels occur when malicious processes covertly send higher level information to lower level processes. For a detailed discussion we refer to [GASS88].

did not go beyond the prototype stage, the research on deductive and intelligent database systems has contributed to the developments in data mining to some extent. However, some applications of deductive database technology are given in [RAMA94].

Two of the architectures that have been examined by deductive database researchers are the loose coupling approach and the tight coupling approach (see, for example, [BROD86, SCHI89, DAS92]). With the loose coupling approach, the DBMS manages the database which is usually relational. The knowledge base consists of rules specified in a logic programming language such as Prolog [KOWA74]. The knowledge base management system (KBMS) manages the knowledge base. The inference engine component of the KBMS examines the rules and makes deductions. The DBMS is accessed to retrieve data. In the tight coupling approach, there is no separation between the DBMS and the KBMS. That is, a module that integrates the functions of a KBMS and a DBMS manages the knowledge base which now consists of both the database and the rules. The architectures are illustrated in figures 2-18 and 2-19.

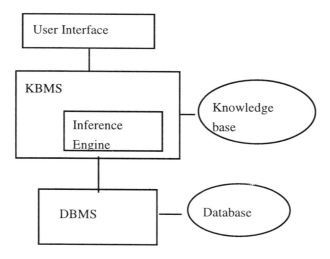

Figure 2-18. Loose Coupling Architecture

We illustrate the concepts with a simple example which has been used in numerous cases. Suppose the database consists of the FATHER relation and there is a rule in the rule base that the father of a father is a grandfather. If the query is to retrieve all the (grandfather, grandchild) pairs, then the inference engine will examine this rule, query the database to get all pairs (X, Y) such that there is a Z where (X, Z) and (Z, Y) are in the FATHER relation. The resulting pairs (X, Y) is the response. Note that in this example, one does not have to explicitly store the relation GRANDFATHER in the database.

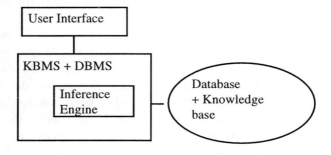

Figure 2-19. Tight Coupling Architecture

2.7.4   Real-time Database Systems

A real-time database management (RTDBMS) system integrates techniques from both DBMSs and real-time operating systems. In RTDBMSs, the data has to have temporal validity. That is, the data may be valid only for a certain time period. In such systems, queries and transactions have to meet timing constraints. Therefore, transactions are assigned priorities and special scheduling algorithms are needed to ensure that the high priority transactions meet the deadlines.[25]

We discuss some of the issues in incorporating timing constraints into real-time transactions. For example, transactions could be assigned priority levels based on their deadlines. That is, a transaction that has a short deadline may have higher priority. The challenge here is resource contention. Suppose there are two transactions T1 and T2. Let T1 have a priority higher than that of T2. Suppose T2 has a lock on an object and now T1 requires a lock on the same object. If T1 does not get the lock, then it may miss the deadline. So, one of the solutions is for T2 to abort and for T1 to get the lock. Another solution is for T2 to inherit the priority of T1 and continue execution hoping that it can finish its job faster so that T1 can have the lock sooner. Numerous concurrency control protocols have been developed for RTDBMSs. However, it is only recently that attempts

---

[25] We are finding that real-time database management is important for command and control applications [BENS95]. For an overview of real-time database management we refer to [RAMA93]. A detailed treatment of real-time database management is beyond the scope of this book. Some concepts in real-time DBMSs are being used in multimedia DBMSs. For example, real-time processing techniques are being applied for the synchronous display of multimedia data such as video and audio. Some of the issues are discussed in chapter 6.

are being made to transfer research to operational systems. There are very few commercial RTDBMS products.

2.7.5   Parallel Database Systems

In a parallel database system, the various operations and functions are executed in parallel. While research on parallel database systems began in the 1970s, it is only recently that we are seeing these systems being used for commercial applications. This is partly due to the explosion of data warehousing and data mining technologies where performance of query algorithms is critical.

Let us consider a query operation which involves a join operation between two relations. If these relations are to be sorted first before the join, then the sorting can be done in parallel. We can take it a step further and execute a single join operation with multiple processors. Note that multiple tuples are involved in a join operation from both relations. Join operations between the tuples may be executed in parallel.[26]

Many of the commercial database system vendors are now marketing parallel database management technology. This is an area we can expect to grow significantly over the next decade. One of the major challenges here is the scalability of various algorithms for functions such as data warehousing and data mining.

2.8   COMPONENT INTEGRATION FOR DATABASE MANAGEMENT SYSTEMS

The recent trends in database management systems design and development include the use of component software for designing various functional modules. For example, consider the functional modules illustrated in figure 2-11. Various commercial products take an all or nothing approach. That is, when we buy a database management system, we get most of the functions. For many applications, we may not need all the modules. For example, one may not need transaction processing for analytical applications.

The idea behind component integration is to put together a system from existing components. Some early work was carried out under the DARPA (Defense Advanced Research Projects Agency) funded initiative called Open OODB and carried out by Texas Instruments [THOM92]. The idea here is that vendors take an all or nothing approach. That is, you get the entire system or none at all. What is needed is a flexible system based on components. This means that the various components, such as query processor and

---

[26]   For a discussion of parallel database management, we refer to [IEEE89].

transaction manager, could be developed by different vendors. A customer gets these components and puts them together. This means that the components have to meet well defined interfaces. This approach is illustrated in Figure 2-20.

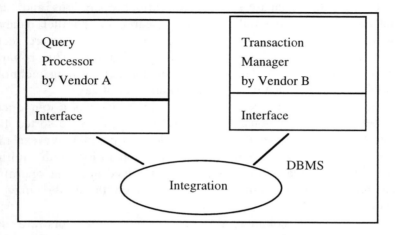

Figure 2-20. Component Integration for Database Management

With the increasing popularity of the Internet and distributed object management technology, it appears that this approach to designing database systems will become a reality. We discuss some of the issues in chapters 4, 5, and 10. Various presentations on this topic have also been given at the Object World conferences (see, for example, [OW96]).

2.9 STEPS TO DATA MANAGEMENT: FROM CONCEPT TO IMPLEMENTATION

Now that we have described some of the major features of database systems technology and provided an overview of the various types of database systems, we will next discuss some essential steps toward installing an operational database system for an enterprise. In particular, the steps from concept to implementation are discussed.

The very first step that has to be carried out is data analysis. An organization has to determine what its data is. That is, the data has to be defined and possibly grouped. An enterprise model representing the data and also the functions has to be developed. This process is an iterative process. That is, the model may have to be revised as more data is identified. Analyzing the quality of the data is also an integral part of this process.

Once an enterprise model is developed, the next step is to determine the approaches to implementing this model. For example, answers to the following questions are needed. What is the infrastructure? What type of data manager should be used? What is the relationship between the infrastructure and the data manager?

If it is determined that some form of data manager is needed, then should it be a database management system or should it be some type of file system to store and manage the data? If it is a database management system, the next step is to refine the enterprise model and develop a data model to capture the data part. At the high level, the data model could be based on some semantic data model.

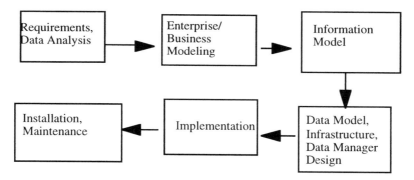

Figure 2-21. From Concept to Implementation

The next step is to determine the type of database management system to be used. This would involve developing a data model specific to the system, identifying the schemas, designing the database, and populating the database. The database management system could be based on a commercial product or it could be home grown, depending on the requirements. The final step is to install the system, develop plans for maintaining the system, and also determine approaches to evolve the system as the requirements evolve.

In order to carry out these steps, the cooperation of several individuals are needed. First of all management commitment and support are essential. Then the application specialist, data administrator, and enterprise modeler have to communicate to carry out the tasks of application design, data analysis, and enterprise modeling. The database administrator, database designer, and database system designer are brought in to design the entire system as well as to conduct data modeling. Finally, the implementors are brought in to develop and install the system.

Figure 2-21 illustrates the steps outlined here. Note that we have discussed only the high level ideas. Details on conducting data analysis as well as designing the database and system are discussed in various texts. Some examples are given in [DMH94, DMH95, DMH96].

2.10 DATABASE SYSTEMS SURVIVABILITY

Much of the discussion in this book is focused on data management technologies for managing the explosion of data and information. That is, techniques for querying the databases, updating the database, and managing the metadata for the databases, as well as maintaining the security and integrity of operations, are discussed.

Another key aspect to information technology is information survivability. That is, the information and data in the databases may not be accurate. They may be incomplete. More importantly, they may be subject to attacks and intrusions. Finally, there may be various faults occurring both externally and internally to the system. In the midst of all these problems, the information has to survive and be preserved in a manner so that users get timely and accurate information that they are authorized to know.

Information survivability is gaining a lot of interest during the recent years [BABA96]. Several technologies have to be integrated to provide coherent techniques for information survivability. Some critical technologies are security, real-time processing, and fault tolerance. Security technology ensures that users get authorized information. However, in the presence of faults, it may not be possible to get accurate information. Therefore fault tolerance techniques integrated with security techniques must ensure that information security is preserved in the midst of system failures. Real-time processing techniques must ensure that the information is brought to the user in a timely manner in the midst of faults and intrusions.

Database systems that integrate security, real-time, and fault tolerance processing techniques will play a critical role in information survivability. While this chapter has focused only on the individual technologies such as database security, database integrity, database fault tolerance, and real-time database systems, integrating all of these features for database management is a major challenge and this challenge must be addressed if we want to ensure information survivability.

CHAPTER 3

CONCEPTS IN DISTRIBUTED DATABASE SYSTEMS

3.1 OVERVIEW

Chapter 2 described concepts in database systems with some emphasis on relational database systems. During the mid-1970s focus shifted toward distributed database systems. This was partly due to the developments in computer networking technology. It was felt that many applications would be distributed in the future. This chapter describes concepts in distributed database systems.

Although many definitions of a distributed database system have been given, there is no standard definition. Our discussion of distributed database system concepts and issues has been influenced by the discussion in [CERI84]. A distributed database system includes a distributed database management system (DDBMS), a distributed database, and a network for interconnection. The DDBMS manages the distributed database. A distributed database is data that is distributed across multiple databases. Figure 3-1 illustrates a distributed database system. As illustrated, each node (which can be regarded to be a machine or a system) has a database attached to it. The various nodes are connected through a network. We will revisit this definition of a distributed database system when we discuss our choice architecture in section 3.2.2.

Distributed database system functions include distributed query management, distributed transaction processing, distributed metadata management, and enforcing security and integrity across the multiple nodes. This chapter provides an overview of distributed database system concepts. Section 3.2 describes architectural issues as well as our choice architecture. Distributed database design is discussed in section 3.3. Query processing, transaction management, replication issues, metadata management, integrity, and security are discussed in sections 3.4, 3.5, 3.6, 3.7, 3.8, and 3.9, respectively. Distributed database administration issues are discussed in section 3.10. A note on other types of distributed database systems such as distributed object-oriented database systems is given in section 3.11. Distributed database management for mobile applications is the subject of section 3.12. We discuss this to show how some of the concepts illustrated in the previous sections could be applied to real-world situations. Finally, some networking issues for distributed databases are given in section

3.13.[27] Numerous articles have been published on distributed database management systems. These include the work reported in [CERI84, BELL92, RAM89, OSZU91, and THUR93c].

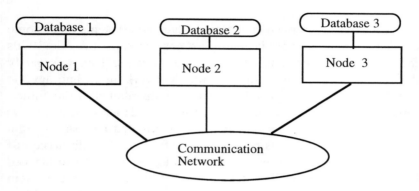

Figure 3-1. Distributed Architecture

It should be pointed out that distributed database systems are useful if the application requires that the database be distributed. For example, many corporations now have multiple sites. Centralizing the employee records for such corporations may cause performance bottlenecks. Therefore records belonging to a site may be stored in a local database at that site. The distributed database is then a collection of the local databases. In contrast, in a heterogeneous database environment, the assumption is that multiple heterogeneous databases already exist and these databases need to interoperate with each other. Heterogeneous database systems is the subject of chapter 4. While there may be more real-world examples that require heterogeneous database integration, distributed databases for homogeneous environments also have some applications. We briefly discuss one such application in section 3.12.

3.2 ARCHITECTURAL ISSUES

3.2.1 Alternatives
There are various architectural alternatives for a distributed database system. Figure 3-2 illustrates an architecture where there is central control. Figures 3-3 and 3-4 illustrate architectures with distributed control. Figure 3-3 takes a multi-database approach. In

---

[27] Networking is an integral part of distributed database systems. However, a detailed discussion of networks is beyond the scope of this book. For details we refer to [TANN90]. We briefly address networking issues in section 3.13.

this approach each database is managed by a local DBMS. These DBMSs are connected through a communication network. Figure 3-4 takes a non-multidatabase approach. In this approach there are no local DBMSs.

Multidatabase architectures have been studied extensively in the literature. They can be grouped according to whether they are based on tightly coupled or loosely coupled approaches. An orthogonal method is to group the multidatabase systems depending on whether they are based on homogeneous or heterogeneous architectures.

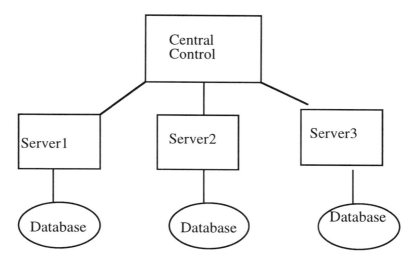

Figure 3-2. Centralized Control and Distributed Data

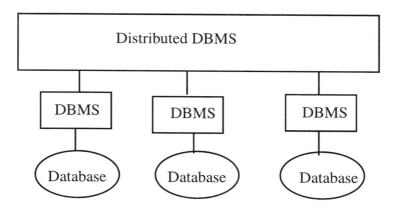

Figure 3-3. Distributed Control and Distributed Data - Multidatabase

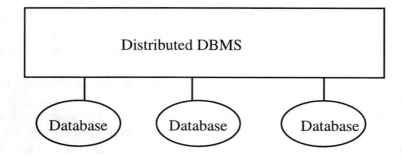

Figure 3-4. Distributed Control and Distributed Data - Nonmultidatabase

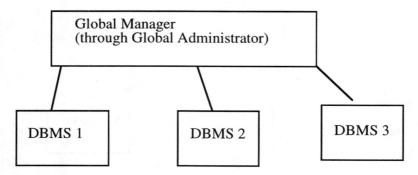

Figure 3-5. Tightly-Coupled Architecture

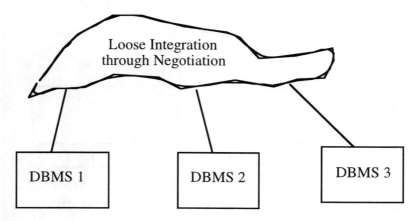

Figure 3-6. Loosely-Coupled Architecture

A distributed architecture, such as the one illustrated in Figure 3-3, could be tightly integrated in which case there is usually a global administrator or it could be loosely integrated in which case there is no global administrator. In a loosely-coupled architecture, the individual DBMSs may have more autonomy than those in a tightly coupled architecture. Whether an architecture is tightly

coupled or loosely coupled, the individual DBMSs could form a
federation. Such a system is called a federated database system.
Figure 3-5 provides a view of a tightly-coupled approach where
there is a global administrator Figure 3-6 provides a view where
there is no global administrator. Figure 3-7 illustrates a federated
database system.

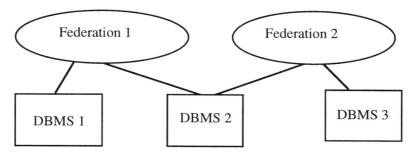

Figure 3-7. Federated Architecture (either Loose or Tight)

In a homogeneous distributed database system based on the
multidatabase approach, one generally assumes that the local
DBMSs are designed and operated identically. In a heterogeneous
environment, the local DBMSs may be different. Note that while
this chapter focuses on a homogeneous environment, Chapter 4
focuses on a heterogeneous environment.

3.2.2   Choice Architecture

Our choice architecture for a distributed database system is the
multidatabase architecture which is tightly coupled. This architecture, which was illustrated in figure 3-3, is elaborated in figure 3-8.
We have chosen such an architecture as we can explain the
concepts for both homogeneous and heterogeneous systems based
on this approach. In this architecture, the nodes are connected via
a communication subsystem. Furthermore, as illustrated in figure
3-9, each node has its own local DBMS which is capable of handling the local applications. In addition, each node is also involved
in at least one global application. That is, there is no centralized
control in this architecture. As shown in figure 3-8, the DBMSs are
connected through a component called the Distributed Processor
(DP). Furthermore, for the discussions in this chapter we assume
that the local DBMSs are homogeneous. In chapter 4 we discuss
heterogeneous database management systems based on such an
architecture. Federation issues are also addressed in chapter 4.

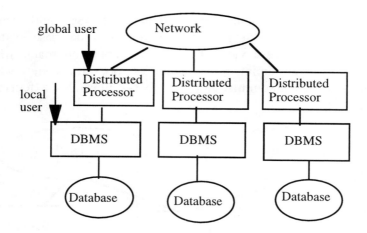

Figure 3-8. An Architecture for a DDBMS

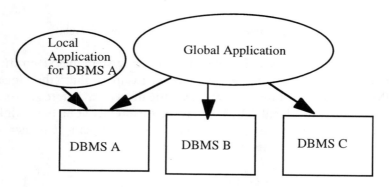

Figure 3-9. Global/Local Applications

Let us revisit the definition of a DDBMS given in section 3.1. Based on the choice architecture, a DDBMS consists of the local DBMS and the DP. The DP is a critical component of the DDBMS. It is this module that connects the different local DBMSs. That is, each local DBMS is augmented by a DP. The modules of the DP are illustrated in figure 3-10. The components are: the Distributed Metadata Manager (DMM), the Distributed Query Processor (DQP), the Distributed Transaction Manager (DTM), the Distributed Security Manager (DSP), and the Distributed Integrity Manager (DIM). DMM manages the global metadata. The global metadata includes information on the schemas which describe the relations in the distributed database, the way the relations are fragmented, the locations of the fragments, and the constraints enforced. DQP is responsible for distributed query processing; DTM is responsible for distributed transaction management; DSM is responsible for enforcing global security constraints; and DIM is responsible for maintaining integrity at the global level.

The DQP, DTM, DSM, and DIM communicate with the DMM for the metadata required to carry out their functions. The DSM and DIM also communicate with the DQP and the DTM as they process security and integrity constraints during query, update, and transaction execution. In our design of the DP we do not have a separate module for update processing. We assume that individual update requests are handled by the DQP. Update requests specified as part of a transaction are handled by the DTM. Since a transaction is a series of query and update requests, we assume that the DQP is invoked by the DTM in order to carry out the individual requests.

Note that the modules of DP communicate with their peers at the remote nodes. For example, the DQP at node 1 communicates with the DQP at node 2 for handling distributed queries. This is illustrated in figure 3-11. As stated earlier, throughout this chapter we have assumed that the local DBMSs are identical. That is, the DDBMS operates in a homogeneous environment.

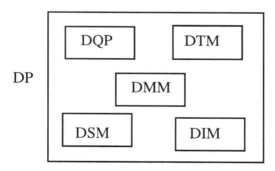

Figure 3-10. Modules of DP

Figure 3-11. Peer-to-Peer Communication

3.3 DISTRIBUTED DATABASE DESIGN

Designing a distributed database includes several steps. These steps are elaborated in [CERI84]. First of all, one needs to determine the schema at the global level. For example, the entire distributed database is viewed as a single entity and the schemas are designed. In the case of a relational system, the schemas would describe the relations and attributes. The next step is to design the fragments. For example, in the case of a relational database, the fragments could partition a relation horizontally or vertically or both. The third step is to allocate the fragments to the various sites. It is at this stage that one determines whether the fragments are replicated or not. Then the last stage is to develop mappings between the global schema and the local schemas utilized by the databases. That is, if the global model is different to the local models, then appropriate mappings have to be developed. In a

SITE 1

EMP1

SS#	Name	Salary	D#
1	John2	0	10
2	Paul	30	20
3	James	40	20
4	Jill	50	20
5	Mary	60	10
6	Jane	70	20

DEPT1

D#	Dname	MGR
10	C. Sci.	Jane
30	English	David
40	French	Peter

SITE 2

EMP2

SS#	Name	Salary	D#
9	Mathew	70	50
7	David	80	30
8	Peter	90	40

DEPT2

D#	Dname	MGR
50	Math	John
20	Physics	Paul

Figure 3-12. Horizontal Fragmentation of a Distributed Database

homogeneous environment, since we assume that all the local DBMSs are identical, it is more meaningful to have global schemas utilizing the same representation model as the local systems. Finally the physical schemas for the local DBMSs are designed.

A distributed database stored at two sites is illustrated in figure 3-12. Figure 3-13 illustrates the global view that the users have of the database. So, in designing the distributed database, one first designs the global schema for the global view in figure 3-13. Then the fragments are determined. The third step is to assign the fragments to the two sites. The fourth step is to provide mappings. Since we assume that both models are relational (i.e., the global and local data models), there are no mappings in this case. The fifth step is to design the physical schemas for the two sites.

EMP

SS#	Name	Salary	D#
1	John2	0	10
2	Paul	30	20
3	James	40	20
4	Jill	50	20
5	Mary	60	10
6	Jane	70	20
9	Mathew	70	50
7	David	80	30
8	Peter	90	40

DEPT

D#	Dname	MGR
10	C. Sci.	Jane
30	English	David
40	French	Peter
50	Math	John
20	Physics	Paul

Figure 3-13. Global Views of relations EMP and DEPT

3.4 QUERY PROCESSING

There are two aspects to query processing in a DDBMS. They are: query transformation and query optimization. The query transformation process transforms a global query into equivalent fragment queries. This process is performed according to transformation rules and does not depend on the allocation of the fragments. In chapter 2 we discussed some rules for query transformation in a centralized system. Additional rules for query transformation have been formulated for distributed database systems to take into account the horizontal and vertical fragmentation.

While query transformation focuses on modifying a query at the logical level, the query optimization process optimizes the query with respect to the cost of executing the query. That is, the alternate execution strategies produced by the query transformation process must be examined by the query optimizer in terms of the cost of executing them. The cost is usually determined by the number of tuples that are transmitted and the number of join or semi-join[28] operations that have to be performed.

---

[28] A discussion of semi-join operation is given in [CERI84].

Figure 3-14 illustrates query processing in a homogeneous distributed environment. In this example, three relational database systems are connected and the employee and department relations are fragmented. As can be seen in this figure, site 1 has 20 employee tuples, site 2 has 30 employee tuples and 20 department tuples, and site 3 has 50 employee tuples and 30 department tuples. The 20 employee tuples at site 1 are also replicated at site 3. The query is to perform a join operation between employee and department relations and is posed from site 1. Since site 3 has the most number of tuples, the fragments are transferred to site 3 and the join is performed there. The result is sent back to site 1. Note that in many cases, multiple query execution strategies are examined and the one with the least cost is generally selected for execution. The cost is determined in terms of the number of tuples to be transferred from one site to another. Significant developments have been made in generating query execution strategies in homogeneous distributed environments.

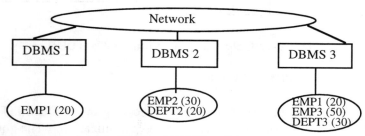

Query at site 1: Join EMP and DEPT on D#

Move EMP2 to site 3; merge EMP1, EMP2, EMP3 to form EMP
Move DEPT2 to site 3; merge DEPT2 and DEPT3 to form DEPT
Join EMP and DEPT; move result to site 1

Challenges: Transferring data between sites may not be possible; query optimization techniques

Figure 3-14. Query Processing

3.5 TRANSACTION MANAGEMENT

3.5.1 Overview

Transaction management in a DDBMS involves the handling of distributed transactions. By a distributed transaction we mean a transaction which executes at multiple sites. The portion of the transaction which executes at a particular site is a subtransaction associated with that site. A coordinator controls the execution of the subtransactions.

Two types of log files are maintained at each node; one is the local log file which records the subtransaction execution and the other is the global file which records the actions of the coordinator of all of the subtransactions. When a transaction commits, either all of the local subtransactions must commit or none should commit in which case the transaction aborts. The technique used to ensure this requirement is the two-phase commit protocol.

As stated in chapter 2, if transactions are executed serially, then there will be a performance bottleneck. Therefore, transactions usually execute concurrently. As a result, it must be ensured that the multiple transactions maintain the consistency of the distributed database. Concurrency control techniques ensure the consistency of the distributed database when transactions execute concurrently. There are additional problems in a DDBMS because of the replication of files. It has to be ensured that all of the copies of a file are consistent. The techniques of locking, time-stamping, and validation have been proposed for concurrency control in a DDBMS. An additional problem of transaction management in a distributed environment is ensuring the consistency of the data in the presence of network partitions. Network partitions occur when certain nodes and/or links fail.

We will first describe the various concurrency control techniques used in a DDBMS and then discuss the recovery and reliability issues.

3.5.2   Concurrency Control

In order to ensure consistency, the transaction has to be serializable. Conditions have been formulated for distributed transactions. Furthermore, concurrency control techniques such as locking, time-stamping, and validation methods have been extended for distributed transactions. We discuss some of the essential points.

Distributed Locking: In a distributed environment, due to multiple copies of the data, it may be necessary to obtain locks on more than one copy. Three of the schemes to obtain locks are the following.

- Exclusive locks are obtained for all copies of the data item. Shared locks are obtained for only one copy.
- Both shared and exclusive locks are obtained for a majority of copies of the data item.
- Only the primary copy of the data item is locked.

As in a centralized system, locking can cause deadlocks. Various techniques have been proposed to detect and prevent deadlocks in a DDBMS.

Distributed Time-stamping: In a distributed database system there are some additional considerations for the time-stamping algorithm discussed in chapter 2. For example, the time-stamps assigned to the transactions are global time-stamps. Since it is difficult to keep the system clocks at each node synchronized, other techniques to assign global time stamps have been devised.

Distributed Validation: In the validation technique, each local transaction is validated first. During this validation certain checks are performed. If it does not pass the validation test, the subtransaction is aborted. This in turn will cause the global transaction to be aborted. If a subtransaction passes the validation test, then it enters a global validation phase. If it fails the global validation, then it is aborted. Otherwise, a message is sent to the coordinator that it has passed the global validation. If all the subtransactions have passed the global validation, then the transaction is committed.

3.5.3 Recovery

A popular recovery technique for distributed transaction is the two-phase commit protocol. In this protocol, one site (usually the site of origin) acts as the coordinator, and other sites where the transaction executes act as participants. The coordinator as well as the participants maintain log records and write all their actions on the records. First the coordinator sends a message to the participants to prepare to commit. Each participant sends a message to the coordinator as to whether it is ready to commit. If all of the participants have answered positively, then the coordinator sends a commit message to all participants. Otherwise, the coordinator sends an abort message to the participants. If a participant receives a commit message, then the subtransaction at that site is committed. If an abort message is received, the subtransaction is aborted.

Figure 3-15 illustrates transaction processing in a distributed environment. The coordinating site, which may or may not be the site at which the transaction request was issued, sends the request to the participating sites for the subtransactions to execute. The transaction is committed according to a protocol. In the case of the two-phase commit protocol, the coordinator queries the participants as to whether they are ready to commit. If all participants agree, then the coordinator sends a request for the participants to commit.

While significant developments have been made in distributed transaction processing, and commercial products are now available, there are still some issues in ensuring the consistency of replicated copies, handling a large number of sites, and developing commit protocols to handle network and site failures. The two-phase commit protocol has been extended (e.g., three-phase commit, voting protocols) to accommodate various types of failures such as site failures and network partitions. Details are given in [CERI84].

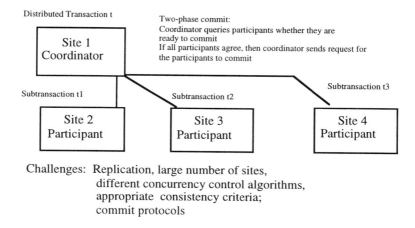

Distributed Transaction t

Site 1
Coordinator

Two-phase commit:
Coordinator queries participants whether they are ready to commit
If all participants agree, then coordinator sends request for the participants to commit

Subtransaction t1

Subtransaction t2

Subtransaction t3

Site 2
Participant

Site 3
Participant

Site 4
Participant

Challenges: Replication, large number of sites,
             different concurrency control algorithms,
             appropriate consistency criteria;
             commit protocols

Figure 3-15. Transaction Processing

3.6 REPLICATION

Replication technology is becoming a major area in distributed database systems. Commercial database system vendors are providing support for handling replication. Simply stated, the database relations are often replicated across the different sites. Replication is needed for availability. For example, if a remote site is down, then the relations at that site cannot be accessed. So, the relation may be replicated at multiple sites. The issue is whether to replicate all of the relations or some of the relations.

If the relations are replicated, then the copies have to be kept in a consistent state when the database is updated. Numerous strategies have been proposed to handle replication. One strategy is to do the update in the master copy and then the master server will propagate the updates to the other copies. With this approach, there might be inconsistency for a certain period. Another approach is to lock all the copies until all of them are updated. With this approach, while consistency is maintained, it may take some time to update all the copies. The solution adopted will depend on the application requirements to a great extent.

3.7 METADATA MANAGEMENT

Metadata in a distributed environment includes information about the relations, fragmentation of the relations, allocation of the relations, and the local schema information. It is usually maintained at two levels. One is the global metadata and the other is the local metadata. Local metadata is the metadata associated with the local DBMS. We only discuss the global metadata here.

The global metadata includes information on the global schema, fragmentation schema, allocation schema, and all the mappings. These schemas are used for the various DDBMS functions such as query processing and transaction management. Constraints such as global integrity constraints and security constraints are also part of the metadata. In addition to the schema and constraint information, the metadatabase may also contain information on statistics of the database. The statistics include profiles of the database, access patterns, and history information.

As in the case of the centralized database system discussed in chapter 2, efficient strategies for querying and updating the metadatabase are needed. In addition, in the case of a DDBMS, distributing the metadata is also an issue. For example should the metadata be replicated, partially replicated, or not replicated at all?

For many applications, the distributed environment is becoming more and more complex. For example, with respect to Internet database management, metadata may include the various policies and procedures as well as information about the resources in the network. Metadata may also be used to guide the navigation/browsing process. That is, the metadata here may be dynamic with information about the user's browsing patterns. Metdata may also include repository information needed to develop a global schema of the entire distributed system. That is, the various local schemas may have to be integrated to provide a global schema for the users. Since metadata is a critical technology, we have discussed its role in many of the chapters in this book.

3.8 INTEGRITY

As stated in chapter 2, there are various types of integrity enforcement mechanisms. These include traditional database integrity techniques such as concurrency control, recovery, and enforcing application independent and application specific integrity constraints. Integrity mechanisms also include techniques for determining the quality of the data. In this section, we focus on enforcing integrity constraints in a distributed environment.

Integrity issues in a DDBMS include enforcing integrity constraints across multiple DBMSs. For example, consider the relational database of figure 2-2. In this example, the EMP relation could be at site 1 and the DEPT relation could be at site 2. If referential integrity is to be maintained, then when a D# value is inserted into EMP, the system must query the remote DBMS to ensure that the D# value is referenced in DEPT. In the case of ensuring the uniqueness of primary keys, if a relation is horizontally fragmented across the sites (for example, some of the tuples of the EMP relation could be at site 1 and the rest could be at site 2), then when a tuple is inserted into a fragment, the remote DBMS must be queried as to whether a tuple with the same primary key already exists.

In the case of application specific integrity constraints, they could be enforced across the multiple databases. For example, consider the constraint "the total salary of the employees cannot exceed two million". If the relation EMP is fragmented, then whenever an employee tuple is entered, the remote DBMSs must be queried to obtain the salaries of the employees. Another issue with application specific constraints is distribution. That is, should the constraints be distributed across sites, should they be replicated, or should they be stored in one location? One could treat the application specific integrity constraints as part of the metadata and therefore the approach taken to store the metadata could be used for such constraints.

3.9 SECURITY

3.9.1   Discretionary Security

Security controls must ensure that users access only authorized information. These include discretionary security as well as multilevel security controls. Discretionary security mechanisms enforce rules which specify the types of access that users or groups of users have to the data. Multilevel security controls ensure that users cleared at different security levels access and share a distributed database in which the data are assigned different sensitivity levels without compromising security. In this section we describe both types of security.

In a distributed environment, users need to be authenticated with respect to the local system as well as the global environment. An issue here is whether the authentication mechanism should be centralized or distributed. If it is centralized, then the authenticator needs to have information about all of the users of the system. If the authenticator is distributed, then the various components of the authenticator need to communicate with each other to authenticate a user.

The access control rules enforced in a distributed environment may be distributed, centralized, or replicated. If the rules are centralized, then the central server needs to check all accesses to the database. If the rules are distributed, then appropriate rules need to be located and enforced for a particular access. Often the rules associated with a particular database may also be stored at the same site. If the rules are replicated, then each node can carry out the access control checks for the data that it manages.

3.9.2   Multilevel Security

As described in [THUR91], in a multilevel secure distributed database management system (MLS/DDBMS), users cleared at different security levels access and share a distributed database consisting of data at different security levels without violating security.[29] A system architecture for an MLS/DDBMS is shown in figure 3-16. This architecture has been derived from the architecture for a DDBMS (given in figure 3-3). In this architecture, the MLS/DDBMS consists of several nodes that are interconnected by a multilevel secure network.[30] In a homogeneous environment, all of the nodes are designed identically. Each node is capable of handling multilevel data. Each node has an MLS/DBMS which manages the local multilevel database. Each node also has a distributed processing component called the Secure Distributed Processor (SDP).

The modules of the SDP, illustrated in figure 3-17, are similar to those of the DP described in section 3.2. These modules are the Secure Distributed Query Processor (SDQP), the Secure Distributed Transaction Manager (SDTM), the Secure Distributed Metadata Manager (SDMM), the Secure Distributed Security Manager (SDSM), and the Secure Distributed Integrity Manager (SDIM).

---

[29]   To be consistent with the terminology, a multilevel secure distributed database system includes a MLS/DDBMS and a multilevel distributed database.

MLS/DDBMS manages the multilevel distributed database.

[30]   For a discussion on multilevel secure networks we refer to the Trusted Network Interpretation [TNI87].

Multilevel security must be taken into consideration during all of the processing. Some of the issues are described below. A more detailed discussion of multilevel security in distributed database systems can be found in [THUR91].

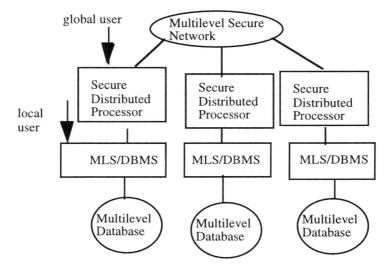

Figure 3-16. System Architecture for a MLS/DDBMS

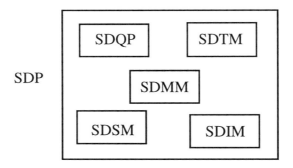

Figure 3-17. Modules of the Secure Distributed Processor

First of all, an appropriate security policy has to be formulated. This policy will depend on the policies of the local DBMS, the network, and the distributed processor. The algorithms for query, update, and transaction processing in a DDBMS have to be extended to handle multilevel security. As stated in chapter 2, locking techniques could cause covert channels. Therefore, algorithms for MLS/DBMSs have to be integrated with algorithms for DDBMSs to handle MLS/DDBMSs. These algorithms are implemented by the SDTM. Finally, security and integrity processing techniques for MLS/DBMSs and DDBMSs have to be extended for MLS/DDBMSs. For example, in the case of the SDSM, it has to consider multilevel security in its functions such as identification, authentication, and enforcing discretionary security controls.

3.10 ADMINISTRATION ISSUES

Administering a distributed database management system is a challenge. Since the idea here is that a global database is distributed across multiple nodes, there must be a global administrator for the system. Each of the local databases may have its own administrator. The global administrator must coordinate the administration of the local databases with the local administrators. Administration functions include creating and deleting the databases, performing security functions such as auditing the databases, integrating the schemas to provide a global view, enforcing various policies, and performing appropriate backup and recovery procedures. The administrator should also determine how the relations are fragmented, replication of the data, and many other features such as enforcing integrity and security constraints as well as defining standards.

Sharing of the functions between the global administrator and local administrators is usually done on a case by case basis. That is, there is no standard way to allocate the responsibilities of database administration. It depends on the application which utilizes the distributed database system as well as on the administrators. While much of the work in distributed database systems has focused on developing technology, it is only recently that administration issues are being given serious consideration. This may be due to the fact that operational distributed database systems are not quite mature.

3.11 OTHER TYPES OF DISTRIBUTED DATABASE SYSTEMS

3.11.1 Overview

In chapter 2, in addition to relational database systems, we described various other types of database systems. These included object-oriented database systems, deductive database systems, real-time database systems, and parallel database systems. There is research on extending these systems to distributed environments. Many of the issues for DDBMSs based on relational systems have to be handled for these new generation systems. In section 3.11.2, we discuss distributed object-oriented database systems. Distribution issues for multimedia database systems will be discussed in chapter 6. In this section we provide a brief overview of some other types of distributed database systems.

Consider the case of distributed deductive database systems where the logic database may be distributed across sites. The inference engine (the module that is responsible for making deductions) has to access the rules (or logic clauses) across the various sites and make deductions. For example, a parent-child relation may be distributed across multiple sites. The fact that X is the parent of Y may be at site A while the fact that Y is the parent of Z may be at site B. If the query is to extract all the (grandparent, grandchild) pairs, then the inference engine has to access both sites and deduce that X is the grandparent of Z. There are similar issues for distributed active database systems where the rules may be distributed across sites. When an event occurs, the rules are triggered and certain actions may be taken. In the case of distributed real-time database systems, the distributed concurrency control algorithms as well as the commit protocols have to take timing constraints into consideration.

A discussion of all types of distributed database systems and the issues involved are beyond the scope of this book.

3.11.2   Distributed Object-Oriented Database Systems

Much of the previous discussions have focused on distributed relational database systems. While relational database systems are becoming common practice, since object-oriented database systems are now commercially available, distributed object-oriented database systems need to be given some consideration.

A distributed object-oriented database system includes a distributed object-oriented database management system (DOODBMS) and a distributed object-oriented database. A DOODBMS manages a collection of object-oriented databases.[31] That is, an object-oriented database is distributed for the reasons we have described earlier. The functions discussed for distributed relational database management systems have to be developed for distributed object-oriented database management systems also. These include data distribution, query processing, transaction

---

[31]   Note that we differentiate a DOODBMS from a distributed object management system (DOMS). A DOODBMS manages a distributed database which is based on the object-oriented model, while a DOMS integrates various components by encapsulating them as objects. Note that OMG's CORBA is an example of a DOMS.

management, metadata management, integrity, and security, as well as administration. These functions manipulate objects and not relations.

Distributing objects is still a research issue. For example, can a class be stored at one node and its subclasses be stored at another node? Should all of the instances of a class be stored at one node or could they be distributed? How are relationships between objects stored and distributed? Can an object be stored at one node and its components (in the case of an aggregate object) be stored at another node? These are some of the questions that need to be answered before designing a distributed object-oriented database management system. Figure 3-18 illustrates a situation where some employee objects are stored at one node while some others are stored at another node.

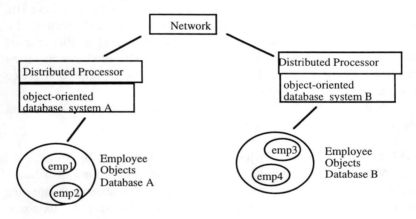

Figure 3-18. Distributed Object-Oriented Database Management System

3.12   DISTRIBUTED DATABASE SUPPORT FOR MOBILE COMPUTING APPLICATIONS

Some investigations have been reported on distributed data-bases issues for mobile computing applications (see, for example, [IMIE92]). In this section we discuss some of the issues to illustrate how the various concepts described in the previous sections could be utilized.

In a mobile computing environment, it is assumed that the users could be traveling across different sites with each user carrying a personal computer (PC). The network that connects the different users' PCs is a wireless network. However there may be base stations that connect the different users. That is, each user may be attached to a base station. There is communication between the base stations. As a user moves from one site to another, the base station that he is attached to may change. Such an environment is illustrated in figure 3-19.

Each base station may have a local database attached to it. All of the local databases together would form the distributed database. The local databases are dynamic as they maintain information about the mobile users. Users' movements have to be recorded in these databases. These local databases could also contain, say, travel information such as the various routes and maps to guide the users, or the base stations may be connected to some central station which stores more permanent information. A configuration connecting base stations to central stations is illustrated in figure 3-20.

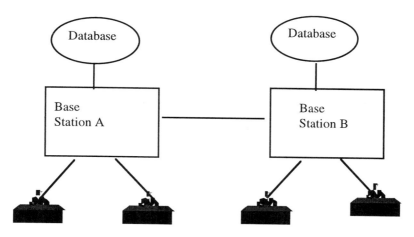

Figure 3-19. Configuration I for Mobile distributed database management

Distributed database system functions will have some impact on the mobile nature of the environment. For example, a user may pose a query while at location A and may be traveling to location B. This means that his base station would have changed. So, the responses have to be routed to the base station associated with location B so that they are given to the user. The query optimization algorithms may be impacted by this need.

Commercial database system vendors are now marketing products for mobile environments. We expect this market to grow with the increasing number of users having PCs. There are many domain application areas that would need mobile computing support. These include medical applications where physicians may be traveling from place to place visiting patients, defense applications where soldiers may be traveling to multiple bases, or in general for those working in sales and marketing.

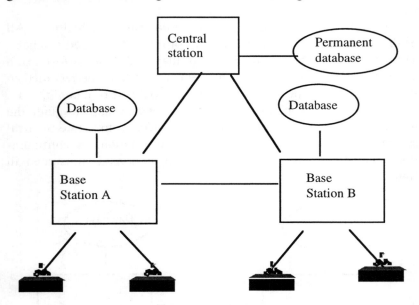

Figure 3-20. Configuration II for Mobile Distributed Database Management

3.13 NETWORKING ISSUES FOR DISTRIBUTED DATABASES

Networks play a major role in distributed database management systems. This is because a network connects the different nodes in a distributed environment. Distributed database systems may utilize long haul networks or local area networks. The bandwidth of the network will impact the design of the architecture of the distributed database system. Furthermore, many of the algorithms, such as the commit protocols, depend on the reliability of the network.

It appears that distributed database systems research has proceeded more or less independently of the networking issues. There are some papers that have been published on the impact of network protocols, network topology, and the design of networks on distributed databases (see, for example, [LARS84]). Various performance studies have also been conducted. For example, replicating relations in a distributed database as well as computing costs of various query optimization strategies have some dependency on the network topology [CERI84, OSZU91]. As distributed and heterogeneous database systems become common practice, integration with networking technology will play a major role.

Figure 3-21 illustrates three types of networks that are interconnected to form some sort of super network. Each circle is a node and could host a DBMS. These various DBMSs may be interconnected to form a DDBMS. In network A, the nodes are connected through a single node. It can be regarded as a star network. In network B, all the nodes are connected to one another. The DDBMS based on our choice architecture is assumed to be hosted on such a network. In network C, some of the nodes are connected to one another.

Some applications that require distributed database support may also have special requirements for the network. For example, in the case of mobile applications discussed in section 3.12, it is important that the network be secure and reliable. Details of networking support for distributed database systems are beyond the scope of this book.

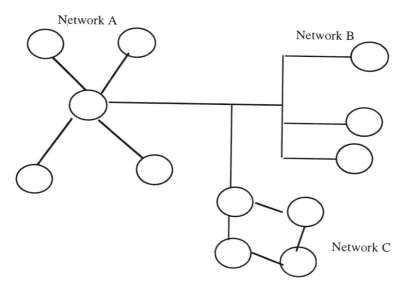

Figure 3-21. Different Types of Networks

CONCLUSION TO PART 1

We have discussed database systems and distributed database systems technology mainly focusing on the relational model. Now let us examine how the contents of part I relate to the framework. At each layer of the framework we get technologies that can be used to build more sophisticated technologies belonging to a higher layer. With the technologies of layer 1, one could develop database systems and distributed database systems functioning in a homogeneous environment. Users could query, update, as well as execute transactions on the database and distributed database systems. At this stage, there are no sophisticated user interfaces. Languages such as SQL as well as application programming languages may be utilized. The technologies in part I make use of some supporting technologies such as networking and distributed processing.

It should be noted that the distributed database systems technology discussed in chapter 3 builds on the database systems technology discussed in chapter 2. The architecture of a distributed database system includes local DBMSs. The functions of a distributed database system such as query processing and transaction management build on the query processing and transaction management functions of a database system.

In summary, with respect to the data management systems framework, the technologies discussed in part 1 provide basic database management and homogeneous distributed database management capabilities.

Database Systems Interoperability and Migration

Part II

INTRODUCTION TO PART II

Part II consists of four chapters addressing the developments in system interoperability and migration. That is, with respect to the data management systems framework illustrated in figure 1-7, these four chapters describe the Interoperability and Migration layer. The contents of these chapters build on the basics discussed in chapters 2 and 3.

Chapter 4 describes the concepts in heterogeneous database integration with a special focus on federated data management. Various aspects of heterogeneity and federated database management are examined first. Then each type of heterogeneity is addressed in more detail. In particular, data model heterogeneity, schema integration and transformation, solutions based on object-oriented approach, semantic heterogeneity, query processing, transaction management, integrity, security, and administration issues are discussed. Heterogeneity with respect to handling multiple data types is briefly examined. Some of the new developments in mediator technology for interoperability, as well as distributed object management approach for interoperability, are also discussed. Finally, some of the practical developments with the research prototypes on the interoperability of heterogeneous database systems are discussed.

While federated data management is one way of integrating heterogeneous databases, client-server based interoperability is another way. This approach is discussed in chapter 5. An overview of client-server based interoperability, with a discussion of some of the emerging standards and products, is discussed. Some of the technical challenges in query processing, transaction management, and security as well as architectural issues for client-server systems, are described. Finally, some example approaches are given: one is based on the ISO (International Standards Organization) standard called Remote Database Access (RDA), the other is based on Microsoft's Open Database Connectivity (ODBC), and the third is based on OMG's CORBA.

Chapter 6 will discuss some of the essential concepts in handling multimedia data. That is, handling heterogeneous data types is addressed in this chapter. In particular, multimedia database system issues are described. First, various architectures and data models for multimedia database systems are proposed and then the functions such as data manipulation, transaction processing, metadata management, distribution, security, and integrity are described.

While chapters 4, 5, and 6 focus on interoperability, migration is given some consideration in chapter 7. In particular, legacy system migration issues are addressed in this chapter. Although integrating heterogeneous database systems, which may include legacy databases, is important for many enterprises, in many cases, one may want to migrate the legacy databases to new platforms. There are several issues that need to be considered in migrating legacy databases. In addition, the database should still be accessible to the heterogeneous database environment during the migration process. That is, one cannot simply state that the legacy databases cannot be accessed until the migration is complete. This remains a challenge. We describe two approaches to migration and then focus on evolvable systems. Finally, a brief discussion of some of the issues, as well as the cost of evolving these systems, is provided.

CHAPTER 4

HETEROGENEOUS DATABASE SYSTEMS INTEGRATION

4.1 OVERVIEW

Chapter 3 described concepts in homogeneous database systems where it was assumed that the local database systems were designed identically. While homogeneous distributed database systems provided many research challenges in the late 1970s and early 1980s, they have limited practical use.[32,33] In the real world, different database management systems will continue to exist. Interoperability between these systems will be the major issue. However, work on homogeneous distributed database systems provided the foundations for the interoperability of heterogeneous database systems. For example, the query processing, transaction management, and metadata management algorithms provide the base line for developing solutions toward query processing, transaction management, and metadata management in interoperable database systems.

Autonomy is also a major consideration in accessing remote databases. The owner or an administrator of a database system would want to have as much autonomy as possible to carry out his operations. At the same time he would want to gain maximum access to remote databases. That is, the administrators of the different database systems would have to cooperate with one another to share each others' data. Autonomy and cooperation are conflicting goals and therefore a balance between the two has to be achieved.

Research into handling heterogeneity and autonomy has led to the development of federated database systems (FDS). Such a system has been defined to be a collection of cooperating database systems which are possibly autonomous and heterogeneous (see the discussion in [SHET90]). The intent is for a database system to continue its local operation and at the same time participate in a federation if it wants to. While heterogeneity brings about complexities not present in a homogeneous environment, autonomy, which enables a database system to join or leave a federation whenever it wishes to, makes the

---

[32] It should be noted that due to the complexities involved in connecting heterogeneous database systems, new initiatives may choose to implement a homogeneous distributed database system.

[33] This does not mean that there are no applications requiring the support of distributed databases. An example application, mobile computing, was discussed in section 3.12. Another application, collaborative computing, will be the subject of chapter 11.

task of developing an FDS even more difficult. Recently several research and development activities on FDSs have been reported [IEEE87, ACM90]. Although some promising results have been obtained, several tasks, such as multiuser updates, are yet to be carried out successfully.

This chapter describes concepts in heterogeneous database systems integration. Various types of heterogeneity are described in section 4.2. Issues on autonomy are described in section 4.3. Notion of a federated database system is given in section 4.4. Some of the essential points in heterogeneous database integration such as data model heterogeneity, schema integration and transformation, object-oriented approach to schema transformation, semantic heterogeneity, query processing, query language, transaction management, integrity, security, multimedia data types, and database administration issues are discussed in sections 4.5-4.13. Some approaches to interoperability such as the use of mediators, agents, repositories, as well as distributed object management technology, are discussed in section 4.14. The role of metadata is the subject of section 4.15. Finally, a discussion of some of the practical developments with the research prototypes on distributed heterogeneous database systems is given in section 4.16.

4.2 HETEROGENEITY

4.2.1   Types of Heterogeneity
In discussing query processing, transaction management, and metadata management for a homogeneous environment, we assumed that the local DBMSs were relational and that they used the same algorithms. In a heterogeneous environment, the DBMSs may not be the same. For example, one DBMS could be relational and another could be object-oriented. This feature was illustrated in figure 1-6. Even if the DBMSs are based on the relational model, they could use different query languages and algorithms. Providing solutions to interconnecting different DBMSs is difficult. In this section we discuss the issues involved in interconnecting heterogeneous components. These issues have been discussed in [SCHE90].

(i) Schema (or data model) Heterogeneity: Not all of the databases in a heterogeneous architecture are represented by the same data model. Therefore, the differences between the multiple data models utilized have to be reconciled. In order to do this, translators which transform the constructs of one data model into those of another are being developed. A closely related issue is handling the different schemas of the local database systems. These schemas have to be integrated so that users have a uniform view of the global system. Transformations between these different schemas are also necessary.[34]

(ii) Semantic Heterogeneity: Data may be interpreted differently at different component sites. For example, the entity address could mean just the country at one component while another component could interpret it to be the number, street name, city name, and country. That is, the same object could be interpreted differently at different sites. These semantic differences have to be reconciled. Semantic heterogeneity is rather difficult to handle.

(iii) Query Processing Heterogeneity: Different DBMSs utilize different query processing and optimization strategies. One of the research areas here is to develop a global cost model for distributed query optimization.

(iv) Query Language Heterogeneity: Different DBMSs will utilize different query languages. Even if the DBMSs are based on the relational model, one could use SQL and the other could use relational calculus. Standardization efforts are being explored to develop a uniform interface language.

(v) Transaction Processing Heterogeneity: Different DBMSs may utilize different algorithms for transaction processing. The various transaction processing mechanisms have to be integrated to provide consistency. For example, techniques that integrate locking, time stamping, and validation mechanisms are needed. It has been suggested that the notion of strict serializability may have to be sacrificed for a heterogeneous environment. That is, one may have to contend with a weaker form of serializability.

(vi) Constraint Heterogeneity: Different DBMSs enforce different integrity constraints which are often inconsistent. For example, one DBMS could enforce a constraint that all employees must work at least 30 hours while another DBMS may not enforce such a constraint.

(vii) Security Policies: Different nodes may enforce different security policies. These policies have to be integrated. Multilevel

---

[34] The object-oriented approach is also being investigated for handling schema heterogeneity. The idea here is for the users to have a generic view of the entire system. Translators are then necessary to translate the constructs from/to the generic representation to/from an individual representation. We discuss this in section 4.5.

security also has an impact on all of the other features discussed here.[35]

(viii) Heterogeneous (Multimedia) Data Types: The data types may be heterogeneous in nature. For example, one node may process text and images while another node may process video data. An approach to integrate the different data types has to be formulated.

Work is being conducted on providing solutions to the interoperability of heterogeneous database systems. The problems become even more complex if there are several types of heterogeneity to be handled. For example, the various systems could not only utilize different data models but also different algorithms. Handling all types of heterogeneity will be extremely difficult. Therefore, solutions to handle different combinations of heterogeneous features are needed.

4.2.2 Architecture

As stated in chapter 3, we chose the multidatabase architecture with tight integration to explain the concepts in distributed database systems. We mentioned that this architecture could be used to explain the concepts in a heterogeneous database system also. We have adapted this architecture for a heterogeneous environment and it is illustrated in figure 4-1. As shown in this figure, different database management systems are connected through a distributed processor. However, unlike in the case of a homogeneous environment, the distributed processor's functions are different at each node. This is because of the differences in the local DBMSs. We call such a distributed processor to be a heterogeneous distributed processor (HDP).

Figure 4-2 illustrates the components of the HDP. Note that while we still have the components DQP, DTM, DMM, DSM, and DIM, they all have a DBMS specific part and a DBMS independent part. The DBMS independent parts of the corresponding modules at the various nodes are identical. However, the DBMS specific parts of the modules depend on the local DBMSs. For example, in the case of query processing, the DBMS specific component of DQP will be specific to the data model utilized by the local DBMS while the DBMS independent part of the DQP will be based on some generic representation of the schemas. These ideas will be clearer when we discuss schema integration and transformation in section 4.5.

---

[35]   A discussion of security issues for federated database systems is given in [THUR94]. Some aspects are also discussed in [THUR95b]. Security is addressed in section 4.11.

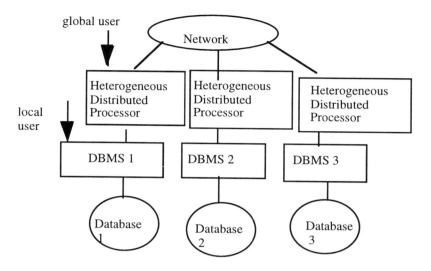

Figure 4-1. Architecture for a Heterogeneous Database System

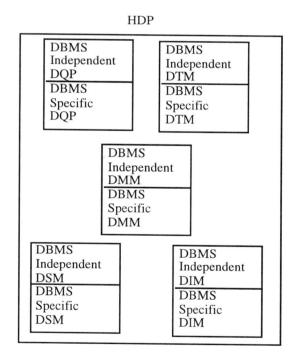

Figure 4-2. Modules of the Heterogeneous Distributed Processor

4.3 AUTONOMY

Although the different DBMSs in the network should cooperate so that users of one DBMS could access remote data, it is also desirable that the local DBMSs have some degree of autonomy. Cooperation and autonomy have conflicting goals. In most cases the database administrators of the DBMSs have to negotiate with one another to cooperate, but at the same time maintain some degree of autonomy. Sheth and Larson [SHET90] have identified various types of autonomy. These include: Design autonomy, Communication autonomy, Execution autonomy, and Association autonomy. We discuss each type.

Design Autonomy: This implies that each component will have the ability to choose its own design. For example, it could determine (i) the data to be managed, (ii) the policies to be enforced, (iii) the query processing and transaction management algorithms to be used, and (iv) the semantic interpretation of data.

Communication Autonomy: This implies that a component will determine with whom it wishes to communicate.

Execution Autonomy: This implies that the local operations of a component are not affected by the global users in any way.

Association Autonomy: This implies that a component can decide when and what information to share with the others.

Note that autonomy is not restricted to a heterogeneous environment. Even in a homogeneous distributed database system, the identical local DBMSs could be autonomous as well as belong to a federation. However, as mentioned earlier, in the real-world, many applications require the interoperability of heterogeneous database systems. Therefore, autonomy is usually discussed within the context of heterogeneity.

Figure 4-3 illustrates a situation where there is less autonomy as there is an integration module that is responsible for integrating the different DBMS components. Figure 4-4 illustrates a situation where

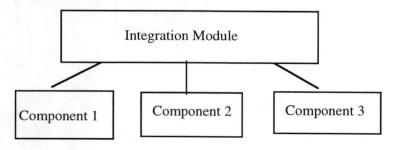

Figure 4-3. Less Autonomy

there is more autonomy as there is no such integration module. That is, in the latter case, the individual DBMS components are responsible for integration.

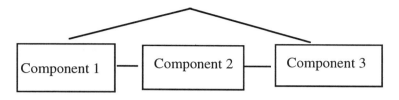

Figure 4-4. More Autonomy

4.4 FEDERATED DATABASE SYSTEM

As stated by Sheth and Larson [SHET90], a federated database system is a collection of cooperating but autonomous database systems belonging to a federation. That is, the goal is for the database management systems which belong to a federation to cooperate with one another and yet maintain some degree of autonomy. Note that to be consistent with the terminology, we distinguish between a federated database management system and a federated database system. A federated database system includes both a federated database management system, the local DBMSs, and the databases. The federated database management system is that component which manages the different databases in a federated environment.

Figure 4-5 illustrates a federated database system. Database systems A and B belong to federation F1 while database systems B and C belong to federation F2. We can use the architecture illustrated in figure 4-1 for a federated database system. In addition to handling heterogeneity, the HDP also has to handle the federated environment. That is, techniques have to be adapted to handle cooperation and autonomy. We have called such an HDP an FDP (Federated Distributed Processor). An architecture for an FDS is illustrated in figure 4-6.

Figure 4-7 illustrates an example of an autonomous environment. There is communication between components A and B and between B and C. Due to autonomy, it is assumed that components A and C do not wish to communicate with each other. Now, component A may get requests from its own user or from component B. In this case, it has to decide which request to honor first. Also, there is a possibility for component C to get information from component A through component B. In such a situation, component A may have to negotiate with component B before it gives a reply to component

B. The developments to deal with autonomy are still in the research stages. The challenge is to handle transactions in an autonomous environment. Transitioning the research into commercial products is also a challenge.

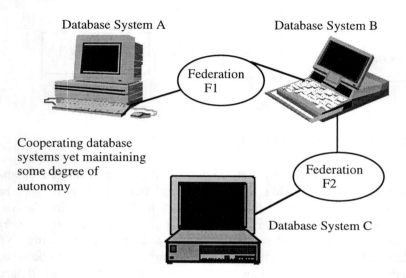

Figure 4-5. Federated Database Management

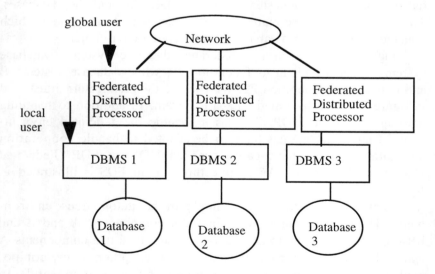

Figure 4-6. Architecture for a Federated Database System

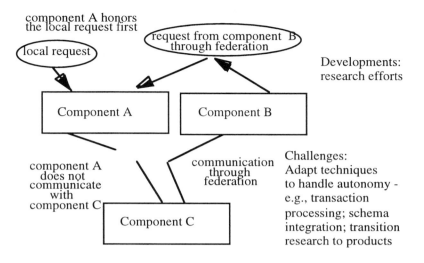

Figure 4-7. Autonomy

4.5 DATA MODEL HETEROGENEITY

4.5.1 Overview

As stated earlier, there are various types of heterogeneity. One type of heterogeneity, known as data model heterogeneity, arises due to different types of database systems. Figure 4-8 illustrates data model heterogeneity. There are four database systems utilizing relational, network, hierarchical, and object-oriented data models, respectively. The goal is for users to access these heterogeneous databases without having to be concerned about the type of database system that is being accessed.

The developments include tools for handling heterogeneity with respect to data models. Commercial products are now available, and many of these products transform one representation scheme into another. For example, if a user of a relational database management system had to access a network database management system, then the translator will translate the relational database request into an appropriate network database request. To avoid the multiple transla-tors that are necessary to provide transparent access, one approach is to utilize a global data model. That is, an intermediate representa-tion is used and there are transformations between the individual database schemes and the intermediate representation. The challenge here is to develop a global data model. Some of the challenges and an approach for a global model are discussed in the next two subsections.

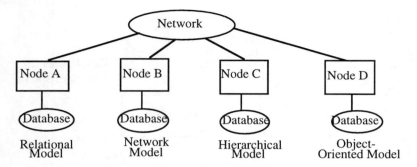

Developments: Tools for interoperability; commercial products
Challenges: Global data model

Figure 4-8. Different Data Models

4.5.2   Schema Integration and Transformation

Figure 4-9 illustrates a framework for schema integration and transformation in a heterogeneous environment. Such a framework was also proposed by the Distributed Database Testbed System (DDTS) project at Honeywell Inc. (see, for example, [DEVO82]). At the lowest level, one describes the schemas of the individual databases. To facilitate the development of a global unified schema, the individual schemas have to be transformed into some generic representation. Then the generic schemas are integrated to provide a global view of the heterogeneous database system. One could provide multiple external schemas if necessary for different classes of users. For example, the

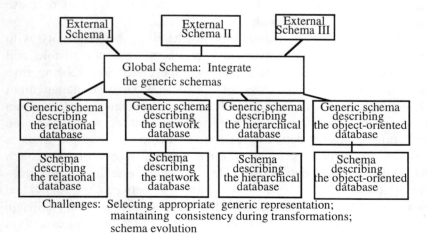

Figure 4-9. Schema Integration and Transformation

information necessary for a president to carry out his tasks may be different from that of a department manager.

An approach for schema integration and transformation in a federated environment that is becoming extremely popular is illustrated in figure 4-10. This approach was proposed by Sheth and Larson [SHET90]. It appears that this approach also evolved from the five-schema architecture proposed in the DDTS project [DEVO82]. In Sheth and Larson's approach, each component system

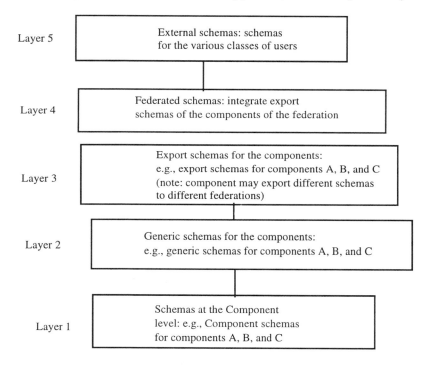

Figure 4-10. Schema Integration and Transformation in a Federated Environment

has a component schema.[36] The component schemas are trans-formed into generic schemas to facilitate integration. Due to auton-omy, not all of the generic schema of a component may be exported to a federation. That is, the export schema is the schema that a component decides to export to a federation. As illustrated in this figure, component B which belongs to two federations may export

---

36   Note that each component itself could also be a federated database system, a distributed database system, or a heterogeneous database system. But for the purposes of the federated environment under discussion here it is assumed that each component's schema has been generated.

different export schemas. The export schemas exported by the individual components are integrated into a federated schema. Finally, depending on the classes of users, different external schema are generated.

4.5.3   Object-Oriented Approach to Schema Integration and Transformation

The object-oriented approach to schema integration and transformation has been examined by various efforts. In this approach, the generic schema is based on an object-oriented data model. By having a generic representation, transformations between individual representations are not necessary. For example, if there are N different database management systems utilizing different representations, then order of N squared translators are needed to transform one scheme into another. However, by having a generic scheme, only order of N translators are needed. That is, the constructs of local models have to be transformed into that of the generic model. Object-oriented data models are popular for the generic model as many of the constructs of the local models can be transformed into those of the object model.

Document

Document#	Name	Author

Book

Document#	ISBN#

Journal

Document#	Vol#

Figure 4-11. Representation of Inheritance in a Relational Model

We will briefly examine the transformations between the relational and object-oriented data models. In one approach, each relation can be transformed into a class. The attributes of the relation transform into the instance variables of the class. The rows of the relation transform into instances of the class. See for example the information in figures 2-2 and 2-5 in chapter 2, where EMP relation transforms into EMP class and DEPT relation transforms into DEPT class.

Not all of the constructs of an object model can be transformed into those of a relational model. For example, there is no notion of object-ID in the relational model. Although there is the notion of tuple-IDs in the relational model, these tuple-IDs are not visible to the user while object-IDs are visible. Also, in the basic relational model, one cannot represent composite (or aggregate) objects. However, inheritance concept can be represented by relations. For example, consider the document class and its subclass illustrated in figure 2-6. The three classes transform into three relations Document, Book, and Journal, respectively as shown in figure 4-11. Document# is an attribute both in the relations Book and Journal. That is, Document gives the association between Book and Document as well as between Book and Journal. Furthermore, Book and Journal have additional attributes. That is, Book has attribute ISBN number while Journal has attribute Volume#.

Other models have also been examined for the generic model. These include the ER model and its extensions. It should be noted that having a generic representation is not accepted by everyone. Some believe that a generic representation is not needed. In other words, a loose integration of the heterogeneous database systems is preferred. If this is the case, then it is up to the user to maintain the mappings between the different systems.

4.6 SEMANTIC HETEROGENEITY

Semantic heterogeneity is a major challenge in a heterogeneous environment. For example, semantic heterogeneity occurs when different sites do not agree about the meaning of some data. Figure 4-12 illustrates the case where sites A and B interpret the same object differently. There is also a problem of different objects being interpreted identically. There are various efforts to handle semantic heterogeneity. Some are proposing to standardize different data elements. Some are proposing to build repositories to store the different interpretations of the same data. Some are proposing a combination of standardization and building repositories. Appropriate logics to capture the different semantics are also being investigated.

There is much research on handling semantic heterogeneity. Repositories are being built to accommodate the different names given to an object. For example, an object with name A could also be referred to as X, Y, and Z at the various sites. The repository will have an entry for this object with name A and alias names X, Y, and Z. Techniques are also being developed to process the entries in the repository efficiently and resolve the various conflicts that could occur. Application of repository technology is illustrated in figure 4-13.

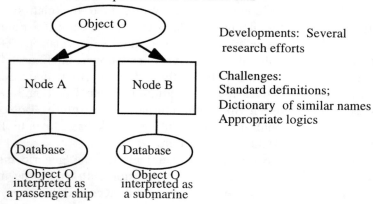

Figure 4-12. Semantic Heterogeneity

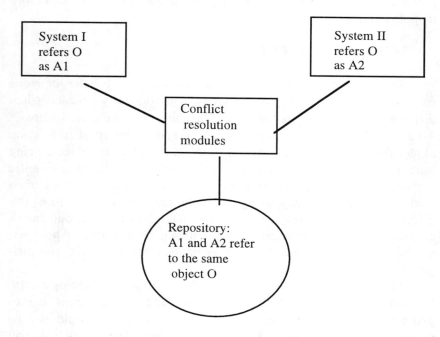

Figure 4-13. Application of a Repository

4.7   QUERY PROCESSING

Section 3 described techniques for processing queries in a distributed environment. In a heterogeneous environment, the databases may not utilize the same data model. Therefore the local database management systems may implement entirely different query processing strategies. Even if the data models utilized are identical, different optimization techniques may be utilized by the different systems. Coming up with global query processing strategies in a heterogeneous environment is a challenge. Often in a federated environment, information about a particular node may not be available at the global level. Certain assumptions have to be made to handle such a situation.

Another issue in heterogeneous query processing is transferring data between sites. In the example described in section 3, the relation fragments were transferred between sites for efficient join processing. This may not be possible in an autonomous environment without negotiating ahead of time.

4.8   QUERY LANGUAGE

Query language heterogeneity is another issue. If the database management systems are based on different data models, then the languages used to access the systems are usually different. There has been some research toward developing multidatabase languages. For example, object-based languages for accessing multiple databases are being examined. Even if the database management systems are based on the same model, say relational, different systems may use different versions of relational languages. One advantage here is the standard language ANSI SQL [SQL3]. As stated earlier, there is widespread acceptance of this language. Extensions to SQL are also being proposed for object definition and manipulation as well as for handling multimedia data types. Also, standards for object databases such as ODMG's specifications are also being developed.

A standard query language for a heterogeneous database system will depend on the generic data model utilized. If it is a relational model, then one could use a language such as SQL. If it is an object-oriented data model as discussed in section 4.5.3, then an object-oriented query language is needed. As mentioned in the previous paragraph, SQL extensions for objects or ODMG's object language may be used for this purpose.

4.9 TRANSACTION MANAGEMENT

This section examines the impact of handling heterogeneity and autonomy during transaction management. While research on transaction processing in heterogeneous and autonomous environments is fairly recent, several efforts have now been reported. Much of the focus has been on investigating serializability for autonomous environments. In addition, work on integrating different concurrency control protocols such as locking and time stamping has also begun.

To handle the new types of application environments, advanced transaction models have been proposed [ELMA92]. As stated by Elmagarmid et al., in an autonomous environment, each database system may often process the local requests first before the global requests. Therefore, the global transactions could be of long duration. In addition, since each local system is autonomous, it may be difficult to detect and resolve conflicts between global transactions and, as a result, serializability conditions would be difficult to meet. Due to these problems, the traditional transaction model, where each transaction satisfies the ACID properties, may not be suitable for heterogeneous and autonomous environments. That is, weaker forms of serializability which do not enforce strict consistency may be needed.

Various new models that enforce weaker forms of serializability have been proposed. These include models such as the DOM transaction model [BUCH92], Flex transaction model [KUHN92], S-Transaction model [VEIJ92], Polytransactions [SHET92], and Cooperative transaction hierarchy [NODI92]. A detailed discussion of these models is given in [ELMA92].

4.10 INTEGRITY

Enforcing integrity constraints in heterogeneous and autonomous environments has also received much attention recently. There are several aspects to consider and we briefly discuss them in this section.

First of all, constraints may be specified in different languages. One system may use the structured query language to express constraints while another may use first order logic clauses. A solution to this problem is either to specify transformations between one representation to another or mandate the use of a standard language such as SQL.

In the case of data model heterogeneity, different data models may be utilized by the different systems. This means that the specification of the integrity constraints may vary with the model.

For example, in a relational DBMS, one could enforce the constraint that "the salary attribute value of the employee relation must be positive". In an object-oriented DBMS, one could enforce this same constraint as "the salary instance variable value of the employee class must be positive". Techniques to handle data model heterogeneity must ensure that the constraints are transformed correctly.

The problem is more complex if the constraints themselves are heterogeneous regardless of the model. That is, different DBMSs may enforce different integrity constraints which are often inconsistent. For example, one DBMS could enforce a constraint that all employees must work at least 30 hours while another DBMS may enforce a constraint that all employees must work 40 hours. If an employee relation is updated, then both constraints are triggered. The administrators of the two systems may have to resolve the conflict possibly through negotiation.

Semantic heterogeneity, addressed in section 4.6, could also cause integrity problems. As stated earlier, the same attribute, say salary of an employee, may be interpreted differently by different DBMSs. One system may consider the salary to be the hourly wage of an employee while another system might interpret it to be the weekly wage. Another example of heterogeneity is the use of different names to denote the same object. The word "aircraft" may be interpreted as "plane" or as "aviation vehicle". One approach to handling semantic heterogeneity is to agree upon standard notions. This is often infeasible as different groups may not agree on common definitions. Therefore, an alternative approach will be to accept semantic heterogeneity, but to have a repository which specifies all the names that may be used to denote an object and to check this repository to handle conflicts.

Enforcing integrity constraints in an autonomous environment is difficult if the information about a remote database is not known. For example, there could be a constraint that the total salary of an organization cannot exceed one million. If the organization consists of different groups, each having its own database, then enforcing such a constraint is difficult if a remote group does not make its data available. In such a situation, the system has to reason with partial information, making some guesses possibly based on previous experience. Some techniques for enforcing integrity constraints in heterogeneous and autonomous environments are given in [RAM93].

4.11 SECURITY

4.11.1 Overview

Secure interoperability of heterogeneous database management systems is important for a variety of applications. Few efforts have been reported on security issues concerning the interoperability of heterogeneous database systems in general and secure federated data management in particular. An early investigation was reported in [THUR94] where multilevel security issues were described for federated database management systems. More recently, the Secure Federated Data Management project at the MITRE Corporation has been investigating issues involved in allowing cooperating organizations to share sensitive data across jurisdictional boundaries in a federation, even when organizations have different confidentiality and handling requirements. Some of the key technical developments resulting from this effort are discussed in [BLAU95].

Security has an impact on the various types of heterogeneity discussed in this book. For example, the query and transaction processing algorithms have to take the security policies into consideration. Efficient techniques are needed to enforce the various access control rules. In a heterogeneous environment, where different data models may be utilized by the different systems, the access control rules enforced on one representation scheme may have to be transformed into those of another representation scheme. In addition to all these issues, in a heterogeneous environment, the different security policies enforced by the different systems have to be integrated. This aspect is discussed in section 4.11.2. Also, a multilevel heterogeneous environment introduces additional complexities such as handling different accreditation ranges. This is addressed in the section 4.11.3. Other aspects are discussed in section 4.11.4.[37]

In summary, while many of the commercial database management system vendors are marketing multilevel secure database system products, the secure interoperability between these database systems is a challenge. However, the recent developments on commercial database interoperability products are showing a lot of promise and should help toward the secure interoperability between the multilevel database system products. Furthermore, through the various workshops on trusted database interoperability, there is increased interactions between the research and vendor communities. This will also facilitate the development of solutions for the secure interoperation of heterogeneous database systems.

---

[37]   These security issues for federated databases are also discussed in [THUR94, THUR95b].

4.11.2   Handling Heterogeneous Security Policies

There are many parallels between integrating security policies and schemas for federated database systems. The schema architecture illustrated in figure 4-10 can be adapted for security policies as shown in Figure 4-14.

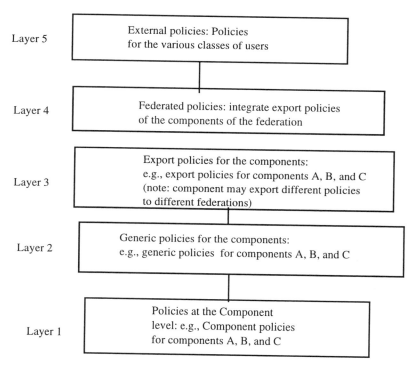

Figure 4-14. Policy Integration and Transformation

Here, the component security policies describe the security policy for each component. If a component database system consists of multiple database systems, the policies of the individual local systems have to be integrated. The component policies are transformed into generic policies. Each system may export a certain policy. For example, additional restrictions on data access may be imposed for remote users. The export policies have to be integrated to form a federated security policy. For example, one site may grant a user access to a particular data object while another site may deny access. Such inconsistencies have to be resolved at the federation level. On the other hand, if such an inconsistency is not related to multilevel data access (e.g., due to different representations of labels and clearances), then it is possible for such differences to be a valid part of the systems' policies. In that case, one might not want to force them to be eliminated in the federated policy. In any case, negotiations between the administrators of the different sites may be necessary to resolve conflicts in general.

4.11.3   Handling Heterogeneous Accreditation Ranges

In a heterogeneous environment, the different sites may handle different accreditation ranges. That is, the range of security levels handled by the different sites may not be the same. An example is illustrated in figure 4-15. In this example, site A is accredited to handle Confidential to TopSecret data, site B is accredited to handle Unclassified to Secret data, and site C is accredited to handle only Unclassified data. If a TopSecret user queries from site A to retrieve Unclassified, Confidential, and Secret data from site B, then the request has to be downgraded first to the Secret level and then sent to site B. Now, if this TopSecret user from site A queries to retrieve Unclassified data from site C, then this request from site A cannot be sent directly to site C as there are no overlapping security levels between these two sites. In such a situation, the request may have to be sent via site B. This would involve two downgrade operations as shown in figure 4-15.

Handling Different Accreditation Ranges

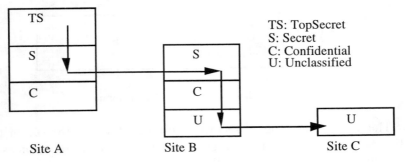

Figure 4-15. Accreditation Ranges

Whenever there is communication between sites accredited to handle different ranges of security levels, there is a potential for covert channels. Furthermore, the downgrade operations have to be trusted. The problem is even more serious as the situation described here with sites A, B, and C directly takes advantage of the cascading problem identified in the Trusted Network Interpretation, a document published by the Department of Defense in 1987.

4.11.4   Other Aspects of Security

As discussed in [THUR95b], in a heterogeneous environment, the security labels may have different interpretations at different sites. This is a form of semantic heterogeneity. Also, an object could have different security labels at different sites. That is, at one site it could be Unclassified while at another site it could be Secret. The problem with this is to determine whether this is legitimate (i.e., the difference is contextually based and meaningful, and therefore necessary to preserve), or it is due to an inconsistency. If it is due to the latter, then the inconsistency has to be resolved possibly through the interoperability layer.

Another problem with a multilevel environment is that the different sites may utilize different multilevel data models. For example, one relational database system could classify the rows of a relation, another relational database system could classify the individual data elements which comprise the row, and a third relational database system could classify the attributes of a relation. The differences between these models will have to be resolved for the interoperability of multilevel database systems. The problem may be harder if different types of data models are utilized at different sites. For example, one site may utilize a multilevel relational data model while another site may utilize a multilevel object-oriented data model. Some of the issues involved are addressed in [THUR94].

4.12 DATA TYPE HETEROGENEITY

Much of the previous discussion has assumed that the data is structured. As more and more information gets digitized, the data in the databases may be unstructured. For example, there is an increasing need to store multimedia data such as voice, text, images, and video. Integrating these heterogeneous data types is becoming a challenge for many applications.

Figure 4-16 illustrates an example of a heterogeneous database system with multimedia data types. Issues on integrating such heterogeneous data sources are addressed in chapter 6. The challenges include developing an appropriate data model, architecture for managing structured as well as unstructured databases, distribution issues, and synchronization of multimedia data such as video and audio, particularly from different databases.

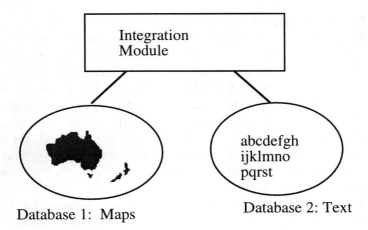

Figure 4-15. Heterogeneous Data Types

4.13 HETEROGENEOUS DATABASE ADMINISTRATION

In chapter 3, we described distributed database administration. Administering heterogeneous databases is even more complex. This is partly due to the fact that the local databases may have some degree of autonomy. Therefore the cooperation between the local administrators as well as between the local and global administrators may not be straightforward. In some cases, there may not be a global administrator.

As in the case of distributed databases, the administration functions include enforcing backup and recovery procedures, integrating the schemas, maintaining integrity and security, and enforcing appropriate audit procedures as well as standards. Each of these functions is more complex due to the heterogeneous nature of the databases. Little research has been reported in administering heterogeneous databases. This is an area that needs a lot more investigation.

4.14 EMERGING TECHNOLOGIES FOR INTEROPERABILITY

4.14.1   Overview

Recently some new technologies have been proposed for interoperability. Some of the early ideas were discussed in [WIED92]. Since then various prototypes have been developed. Notable among these technologies are mediators, agents, repositories, and distributed object management. Although we have discussed each of these technologies separately, two or more of them can be combined to produce a solution for interoperability.

This section briefly describes each of these four emerging technologies for interoperability. The use of mediators is described in section 4.14.2. Intelligent agent technology for interoperation is the subject of section 4.14.3. Repository technology is discussed in section 4.14.4. Finally, the distributed object management approach for interoperability is discussed in section 4.14.5.

4.14.2 Mediators

Mediator technology is becoming popular for integrating heterogeneous database systems. Mediators are modules that perform mediation between heterogeneous activities or information sources. For example, schema integration and transformation could be performed by a mediator or a mediator could mediate between different database systems for query processing and transaction management.

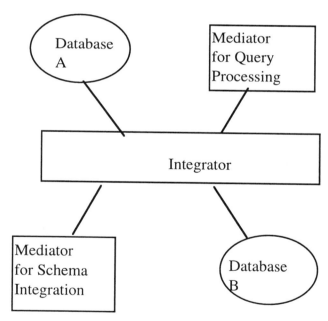

Figure 4-17. Mediators for Interoperability

An issue is the location of the mediators. Should they be located at a particular site or should they be independent of the individual sites. To obtain maximum transparency, at the logical level, the mediators should be independent of the locations of the individual sites. For efficiency, depending on a particular situation, one could place the mediators at particular locations. Figure 4-17 illustrates an architecture which consists of mediation components. For example, the mediator for query processing will ensure that appropriate databases are located, the responses are assembled, and unwanted information is filtered out before giving the response to the user.

4.14.3   Agents

Intelligent agent technology is becoming increasingly popular for integrating heterogeneous databases especially in the Internet environment. Agents are essentially processes performing specific functions. There could be agents for doing mediation. Agents could perform data fusion. Agents could also locate resources and information in the network.

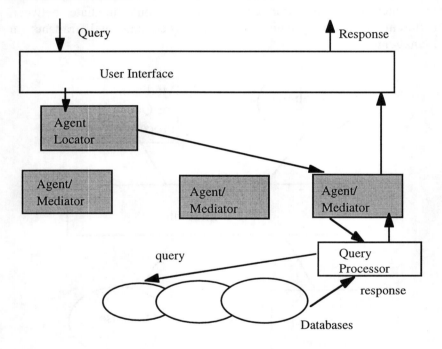

Figure 4-18. Agents for Interoperability

Figure 4-18 illustrates a query processing example using agents. Locator agents locate the resources and database systems. Mediator agents, through the query processing component, query the databases, assemble the responses obtained from the databases, and give the responses to the user. Note that various query languages and message standards have been proposed for agents. For a detailed discussion of agents, we refer to [CIKM95].

4.14.4 Repositories

Repositories were briefly discussed in section 4.8 in addressing semantic heterogeneity. That is, repositories contain information needed for handling the differences between the different databases (see, for example, [RENN95]). For example, the fact that object O means SHIP at node 1 and BOAT at node 2 is in the repository. In addition, as new nodes join the federation and have various interpretations, that information gets updated in the repository. For example, if node 3 joins the federation and interprets object O as a submarine, then this fact is entered into the repository.

Repositories are used by both mediators and agents to get the information to carry out their tasks. This is illustrated in figure 4-19. Managing the repository is an issue. Efficient query and update techniques are needed. In addition, the integrity of the repository has to be maintained. An appropriate data model is also needed to represent the information in the repository. The use of database management systems to manage the repositories is being explored. Repository technology is becoming key not only to interoperability but also to other aspects of data management. For example, this technology is being utilized in building data warehouses. This topic will be addressed in chapter 8.

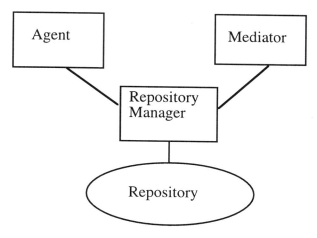

Figure 4-19. Repository Technology for Interoperability

4.14.5 Distributed Object Management Approach

Distributed object management (DOM) technology is becoming increasingly used to interconnect heterogeneous databases, systems, and applications. With this approach, the various systems and applications are encapsulated as objects and the objects communicate with each other through exchanging messages. Figure 4-20 provides a high level view of interoperability based on DOM technology. Here, three components A, B, and C are encapsulated as objects and communicate with each other through the DOM system.[38]

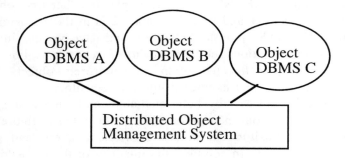

Figure 4-20. Interoperability-based on Distributed Object Management

DOM technology can also be used for finer grained encapsulation. For example, mediators, repositories, and DBMSs can be encapsulated so that different DBMSs interoperate. This is illustrated in figure 4-21. What is key here is that each system must have well defined interfaces using a common interface definition language. What is inside each encapsulated object is transparent to the remote object. This technology is also being used for migrating legacy databases and applications. More details are given in chapters 5 and 7. For a detailed discussion of DOM technology, we refer to [ORFA96].

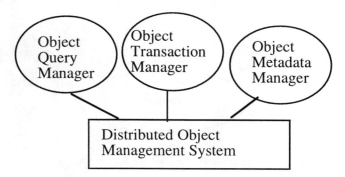

Figure 4-21. Distributed Object Management for Component Integration

---

[38]   Note that component integration was also discussed in section 2.8. Internet-based component integration is discussed in chapter 10.

4.15 THE ROLE OF METADATA

Now that we have described various aspects of heterogeneous database systems integration, let us examine the role of metadata.[39] Metadata is an essential contributor to various aspects of interoperability. First, consider schema integration and transformation. Here, the metadata of the individual data sources have to be transformed into some generic representation and then integrated to form the global schema. This metadata is then used for query processing, transaction management, and maintaining security of the system. Metadata includes information about the various data sources, global access control policies, and other information necessary for query and transaction management.

Metadata also includes the repository information needed for integrating heterogeneous data sources. For example, information required to handle semantic heterogeneity is part of the metadata. Metadata also includes information about the various agents and mediators in the system. In an Internet environment, metadata includes information about the various resources and servers on the networked system.

Metadata management functions include querying and updating the metadata. The facility to update the metadata in a timely manner is needed. Security and integrity of the metadata have to be maintained. Finally, appropriate models to represent the metadata have to be developed.

4.16 PROTOTYPE DEVELOPMENTS

While research was being carried out on various aspects of distributed, heterogeneous, and federated database management, some prototypes of distributed and heterogeneous database management systems were also being developed since the late 1970s. The technology is also being successfully transferred into commercial products. Some of the features provided by the products include transparent distributed query processing, transaction management with concurrency control, and two-phase commit.

As stated in chapter 1, database system prototypes have been influenced by IBM's System R and University of California at Berkeley's Ingres systems developed in the mid-1970s. Both these systems were relational systems and have been extended for distrib-

---

[39] We have discussed various aspects of metadata throughout this chapter. In this section we essentially summarize the discussions.

uted database management during the late 1970s. The distributed version of System R is called System R* and the distributed version of Ingres is called Distributed Ingres. These systems provided distribution transparency, query optimization, transaction management, concurrency control, and recovery (see, for example, the papers in [BROD88]).

Following the developments of these distributed database systems, a series of heterogeneous database system prototypes were developed by the various corporations during the early 1980s, these include Honeywell Inc.'s DDTS (Distributed Database Testbed System), System Development Corporation's Mermaid, and Computer Corporation of America's Multibase. In addition, systems such as Porel and Sirius-Delta were developed in Europe. During the mid to late 1980s developments on systems such as Amoco Corporation's ADDS, General Motors Corporation's DATAPLEX, IMDAS system developed jointly by the University of Florida and the National Institutes of Standards and Technology, Hewlett Packard Company's Pegasus, and GTE Corporation's Calida were reported. More recently, during the early to mid 1990s, various efforts are under way on developing mediators and repositories for integrating heterogeneous database systems [RENN95].

It should be noted that many of these prototypes have implemented a distributed processing layer on top of commercial database management systems. This distributed processing layer is responsible for distributed query processing, distributed transaction management, and distributed metadata management. In addition, various types of heterogeneity are also handled by this layer. Many of these prototypes have utilized the relational model for the generic model. However, some of the prototypes have utilized other models also. For example, DDTS prototype uses an extension of the ER model. This model is called the ECR (Entity Category Relationship) model [ELMA85]. An associated query language for the ECR model was also developed in this project. In the case of Pegasus, the model is an object-oriented data model with an associated query language.

We have not described these prototypes in any detail as some of them are not in use and some have evolved into commercial products. More detailed information about these prototypes is given in [IEEE87, ACM90, IEEE91].

CHAPTER 5

INTEROPERABILITY BASED ON CLIENT-SERVER ARCHITECTURES

5.1 OVERVIEW

Chapter 4 described interoperability between heterogeneous database systems and focused on the federated database systems approach. In this approach, different database systems cooperatively interoperate with each other. This chapter describes another aspect of interoperability which is based on the client-server paradigm.

Major database system vendors have migrated to an architecture called the client-server architecture. With this approach, multiple clients access the various database servers through some network. A high level view of client-server communication is illustrated in figure 5-1. The ultimate goal is for multi-vendor clients to communicate with multi-vendor servers in a transparent manner. A specific example of client-server communication is illustrated in figure 5-2.

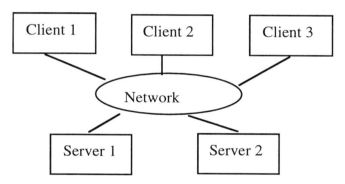

Figure 5-1. Client-Server Architecture-based Interoperability

One of the major challenges in client-server technology is to determine the modules of the distributed database system that need to be placed at the client and server sides. Figure 5-3 shows an approach where all the modules of the distributed processor of figure 3-10 are placed at the client side, while the modules of the local DBMS are placed at the server side. Note that with this approach the client does a lot of processing and this is called the "fat client" approach. There are other options also. For example, some of the modules of the distributed processor could be part of the server in which case the client would be "thinner".

In order to facilitate the communication between multiple clients and servers, various standards are being proposed. One example is the International Standards Organization's (ISO) Remote Database Access (RDA) standard. This standard provides a generic interface for communication between a client and a server. Microsoft Corporation's Open Database Connectivity (ODBC) is also becoming increasingly popular for clients to communicate with servers. OMG's CORBA provides specifications for client-server communication based on object technology. Here, one possibility is to encapsulate the database servers as objects and the clients to issue appropriate requests and access the servers through an Object Request Broker. Other standards include IBM's DRDA (Distributed Relational Database Access) and the SQL Access Group's Call Level Interface (CLI). While much of the developments have been in query processing, the challenges are in transaction processing, semantic heterogeneity, integrity, and security.

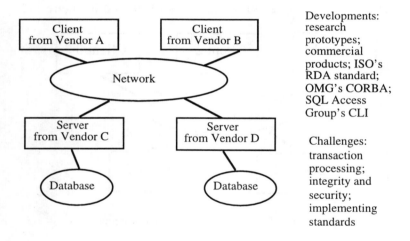

Figure 5-2. Example Client-server architecture

In this chapter we describe various aspects of client-server interoperability. In section 5.2, some of the technical issues for client-server interoperability will be discussed. Architectural approaches will be discussed in section 5.3. Section 5.4 describes three of the standards proposed for communication between clients and servers. They are: RDA, ODBC, and CORBA. The first is an ISO/ANSI standard, the second is becoming extremely popular for client-server database management, and the third is a specification by an industry consortium. Metadata is becoming an important aspect to client-server interoperability. The role of metadata is given some consideration in section 5.5. Quite a few books have been published recently on client-server computing and data management. A good reference is [ORFA94].

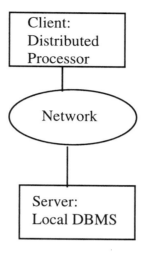

Figure 5-3. An Approach to Place Modules

5.2 TECHNICAL ISSUES

Technical issues for client-server database management include system architectural aspects as well as functions such as caching, query processing, transaction management, metadata management, integrity, and security. The functions depend on the particular system architecture chosen. One of the major issues here is the amount of processing performed by the client and the server. For example, at one end the client could be just a terminal without any processing capability while the server does the entire database management. At the other end, much of the processing is the responsibility of the client while the server simply stores and re-trieves data from the database. We will examine each function and discuss some of the issues when some of the processing has to be done by the client.

Caching: The issue here is how much data should be cached at the client side so that the database is accessed only if necessary. This will depend on the query patterns which include the types and the frequencies.

Query processing: The issues here include developing a query model as well as determining the functions to be carried out by the client. For example, if multiple databases are to be accessed, then should the client perform the merging of the results or should the results be sent to certain servers for processing?

Transaction processing: An issue here is whether the client has to act as a coordinator in client-server transaction processing where multiple databases are to be accessed. Concurrency control and recovery algorithms developed for distributed transaction processing have to be adapted for the client-server architecture chosen.

Metadata management: Should the metadata be maintained by the client or should the servers be responsible for maintaining their own metadata? Even if metadata management is the server's responsibility, what types of information should the client maintain?

Integrity: In addition to concurrency control and recovery issues, should the client enforce application specific integrity constraints? If so, techniques have to be developed to coordinate the activities with the servers.

Security: One of the major issues here is the accreditation ranges handled by the client and the server. If the ranges are the same, then processing could be carried out at the level of the user. If not, then the problems discussed for federated database systems are present for the client-server environment also.

The standards that are being proposed for client-server computing address some of the issues discussed here. Three of the relevant standards will be discussed in section 5.4.

5.3 ARCHITECTURAL ASPECTS

As mentioned in section 5.1, a major challenge is to determine the components that have to be placed on the client and server side. On the one hand one may place all of the applications processing, business rules, and logic at the client side and only have the database at the server side. This is the fat client approach and is illustrated in figure 5-4. Such an approach places a tremendous burden on the client. Current trends are to make the client "thinner" by having it do as little processing as possible.

At the other extreme, one places all of the processing at the server side and only has user interface processing at the client side. This means that all of the business rules and logic also reside at the server side. This is the thin client approach. This places great burden on the server and may cause performance problems. Thin client approach is shown in figure 5-5.

The third alternative, which is becoming increasingly popular, is the three-tiered architecture. The DBMS processing is at the server side. The client side has user interface processing. There is a middle layer which may reside in another machine. The business rules and logic are handled by this layer. This three-tiered architecture is illustrated in figure 5-6. With this architecture, neither the client nor

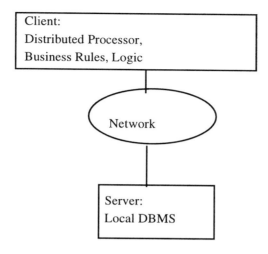

Figure 5-4. Fat Client Approach

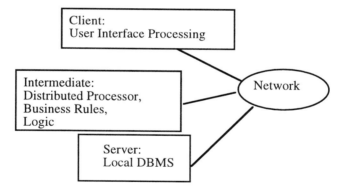

Figure 5-5. Thin Client Approach

the server are burdened. However there is now an additional layer and therefore there is additional communication between the three layers.

We believe that client-server architectures will evolve over the next few years especially with the emergence of the Internet. There has been some discussion as to whether this architecture will "die" due to the Internet [DCI96]. Some argue that it will and some argue that it will not. We address the impact of the Internet on client server architectures in Chapter 10 and give our views.

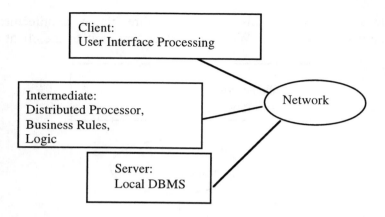

Figure 5-6. Three-tiered Architecture

5.4 STANDARDS FOR CLIENT-SERVER INTEROPERABILITY

5.4.1 RDA

Around December of 1993, ISO's document for Remote Database Access, called RDA, became a standard. It is one of the OSI (Open Systems Interconnection) application standards for multivendor interoperability. The standard consists of two parts. Part 1 specifies the generic model, service, and protocol and part 2 specifies SQL specialization. The RDA standard specifies primitives for communication between a client and a server. It has been influenced by research in distributed and heterogeneous database systems.

Figure 5-7 illustrates interoperability through the RDA protocol. Essentially what happens is that the RDA client and server communicate with each other via the RDA service provider. Five different services are provided. They are the dialogue management service, the transaction management service, the control service, the resource handling service, and the database language service. Essentially these services provide support for creating, deleting, and manipulating databases. Furthermore support for queries and transactions are also provided. As stated by Tang and Scoggins [TANG92], each RDA service element is modeled by an abstract operation. The service parameters are divided into three groups: request group, result group, and the error group. Specialization standards assign values to the parameters. An example of a specialization standard is the SQL specialization standard. For a detailed discussion of the services we refer to [TANG92].

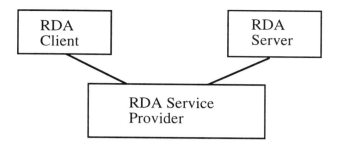

Figure 5-7. Interoperability Through RDA

From our analysis we conclude that RDA's major advantages are support for interoperability between multivendor products and application portability. It also ensures the ACID properties of transactions. In its specification (in the initial version), it appears that RDA does not support location transparency. For example, if a user submits a transaction to an RDA client, he must specify the locations of the servers. One way to overcome this limitation is to use a directory server to locate the DBMS servers that are to execute a transaction. Another issue with RDA is that the SQL specialization standard does not seem to support dynamic SQL. Also, at present, the specialization standard is available only for SQL. As other languages become standards, additional specialization standards have to be developed. Security issues have not received much attention in the RDA standard.

To our knowledge, major database management system vendors are yet to make RDA commercially available. Some third party vendors have developed commercial implementations of RDA. Various prototype developments of RDA have also been reported (see, for example, [IEEE91]).

5.4.2   ODBC

Microsoft Corporation has come up with a specification called Open Database Connectivity (ODBC). The initial idea behind this is for vendors of database management systems to conform to ODBC so that Microsoft applications can access the various database management systems. Figure 5-8 illustrates an example where DBMS vendors A and B build ODBC drivers for their products which are then accessed by Microsoft applications C and D. While the initial focus was on Microsoft applications, ODBC has gone far beyond that and the idea now is for various other applications to access any vendor DBMS using ODBC. That is, ODBC has become a de facto standard for client-server interoperability.

It appears that many of the commercial database management system vendors are showing commitment to ODBC. This will enable the users of various applications to access multiple databases in a transparent manner without having to worry about the details specific to a particular DBMS. Note that the architecture illustrated in figure 5-8 is not a standard architecture. Various vendors have implemented ODBC interfaces in different ways. A discussion of these implementations is beyond the scope of this book. For a discussion of ODBC we refer to [ODBC].

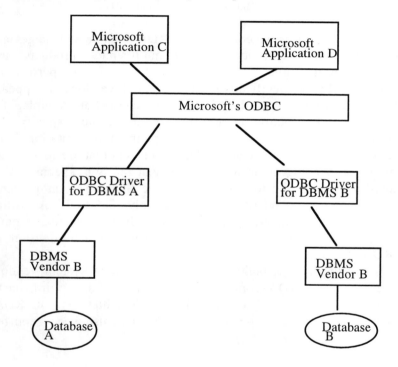

Figure 5-8. Utilizing ODBC

5.4.3   CORBA

An example of a distributed object management (DOM) system that is being used as a middleware to connect heterogeneous database systems is a system based on OMG's CORBA.[40] CORBA is a specification that enables heterogeneous applications, systems, and databases to interoperate with each other. As stated in [OMG95], there are three major components to CORBA. One is the object model

---

[40]   Note that middleware is referred to as the intermediate layer which lies between the operating systems and the applications. This layer connects different systems and applications.

which essentially includes most of the constructs discussed in chapter 2, the second is the Object Request Broker (ORB) through which clients and servers communicate with each other, and the third is the Interface Definition Language (IDL) which specifies the interfaces for client server communication. Figure 5-9 illustrates client server communication through an ORB. Here, the clients and servers are encapsulated as objects. The two objects then communicate with each other. Communication is through the ORB. Furthermore, the interfaces must conform to IDL.

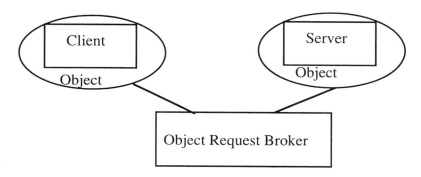

Figure 5-9. Interoperability through ORB

Since heterogeneous database management is of interest to us, our goal is for heterogeneous database systems to interoperate with each other through the ORB. Figure 5-10 illustrates this integration. Essentially nodes A, B, and C are encapsulated as objects. They communicate through the ORB. Note that in this example we have assumed a coarse-grained encapsulation where entire nodes are encapsulated as objects. One could encapsulate portions of the modules. For example, figure 5-11 illustrates a case where the DBMSs and the HDPs are encapsulated separately. Here we have four objects, two for DBMSs and two for the HDPs. One can continue this way and obtain even finer-grained encapsulation where the modules of the DBMS and modules of the HDP are encapsulated.

The advantage of finer-grained encapsulation is that it facilitates migration. That is, one can throw away an HDP and replace it with newer modules. However, the more objects there are, the more messages are sent through the ORB and this will have an impact on the performance.

Various special interest groups and task forces are coming up with specifications based on CORBA. These include specifications for security, real-time processing, and Internet access. In addition, there is also work carried out on developing specifications for vertical domains such as medical, financial, and transportation domains. OMG is also developing specifications for various business objects. It

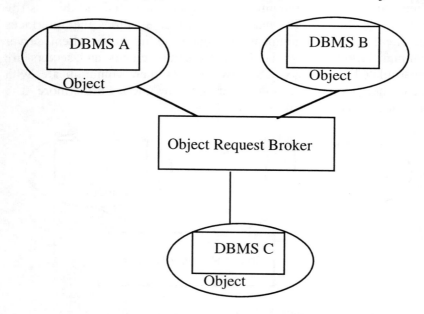

Figure 5-10. Heterogeneous Database Integration through ORB

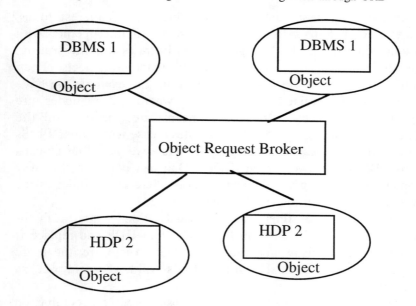

Figure 5-11. Finer-grained encapsulation

appears that this technology is showing a lot of promise for interoperability. A recent workshop addressed issues on the state of CORBA technology and as to whether it was ready for prime time [OOPS94].[41]

5.5 THE ROLE OF METADATA

In the previous sections, we described various architectures for client-server interoperability, provided an overview of some of the technical issues, as well as described various standards. In the discussion of the technical issues, we briefly mentioned metadata management issues. Much of the discussion was influenced by metadata management in a distributed environment.

Metadata in a client-server environment could include many different things. This could be traditional metadata such as global metadata for the data in the servers, or it could include policies and procedures as well as information about the various resources in the network. Metadata may also include repository information needed for semantic interoperability as well as for the interoperability between different systems. Figure 5-12 illustrates a metadata server in the client-server environment. The metadata server is responsible

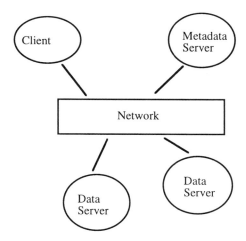

Figure 5-12. Metadata Servers for Interoperability

---

[41] Note that OMG is a consortium of over 700 corporations. Another DOM technology that is becoming increasingly popular is Microsoft Corporation's Distributed OLE (Object Linking and Embedding) and COM (Component Object Model). The future of these technologies will be clearer in the next few years (see, for example, [ORFA96]). In the appendix we provide a brief overview of Microsoft's database access product OLE/DB. Note that the names of the various distributed object management system products are also evolving.

for managing the metadata. Metadata has to be updated in a timely manner so that continuous interoperability is maintained. That is, metadata not only includes information about the data in the data servers, it also facilitates interoperability. In particular, techniques for handling data model heterogeneity, semantic heterogeneity, and policy administration are facilitated by the use of metadata.

In an Internet-based client-server environment, metadata may also include other information such as the access and browsing patterns of the various users. Metadata could act as a guide in the navigation process. Many of the issues are discussed in chapter 10.

CHAPTER 6

MULTIMEDIA DATABASE SYSTEMS

6.1 OVERVIEW

The previous two chapters focused on various aspects of interoperability and heterogeneity. One aspect of heterogeneity is on handling different data types. For many new generation applications, there is a need to integrate different data types such as voice, text, video, and imagery. That is, a multimedia database system is needed to manage the different data types. This chapter describes some of the concepts in multimedia database systems.

A multimedia database system includes a multimedia database management system and a multimedia database. A multimedia database management system (MM-DBMS) manages the multimedia database. A multimedia database is a database which contains multimedia data. Multimedia data may include structured data as well as semi-structured and unstructured data such as voice, video, text, and images. That is, an MM-DBMS provides support for storing, manipulating, and retrieving multimedia data from a multimedia database. In a certain sense a multimedia database system is a type of heterogeneous database system as it manages heterogeneous data types. Heterogeneity is due to the media of the data such as text, video, and voice. An example of an MM-DBMS was illustrated in figure 4-13 when we discussed heterogeneous data types.

An MM-DBMS must provide support for typical database management system functions. These include query processing, update processing, transaction management, storage management, metadata management, security, and integrity. In addition, in many cases, the various types of data such as voice and video have to be synchronized for display and therefore real-time processing is also a major issue in an MM-DBMS.

MM-DBMSs are becoming popular for various applications including C4I, CAD/CAM, air traffic control, and particularly entertainment. Often the terms multimedia and hypermedia have been used interchangeably. We differentiate between the two. While an MM-DBMS manages a multimedia database, a hypermedia DBMS not only manages a multimedia database, but also provides support for browsing the database by following links. That is, a hypermedia DBMS includes an MM-DBMS. We have illustrated both an MM-DBMS and a hypermedia DBMS in figures 6-1 and 6-2, respectively. As illustrated, a hypermedia DBMS includes an MM-DBMS and a linker. The linker module provides support for browsing the multimedia database by following links. This chapter focuses only on MM-DBMSs. Hypermedia issues will be discussed in chapter 10 where we provide an overview of digital library technology and Internet database management.

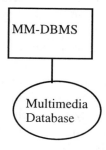

Figure 6-1. Multimedia Database Management System

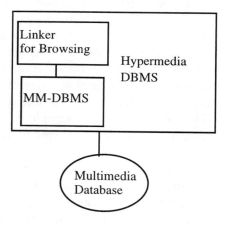

Figure 6-2. Hypermedia Database Management System

Recently there has been much research on designing and developing MM-DBMSs, and, as a result, prototypes and some commercial products are now available (see, for example, IEEE93a, ACM94, IEEE95, IEEE96, NWOS96, CHOR94]). However, as stated in [THUR96a], there are several areas that need further work. Research on developing an appropriate data model to support data types such as video is needed. Some have proposed object-oriented database management systems (OODBMS) for storing and managing multimedia data as they have been found to be more suitable for handling large objects and multimedia data such as sound and video consume considerable storage space (see, for example, [WOEL86]). Although such systems show some promise, they are not sufficient to capture all of the requirements of multimedia applications. For example, in many cases, voice and video data which may be stored in objects have to be synchronized when displayed. The constraints for synchronization are not specified in the object models. Another area that needs research is on developing efficient techniques for indexing. Data manipulation operations such as video editing are still in the early stages. Furthermore, the multimedia databases need to be integrated for many applications as they are distributed. For example, audio data in database 1 has to be integrated with video data in database 2 and displayed to the analyst.

This chapter provides a detailed description of the issues on designing an MM-DBMS. Much of the information has been obtained from our previous work on MM-DBMS [THUR96a]. There were interesting discussions at some recent MM-DBMS workshops on architectural issues.[42] We summarize the discussions at these workshops in section 6.2. Data modeling issues are discussed in section 6.3. Functions of an MM-DBMS are detailed in section 6.4. These functions are: data manipulation (which includes query, update, browsing, and editing), transaction management, metadata management, storage management, data distribution, maintaining, quality of service, user interface management, real-time processing, and maintaining data integrity and security. Finally the chapter is concluded in section 6.5 with a discussion of the current status, developments, and challenges.

6.2. ARCHITECTURES FOR AN MM-DBMS

Various architectures are being examined to design and develop an MM-DBMS. In one approach, the DBMS is used just to manage the metadata and a multimedia file manager is used to manage the multimedia data. Then there is a module for integrating the DBMS and the multimedia file manager. This architecture is based on the loose-coupling approach and is illustrated in figure

---

[42] These discussions are the following: (1) ACM Multimedia 95 Conference Workshop on Multimedia Database Management Systems, San Francisco, CA November 11, 1995. Participants were Bhavani Thuraisingham (co-chair), Peter Paluzzi, Meng Chang Chen, Olav Sandstaa, and Leslie Banach. (2) Panel on Directions for MM-DBMS, at the 1st IEEE Workshop on Multimedia Database Management Systems, August 29, 1995. Panel members included: Bhavani Thuraisingham (Chair), Eric Neuhold, Tom Little, Olivia Liu Cheng, and Bruce Berra.

6-3. In this case the MM-DBMS consists of the three modules: the DBMS managing the metadata, the multimedia file manager, and the module for integrating the two.

The second architecture, illustrated in figure 6-4, is the tight coupling approach. In this architecture the DBMS manages both the multimedia database as well as the metadata. That is, the DBMS is an MM-DBMS. The tight coupling architecture has an advantage because all of the DBMS functions could be applied on the multimedia database. This includes query management, transaction processing, metadata management, storage management, and security and integrity management. Note that with the loose coupling approach, unless the file manager performs the DBMS functions, the DBMS only manages the metadata for the multimedia data.

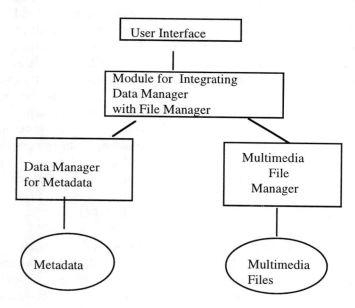

Figure 6-3. Loose Coupling Architecture

Much of the discussion in this section assumes a tight coupling approach. That is, the MM-DBMS manages the multimedia database and performs various functions such as query processing and transaction management. A functional architecture for an MM-DBMS is illustrated in figure 6-5. Note that an MM-DBMS could also be based on a client-server approach. If this is the case, then a DOM system such as the one based on CORBA could be used to integrate the various components. The special extensions for the CORBA IDL to support multimedia data are yet to be specified. A CORBA-based approach to designing an MM-DBMS is illustrated in figure 6-6. An MM-DBMS could also be distributed. An example of a distributed MM-DBMS is illustrated in figure 6-7.

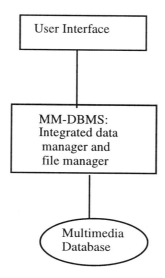

Figure 6-4. Tight Coupling Approach

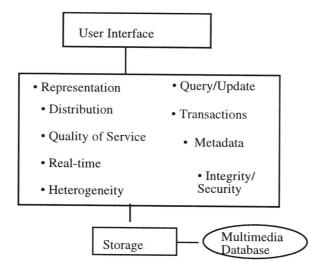

Figure 6-5. Functional Architecture

There are also other aspects to architectures. For example, a multimedia database system could use a commercial database system such as an object-oriented database system to manage multimedia objects. However, relationships between objects and the representation of temporal relationships may involve extensions to the database management system. That is, a DBMS together with an extension layer provide complete support to manage multimedia data. In the alternative case, both the extensions and the database management functions are integrated so that there is one database management system to manage multimedia objects as well as the relationships between the objects. These two types of architectures are illustrated in figure 6-8 and figure 6-9.

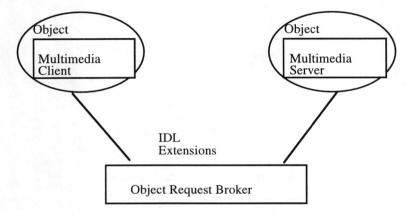

Figure 6-6. An Architecture for Interoperability

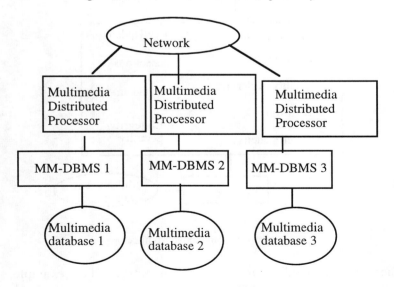

Figure 6-7. Distributed MM-DBMS

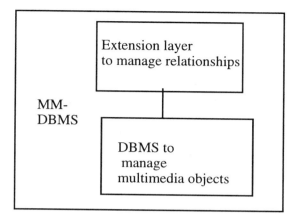

Figure 6-8. DBMS + Extension Layer

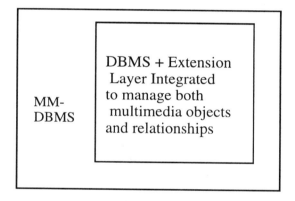

Figure 6-9. DBMS and Extension Layer Integrated

6.3 DATA MODELING

In representing multimedia data several features have to be supported. First of all, there has to be a way to capture the complex data types and all the relationships between the data. Various temporal constructs such as play-before, play-after, play-together, etc. have to be captured (see, for example, the discussion in [OOMO93]). Figure 6-10 illustrates a representation of a multimedia database. In this example, there are two objects: A and B. A consists of 2000 frames and B consists of 3000 frames. A consists of a time interval between 4/95 and 8/95 and B consists of a time interval between 5/95 and 10/95.

An appropriate data model is critical to represent an MM-DBMS. Relational, object-oriented, as well as object-relational, data models have been examined to represent multimedia data. Some argue that relational models are better as they can capture relationships while some others argue that object models are better as they represent complex structures. In the example of figure 6-10, with an object-oriented data model, each object in the figure would correspond to an object in the object model. The attributes of an object may be represented as instance variables and will include time interval, frames, and content description. With the relational model, the object would correspond to an instance of a relation. However with atomic values, it will be difficult to capture the attributes of the instance. In the case of the object-relational model, the attribute value of an instance could be an object. That is, for the instance that represents, say, object A, the attribute value time interval would be the pair (4/95, 8/95). Representing object A with an object model is illustrated in figure 6-11. Representing the same object with an object-relational model is illustrated in figure 6-12. Note that one could build extensions to an existing data model to support complex relationships for multimedia data. These relationships may include temporal relationships between objects such as play together, play before, and play after.

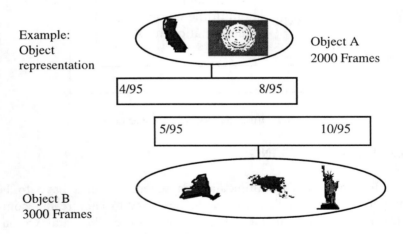

Figure 6-10. Data Representation

Languages such as SQL are being extended for MM-DBMS. Others argue that object-oriented models are better as they can represent complex data types. It appears that both types of models have to be extended to capture the temporal constructs and other special features. Associated with a data model is a query language. The language should support the constructs needed to manipulate the multimedia database. For example, one may need to query to play frames 500 to 1000 of a video script.

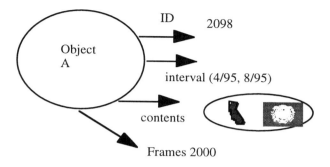

Figure 6-11. Data Representation with Object Model

ID	Interval	Contents	Frame
2098	(4/95, 8/95)		2000

Figure 6-12. Data Representation with ObjecT-Relational Model

In summary, several efforts are under way to develop appropriate data models for MM-DBMSs. Standards are also being developed. This is an area that will become mature within the next few years.

6.4 FUNCTIONS OF AN MM-DBMS

6.4.1 Overview

As mentioned in section 6.1, an MM-DBMS must support the basic DBMS functions. These include data manipulation which includes query/update processing, transaction management, metadata management, storage management, and maintaining security and integrity. All of these functions are more complex as the data may be structured as well as unstructured. Furthermore, handling various data types such as audio and video is quite complex. In addition to these basic DBMS functions, an MM-DBMS must also support real-time processing to synchronize multimedia data types such as audio and video. Quality of service is an important aspect for MM-DBMS. For example, in certain cases, high quality resolution, say, for images may not always be necessary. Special user interfaces are also needed to support different media.

This section provides an overview of the various functions. Data manipulation is the subject of section 6.4.2. Data manipulation includes query/update processing, browsing, and editing. Other functions such as transaction management, metadata management, data distribution, and storage management are described in sections 6.4.3, 6.4.4, 6.4.5, and 6.4.6, respectively. Some of the additional functions such as quality of service, real-time processing, and special user interface management are described in sections 6.4.7, 6.4.8, and 6.4.9, respectively. Finally, maintaining data security and integrity is discussed in section 6.4.10.

6.4.2. Data Manipulation

Data manipulation involves various aspects. Support for querying, browsing, and filtering the data is essential. Appropriate query languages are needed for this purpose. As discussed earlier, SQL extensions show much promise. In addition to just querying the data, one also may want to edit the data. That is, two objects may be merged to form a third object. One could project an object to form a smaller object. As an example, objects may be merged based on time intervals and an object may be projected based on time intervals. Objects may also be updated in whole or in part. Object editing, where the two objects illustrated in figure 6-10 are merged over time intervals, is illustrated in figure 6-13.

In summary, much of the focus on MM-DBMS has been on data representation and data manipulation. Various algorithms have been proposed. Some of these algorithms have also been implemented in various systems [IEEE93a].

6.4.3   Transaction Management

There has been some discussion as to whether transaction management is needed in MM-DBMS [ACM94]. We feel that this is important as in many cases annotations may be associated with multimedia objects. For example, if one updates an image, then its annotation must also be updated. Therefore, the two operations have to be carried out as part of a transaction. Figure 6-14 illustrates an example of transaction management for an MM-DBMS.

Example: Object editing

Edit objects A and B of figure 6-10 by merging them
to form a new object over interval 4/15/95 to 8/15/95

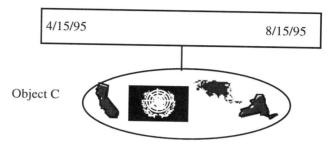

Figure 6-13. Data Manipulation

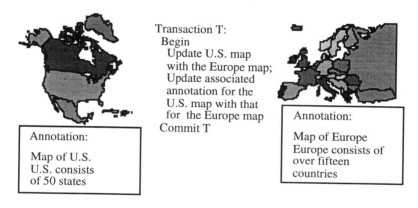

Transaction T:
  Begin
    Update U.S. map
    with the Europe map;
    Update associated
    annotation for the
    U.S. map with that
    for the Europe map
  Commit T

Annotation:

Map of U.S.
U.S. consists
of 50 states

Annotation:

Map of Europe
Europe consists of
over fifteen
countries

Figure 6-14. Transaction Processing

Unlike data representation and data manipulation, transaction management in an MM-DBMS is still a new area. Associated with transaction management are concurrency control and recovery. The issue is what are the transaction models? Are there special concurrency control and recovery mechanisms? Much research is needed in this area.

6.4.3   Metadata Management

Many of the metadata issues discussed for DBMSs apply for MM-DBMSs also. What is a model for metadata? What are the techniques for metadata management?, etc. In addition, there may be large quantities of metadata to describe, say, audio and video data. For example, in the case of video data, one may need to maintain information about the various frames. This information is usually stored in the metadata. An example of a metadatabase for an MM-DBMS is illustrated in figure 6-15. That is, the map of the U.S. is the data while the annotation is part of the metadata.

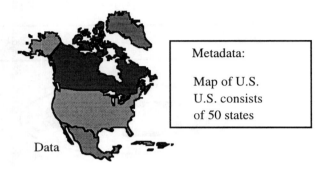

Figure 6-15. Metadata

There are several other considerations. Metadata plays a crucial role in, say, pattern matching. To do data analysis on multimedia data, one needs to have some idea as to what one is searching for. For example, in a video clip, if various images are to be recognized, then there must be some patterns already stored to facilitate pattern matching. Information about these patterns has to be stored in the metadata.

In summary, metadata management in an MM-DBMS is still a challenge. Some ideas were presented in [META96]. The emergence of Internet technologies makes this even more complex. Some of the aspects are discussed in chapter 10.

6.4.5   Storage Management

The major issues in storage management include developing special index methods and access strategies for multimedia data types. Content-based data access is important for many multimedia applications. However, efficient techniques for content-based data access are still a challenge. Other storage issues include caching data. How often should the data be cached? Are there any special considerations for multimedia data? Are there special algorithms? Also, storage techniques for integrating different data types are needed. For example, a multimedia database may contain video, audio, and text databases instead of just one data type. The display of these different data types have to be synchronized. Appropriate storage mechanisms are needed so that there is continuous display of the data. Figure 6-16 illustrates an example for indexing. In this example, an index file is maintained on continents. There is a pointer to the corresponding map. It is assumed here that many of the queries posed pertain to the continents of the world.

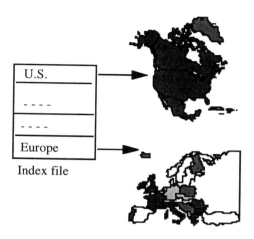

U.S.

- - - -

- - - -

Europe

Index file

Figure 6-16. Indexing

Storage management for multimedia databases is also an area that has been given considerable attention. Several advances have been made during recent years [MDDS94].

6.4.6   Data Distribution

Figure 6-17 illustrates an example of a distributed MM-DBMS. In this example, one node has a map of U.S. while another node has a map of Europe. Such a system must manage the distributed multimedia database. As illustrated in figure 6-17, a distributed MM-DBMS is essentially a collection of MM-DBMSs connected through a network. The multimedia distributed processor module is responsible for handling data distribution issues. For example, how are the objects distributed? Are they distributed based on clusters or related topics? How can different objects be combined in query processing? Are there special mechanisms for distributed transaction management? How is the distributed metadata maintained? In the example of figure 6-17, one could merge the two objects at the two nodes to obtain the result to a query such as "retrieve all the contents of the distributed database". The result will be an object which contains both maps of U.S. and of Europe.

Recently there have been some efforts on distributed MM-DBMSs [IEEE96]. Many of these efforts assume a homogeneous environment except for different data types. Distributed MM-DBMSs could also be heterogeneous with respect to data models and other aspects. Then the issues discussed in Chapter 4 have to be examined for such systems.

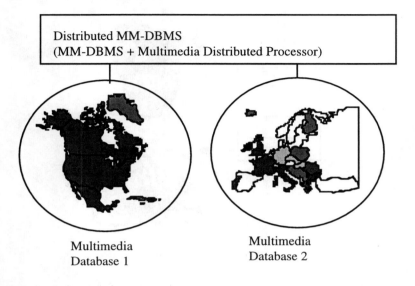

Figure 6-17. Data Distribution

6.4.7   Quality of Service

Not all applications will require high quality data to be displayed. In some cases breaks in display of video data may be tolerated while in some other cases it may not. Figure 6-18 illustrates an example where there is low quality data in a normal mode but higher quality data in a crisis mode.

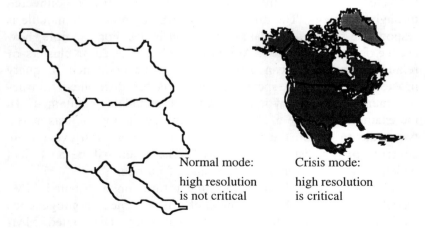

Figure 6-18. Quality of Service

The challenges here include specifying quality of service primitives and implementing these primitives. Formal approaches may help in this area. One needs to develop a model and an associated language for quality of service. The data model for the MM-DBMS may also have to be extended with additional constructs.

6.4.8   Real-time Processing

As discussed in Chapter 2, in a real-time DBMS (RTDBMS), the queries and transactions have to meet timing constraints. There is a strong connection between RTDBMSs and MM-DBMSs. For example, the audio and video data have to be synchronized. This means that certain timing constraints have to be imposed on the data and these timing constraints have to be met. If not, one could hear Jane's voice with Robert speaking on the video script.

The issue is whether the timing constraints are hard, soft, or firm. If they are hard, then they have to be met. Otherwise there could be a catastrophic situation. If they are firm, then they have to be met, but there is no serious consequence. If they are soft, then it will be good to meet the constraints. Once the type of constraints are determined for an application, then techniques are needed to handle these constraints. Real-time scheduling techniques may help here. Real-time multimedia processing is illustrated in figure 6-19.

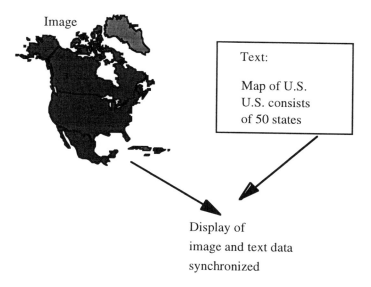

Figure 6-19. Real-time Multimedia Processing

6.4.9   User Interface

Research on user interfaces and database management has been proceeding almost independently. It is only recently that visualization tools are being integrated with database management systems. For multimedia database management, a variety of interfaces have to be provided. These include interfaces for communicating with video, audio, and text databases. In addition, interfaces to support SQL extensions for multimedia data as well as ODMG standards are needed. Figure 6-20 illustrates multiple user interfaces for an MM-DBMS.

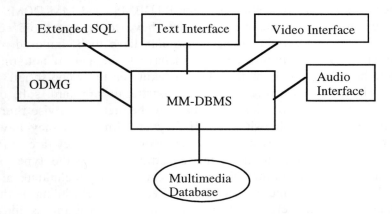

Figure 6-20. User Interface

6.4.10   Maintaining Data Integrity and Security

Integrity: Maintaining data integrity will include support for data quality, integrity constraint processing, concurrency control and recovery for multi-user updates, and accuracy of the data on output. The issues on integrity for database management systems in chapter 2 are present for MM-DBMSs. However, enforcing integrity constraints remains a challenge. For example, what kinds of integrity constraints can be enforced on voice and video data? There is little research to address these issues.

Discretionary Security: Security mechanisms include support-ing access rights and authorization. All of the security issues discussed in chapter 2 apply for MM-DBMSs also. There are also additional concerns. For example, in the case of video data, should access control rules be enforced on entire scripts or frames? Again little research has been done here.

Multilevel security: This type of security is also needed for certain multimedia applications. Some work has been reported on multilevel security [THUR90b]. For example, parts of a document could be classified while other parts may be unclassified. The representation of a multilevel multimedia document is illustrated in figure 6-21. The issue here is for users to read only the documents classified at or below their clearance level.

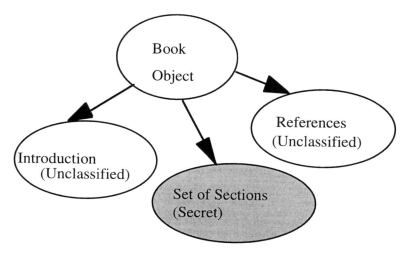

Figure 6-21. Example of a Multilevel Multimedia Document

6.5 CURRENT STATUS AND CHALLENGES

Throughout this chapter, we have discussed the status and challenges for MM-DBMS from architectural, data modeling, and functional view points. This section summarizes much of the discussion plus introduces some additional issues.

Much research has been carried out in recent years in MM-DBMS. As a result, major database system vendors have now developed MM-DBMS products. However, many of these products use limited data management capabilities for multimedia databases. That is, a loose integration approach between a DBMS and a multimedia file manager is utilized. Many efforts have been reported on data modeling research for MM-DBMS, and this field is fairly mature. Various extensions to object and relational models have been proposed to represent multimedia databases and also the relationships between data. Finally, various techniques for query, browsing, and filtering for multimedia data have been developed.

Various research prototypes and commercial products have been developed on multimedia database systems. Some of the recent prototypes include the STORM multimedia database system developed in France [ADIB96] and the VideoStar system developed in Norway [HJEL96]. While there are many similarities between these two systems there are some major differences.

Both STORM and VideoStar systems manage multimedia data and provide support for querying as well as presenting the data. However, STORM uses an object-oriented database system to store the multimedia data and builds layers on top of the database system for various functions. The layer immediately above the database system models temporal relationships between the multimedia data. It is this layer that provides support to queries such as play forward and backward. The layer on top of this modeling layer is the user interface that enables the presentation of multimedia data. In VideoStar, there is no separate database system. That is, the data model captures not only the objects, but also the various relationships including the temporal relationships between the objects. The database system manages these objects. That is, there is no separate layer hosted on top of the database system to capture the temporal relationships. In addition to the two systems discussed here, there are many more systems that have been described in the literature (see, for example, [NWOS96]). A discussion of all of these systems is beyond the scope of this book.

Current challenges in multimedia database management include developing appropriate storage management techniques, transaction management for multimedia databases, security and integrity, as well as metadata management. While various access methods and indexing techniques such as content-based indexing have been developed, there is still a lot of work to be done to handle large video and audio databases. Transaction management research for multimedia databases is just beginning. Security and integrity issues have received little attention. Handling large metadatabases for multimedia databases is still an issue. Integrating real-time data management techniques with multimedia database management is an active research area.

Another major challenge for multimedia database management is the integration with Internet database management technology. There is now a critical need to manage video, image, and audio databases over the Internet. Therefore, additional complexities are introduced with respect to indexing strategies and synchronized display.

Mining multimedia data is also a challenge. Many of the data mining prototypes and products work on structured databases such as relational databases. However, several applications require the management of unstructured data such as text, images, and video. Data mining tools are needed to extract useful information from these unstructured databases. Mining the multimedia data stored in various web servers is also a challenge. Some of the issues involved in mining multimedia data are discussed in chapter 9. A closely related topic is building data warehouses from multiple multimedia data sources. Warehousing is the subject of chapter 8.

Recent research on MM-DBMSs reported in annual multimedia database workshops as well as various publications on MM-DBMSs is showing a lot of promise. However, there are still many challenging problems to be addressed.

CHAPTER 7

MIGRATING LEGACY DATABASES AND APPLICATIONS

7.1 OVERVIEW

Sections 4, 5, and 6 discussed some aspects of interoperability. In particular, heterogeneity issues, federated database systems approach, client-server interoperability, and multimedia data types were discussed. Interoperability also plays a role in system migration. This is because as systems are being migrated to new architectures, they need to interoperate with the old components. This section focuses on system migration with some emphasis on interoperability.

Many database systems developed some ten, twenty, or thirty years ago are becoming obsolete. These systems use older hardware and software. Furthermore, between now and the next few decades, many of today's information systems and applications will become obsolete. Due to resource and, in certain cases, budgetary constraints, new developments of next generation systems may not be possible in many areas. Therefore, current systems need to become easier, faster, and less costly to upgrade and less difficult to support.

Legacy database system and application migration is a complex problem and many of the efforts underway are still not mature. While a good book has been published recently on this subject [BROD95], there is no uniform approach for migration. Since migrating legacy databases and applications is becoming a necessity for most organizations, both government and commercial, one could expect a considerable amount of resources to be expended in this area in the near future. The research issues are also not well understood.

Migrating legacy applications and databases also has an impact on heterogeneous database integration. Typically a heterogeneous database environment may include legacy databases as well as some of the next generation databases. In many cases, an organization may want to migrate the legacy database to an architecture like the client-server architecture and still want the migrated system to be part of the heterogeneous environment. This means that the functions of the heterogeneous database system may be impacted due to this migration process.

This chapter first focuses on two candidate approaches. One is on redoing the system in its entirety and the other is to focus on incremental evolution. The advantages and disadvantages of both approaches are examined. Then the focus will be on evolvable systems. Issues on extracting modules for the legacy system and interoperating with the old system as well as interoperating with the heterogeneous environment are given consideration.

Candidate approaches are described in section 7.2. Overview of evolvable systems is given in section 7.3. Technical challenges for evolving legacy systems are addressed in section 7.4. This discussion also includes the role of metadata in evolving systems. Cost and risk issues are addressed in section 7.5. Finally, in section 7.6, a challenging problem for legacy applications, databases, and software, migration, which is the Year 2000 problem, is discussed.

7.2 CANDIDATE APPROACHES

Two candidate approaches to migrating legacy applications and databases are the following:

- Completely redesign the system and throw away the old system
- Incrementally evolve the old system until the new system is in place.

Figure 7-1 illustrates the first approach where a new system is designed from scratch and the legacy system is thrown away once the new system is in place.

Figure 7-1. Candidate Approach 1

Figure 7-2 illustrates the second approach where the legacy system is evolved in stages. During stage 1 the legacy system is in operation in its entirety. During stage 2, a portion of the legacy system is moved to the new system and communication between the legacy and new system is through a gateway. Stage 3 is similar to stage 2 except some additional progress is made with respect to the new system. During stage 4, the new system is in place in its entirety.

Both approaches have advantages and disadvantages. With the first approach, one has to have some idea of the complete target system. However, this system might be changed upon completion which means the entire effort would not be of much use. However, for systems that are less complex and not dynamic, this approach would be beneficial.

With the incremental evolution approach, some idea of the target system is needed. The target system may also evolve as progress is made with the migration. By incrementally evolving a system, one need not have to wait until the complete system is redone. The challenge here is to determine how to break the complex code and move portions of it to the new system.

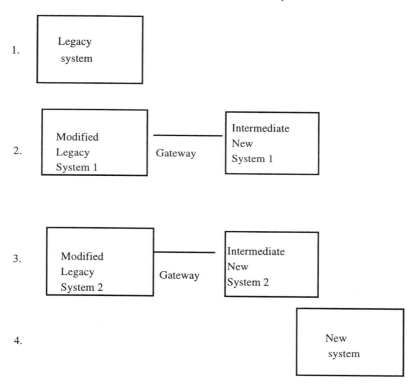

Figure 7-2. Candidate Approach 2

Many of the groups working on migrating legacy databases and applications are focusing on the incremental evolution approach. This is mainly because it is too expensive to throw away a system and rebuild it in its entirety. Therefore, in section 7.3 we focus on evolvable systems. [43]

---

[43] While we are proposing an incremental evolution of legacy systems, there are some who believe that migrating legacy systems will be difficult and that a major rewrite of the system is the only approach. Cost and risk analysis studies have to be carried out to determine the best approach for a particular situation.

7.3 OVERVIEW OF EVOLVABLE SYSTEMS

We need an approach that will evolve a legacy system into a system of the future. To develop such an approach, we need to take advantage of the commercially available hardware and software as well as any product improvements that are planned. For example, many of the products and systems have some funding allocated for improvements. Sometimes these improvements are carried out without any vision for a long-term system. Therefore, we need to make sure that these improvements take the long-term vision into consideration. This means communicating the ideas and the vision to those who control the funding for product improvements. The investment plan should consider incremental evolution of current systems into flexible systems of the future. That is, even if a long-term system has been identified, that is not the end of the whole approach. The end could just be the beginning of another major transition depending on what technology is available at that time. Therefore, the result of the evolution process should be a flexible system that is capable of evolving even in the future as needed. One can expect the extensible system architecture to ultimately replace the current hardware and software architectures.[44]

An evolvable system has many desirable properties. We list some of them. First of all, such a system should be able to incrementally evolve so that user requirements are met in time. This does not mean that all of the requirements are met at once. We would like all of the essential requirements to be met within a feasible time period. The various modules of the system should evolve incrementally. That is, we should not replace all of the modules. We need to determine the modules that have to be replaced and replace them over time. An important point to note is that one does not want the entire system to come to a halt while the system is being upgraded. That is, we need to operate the system as it is being upgraded. This we believe is a major challenge and might require temporary modules as well as simulated modules. Furthermore, the new upgraded portions of the system must interoperate with the old components.

A major rewrite of the entire system is not a desirable feature. That is, parts of the system must be modified with minimal impact on the other modules. Various components of a system may include the operating system, the communication system, the display system, and the data management system. In order to have minimal

---

44 Much of the discussion in this section is influenced by the Evolvable Real-time Systems Initiative carried out at the MITRE Corporation. An overview of this initiative is described in [BENS95].

impact on the rest of the system, it is critical that well defined interfaces are written between the various components. This means that what goes inside a component would not have much impact on the system. Therefore, one could then use commercial off-the-shelf hardware or software for the various components or in some cases it may be necessary to develop some of the components. In any case, an open implementation is essential for the success of an evolvable system project. By having clean interfaces, it is possible for the different components to communicate in a well defined precise manner.

As mentioned earlier, it is critical that an evolvable system be able to support future changes. These changes could be additions to functionality, portability, design, and implementation. In many cases, these future changes will not be known ahead of time and therefore flexibility is very important.

Now that we have described the desirable properties of evolvable systems, the next step is to see what can be done to ensure that a system is evolvable. We believe that designing and developing a software infrastructure is necessary to evolve a system. The infrastructure hosts the evolving system through multiple stages. The infrastructure is a collection of important modules such as the operating system, data management system, and services such as middleware services and scheduling services. Appropriate hardware is needed to build the infrastructure. The applications are hosted on the infrastructure. It is important to clearly define the interfaces between all the components of the infrastructure and also the interfaces between the infrastructure and the applications. The migration path should also be clearly laid out. Figure 7-3 illustrates the infrastructure. As can be seen, the hardware hosts the various infrastructure components such as the operating system and various services. One could consider the middleware and the data manager to be part of these services. Applications are hosted on the infrastructure.

The specific services include memory management, scheduling, file management, data sharing, concurrency control and transaction management, query facility, metadata management, interprocess communication, and enforcing security and integrity constraints. All of the mechanisms for communication between the various components are also provided by the infrastructure.

Now, in evolving a system, one needs to first define the target architecture. One such example is illustrated in figure 7-4. In the ideal case, all of the applications should be hosted on the infrastructure. These applications make use of the infrastructure services such as database management. Database management services enable multiple applications to access and share various databases. In order to host all of the applications of an evolvable system on an infrastructure, one may have to rewrite the entire system at once. This is not desirable. What is needed is an incremental evolution of the system. Furthermore, for many projects the funding is such that a complete rewrite of the system is not feasible. That is, the funding is obtained incrementally for incremental updates. Therefore, the desired approach to evolution is to incrementally migrate the components of an application onto the infrastructure. For example, consider an application with modules A, B, C, and D. During stage 1 module A is hosted on the infrastructure while B, C, and D run on the old legacy system. This means there must be communication between the infrastructure and the old system. Then in stage 2, modules B and C may be hosted on the infrastructure while D still runs on the legacy system. An example of the intermediate architecture during migration is illustrated in Figure 7-5 where one application subsystem is hosted on the new infrastructure and the rest of the system is still a legacy system.

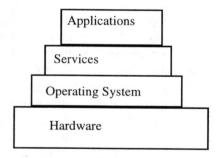

Figure 7-3. Infrastructure

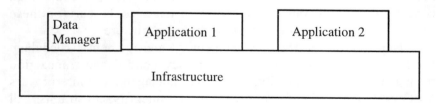

Figure 7-4. Target Architecture

7.4 EVOLUTION ISSUES

In the previous sections we described two candidate approaches for migration and then focused on the incremental evolution approach to migration. This approach has advantages as in many cases the legacy system is complex and the details of the target system are not known ahead of time. This section focuses on some of the evolution issues, the impact of existing heterogeneous database systems, and the use of various technologies such as distributed object management in the evolution process.

One of the key issues in evolving systems is determining which portions to migrate first. In addition, there has to be a clear idea of the evolution path as well as the design of the intermediate system. One need not have the complete description of the target system. Once the portion that has to be taken out of the legacy system is determined, the next question is how to encapsulate the appropriate modules. If the legacy system is well documented with good interfaces, then this may not be very difficult to do. But in many cases the legacy system is not well documented and the person who designed the system may not be with the organization. Identifying the interfaces could also be difficult. In such situations, reverse engineering tools could play a major role. One needs to determine the type of reverse engineering tools to use. Once these tools have been applied, then the modules are extracted and migrated to the new system. The question then is what happens to the old system? Do you rearchitect the old system also or just focus on the new system? This depends on the particular situation. Sometimes redoing the old system may not give any benefits.

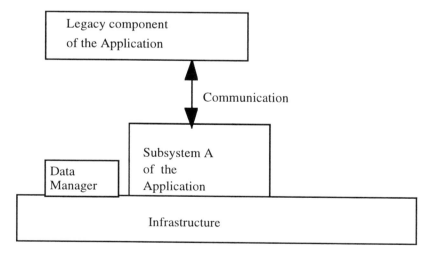

Figure 7-5. Evolvable Architecture

At this stage, we have determined the modules to pull out of the old system. The question then is can these modules be reused? It may be desirable for these modules to be reused by many other systems. If this is the case, one could wrap these modules as objects and use a distributed object management approach to migration. This is illustrated in figure 7-6. The modules that are extracted from the legacy system are reused by different target systems. This evolution process continues until a satisfactory target system is obtained. Note that appropriate IDL interfaces are needed for the modules that are extracted and encapsulated as objects.

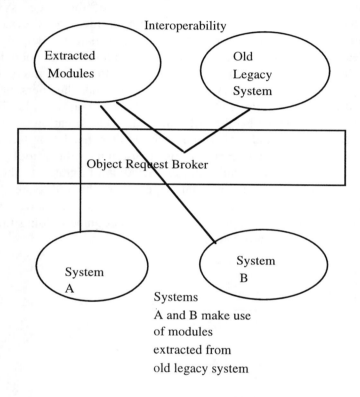

Figure 7-6. Reuse of Extracted Modules

A major issue is the interoperation of the legacy system with other systems in the heterogeneous environment after the changes are made. For example, if some of the modules are taken from the legacy system, can it still interoperate with the heterogeneous environment? Here again object technology can help. Once the modules are extracted and wrapped as objects, then the legacy system, the objects, and the remaining systems can interoperate (see figure 7-7). Many of the issues are largely unexplored and the details are yet to be worked out.

Metadata is an important resource in the evolution of legacy systems. Metadata may include information about the legacy systems, evolution procedure and plans, as well as information on the status of evolution. The metadata repository may be consulted by the various system components in the evolution process. History information about the evolution may also be maintained in the repository. Note that the metadata repository may also be encapsulated as an object in the distributed environment.

Software reverse engineering tools will play a major role in the evolution process. For example, with some of these tools, one may extract the design of the complete system from the legacy modules and then this design may in turn be used to aid in the evolution process.

We have stated some of the issues in system migration. We believe that coarse-grained encapsulation of legacy objects, where an entire legacy application or system is encapsulated as an object, is less complex. The challenge is fine-grained encapsulation. That is, a legacy system or module has to be broken into pieces and the individual pieces have to be encapsulated. As mentioned earlier, appropriate IDL interfaces are needed for the individual pieces.

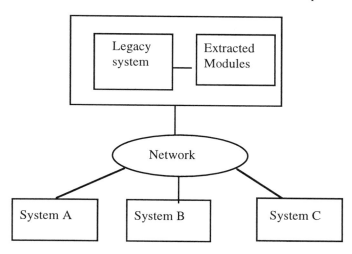

Figure 7-7. Heterogeneous Environment

7.5 COSTS/RISKS OF EVOLVING SYSTEMS

One of the major issues that has been given little consideration is the cost of evolving the legacy systems. For example, before starting any project one needs to determine whether it is better to evolve the system or to build wrappers around the system and let it interoperate with the new systems. That is, a detailed risk analysis has to be carried out. For example, what are the risks involved? Will the project succeed? If it is determined that it is more beneficial to evolve a system, then the cost of the migration plan has to be determined. For example, should the entire system be migrated at one time or should the migration be done in incremental stages as discussed in the previous sections?

Various cost models have been proposed for information systems design and development. The parameters being considered include hardware and software costs, man power, understanding of the technology, and the risks involved. With legacy system migration, since this is still not a mature technology area, the risks involved may be high. Only a few experiences have been reported. Furthermore, since object technology is showing a lot of promise for legacy migration, we need personnel qualified in this technology area. However, there is a significant shortage of object-oriented programmers and these programmers are in high demand. We are also finding that educating structured programmers in object technology is not as straightforward. Also, use of COTS technology might reduce the migration costs. However, not many tools exist for migrating systems.

Another issue is whether the cost models developed for information systems design and development are sufficient for modeling the cost of legacy system migration and interoperability. Little research has been reported in this area. Therefore an active program is needed to determine the cost of system evolution and migration. First of all, the current models have to be examined to determine their suitability. Then appropriate models have to be developed. Finally, these models have to be tested on some real-world applications. Some systems have to be migrated to determine the correctness of the results produced. In summary, the cost analysis of system evolution, interoperation, and migration is still a new area and much research and development work remains to be done.

7.6 EXAMPLE APPLICATION: YEAR 2000 PROBLEM

One of the major challenges faced by several organizations, both the commercial and government sectors, is the Year 2000 problem. Essentially this problem is the following. Most legacy systems and applications use two digits to represent the year. So, for example, 96 means 1996 and 00 mean 1900. So, when the day changes from December 31st 1999 to January 1, 2000, the year in the computer system will change from 99 to 00. However, 00 means 1900 and not 2000. This is expected to cause a major catastrophe with many applications. Organizations could lose billions of dollars all over the world due to this problem. Intense research is now being carried out to determine how this problem can be overcome. Numerous conferences are now taking place to address this challenge [YEAR96].

The question is, what are the solutions? The tedious method is to take each application that uses the year variable and make changes so that 00 does not mean 1900. This is almost impossible to do for complex applications. Another approach is to have a program that automatically tracks down these programs that have the year variable and make appropriate changes. This is also a challenge. Various reverse engineering tools are also being developed to address the Year 2000 challenge. Essentially these tools will reengineer the program so that the modules referencing the year variable are encapsulated. This way, the impact on the rest of the programs may be minimized. It has also been discussed that metadata will play a major role in the Year 2000 problem. One needs to capture the metadata about the various programs and use this metadata in determining the solutions to reengineering. However, it appears that the specific details on how metadata may be captured and used are yet to be determined. That is, it seems that there are still no viable solutions to the Year 2000 problem and we are operating now under a hard timing deadline to solve this problem. However, there is intense work now to address the issues and one can expect some solutions to be developed over the next couple of years.

CONCLUSION TO PART II

Now let us examine how the technologies described in part II relate to the framework. Here, we have technologies for integrating heterogeneous database systems, handling multimedia data types, interoperability based on federated and client-server architectures as well as migrating legacy database applications.

All of the technologies described in chapters 4, 5, and 6 are built upon database and distributed database technologies described in part I. That is, chapters 2, 3, 4, 5, and 6 provide the foundations for developing heterogeneous database systems handling multimedia data both based on client-server and federated architectural approaches.

The technology described in chapter 7 cuts across all of the other technologies. That is, migrating legacy databases and applications is applicable to centralized database systems, distributed database systems, heterogeneous database systems, as well as multimedia database systems. In addition, interoperability issues relating to migration are also addressed. While chapter 7 has discussed migration and system evolution at a general level, the issues specific to a particular system such as heterogeneous multimedia legacy databases are largely unexplored.

Information Extraction and Sharing for Data Management Systems

Part III

INTRODUCTION TO PART III

While part I described concepts and developments in database and distributed database systems and part II described issues on interoperability and migration, during recent years several technologies have emerged to support the efficient access to database systems as well as extracting and sharing the information from the data in the databases. These include data warehousing, data mining, digital libraries, Internet databases, and database support for collaboration. The goal of the four chapters in part III is to give a broad overview of these emerging technologies for data access, sharing, and information extraction. These technologies build on the technologies discussed in parts I and II. With respect to the Data Management Systems Framework, the chapters in part III describe the Information Extraction Layer. Several references are cited in part III should the reader need in-depth coverage of a particular topic.

Data warehousing is the topic of chapter 8. The idea behind data warehousing is that it is often cumbersome to access data from the heterogeneous databases. Several processing modules need to cooperate with each other to process a query in a heterogeneous environment. So, a data warehouse will bring together the essential data from the heterogeneous databases. This way the users need to query only the warehouse. The challenges include designing the warehouse and, in the case of updates to the individual databases, propagating the updates to the warehouse.

Chapter 9 addresses data mining. Data mining is the process of posing multiple queries and extracting often previously unknown information from the data. Multiple technologies have to be integrated to develop data mining tools. These include database management, statistics, machine learning, visualization, and high performance computing. Chapter 9 describes the approaches to data mining and the challenges. Security implications of data mining are also discussed.

Chapter 10 focuses on digital libraries and Internet database management. This is an extremely popular topic with the explosion of the users on the Internet. World wide web sites are now all over the world. Many of these servers are heterogeneous in nature and contain multimedia data such as voice, text, images, and video. Many of the techniques discussed in earlier chapters have to be integrated to provide access to these large quantities of information distributed throughout the world. The topics addressed in chapter 10 include digital library functions as well as the role of one of today's hottest technologies, Javasoft's JAVA, for Internet database management.

Chapter 11 describes database support for collaborative applications. Note that as mentioned in chapter 1, we consider collaborative systems, expert systems, and visualization systems to be part of application technologies. However, many of these systems have to utilize data management systems. It is this utilization that is addressed in chapter 11. We discuss architectural as well as modeling issues and discuss support for transaction management, security, and other database functions for collaboration and data sharing.

CHAPTER 8

DATA WAREHOUSING

8.1 OVERVIEW

Data warehousing is one of the more popular topics in data management. Several organizations are building their own warehouses. Commercial DBMS vendors are marketing warehousing products. In addition, some companies are specializing only in developing data warehouses. What then is a data warehouse? The idea behind this is that it is often cumbersome to access data from the heterogeneous databases. Several processing modules need to cooperate with each other to process a query in a heterogeneous environment. Therefore, a data warehouse will bring together the essential data from the heterogeneous databases. This way the users need to query only the warehouse.

As stated by Inmon [INMO93], data warehouses are subject-oriented. Their design depends to a great extent on the application utilizing them. They integrate diverse and possibly heterogeneous data sources. They are persistent. That is, the warehouse is very much like a database. They vary with time. This is because as the data sources from which the warehouse is built get updated, the changes have to be reflected in the warehouse. Essentially data warehouses provide support to decision support functions of an enterprise or an organization. For example, while the data sources may have the raw data, the data warehouse may have correlated data, summary reports, and aggregate functions applied to the raw data.

Figure 8-1 illustrates a data warehouse. The data sources are managed by DBMSs A, B, and C. The information in these databases are merged and put into a warehouse. There are various ways to merge the information. One is to simply replicate the databases. This does not have any advantages over accessing the heterogeneous databases. The second case is to replicate the information, but to remove any inconsistencies and redundancies. This has some advantages as it is important to provide a consistent picture of the databases. The third approach is to select a subset of the information from the databases and place it in the warehouse. There are several issues here. How are the subsets selected? Are they selected at random or is some method used to select the data? For example, one could take every other row in a relation (assuming it is a relational database) and store these rows in the warehouse. The fourth approach, which is a slight variation of the third approach, is to determine the types of queries that users would pose; then analyze the data and store only the data that is required by the user. This is called on-line analytical processing (OLAP) as opposed to on-line transaction processing (OLTP). Note that much of the discussions in chapters 2, 3, and 4 focused on OLTP applications.

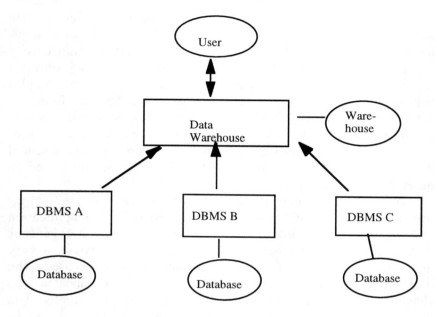

Figure 8-1. Data Warehouse Example

With a data warehouse, data may often be viewed differently by different applications. That is, the data is multidimensional. For example, payroll department may want data to be in a certain format while project department may want data to be in a different format. The warehouse must provide support for such multidimensional data. Multiple views of the same data are illustrated in figure 8-2.

In integrating the data sources to form the warehouse, a challenge is to analyze the application and select appropriate data to be placed in the warehouse. At times, some computations may have to be performed so that only summaries and averages are stored in the data warehouse. Note that it is not always the case that the warehouse has all the information for a query. In this case, the warehouse may have to get the data from the heterogeneous data sources to complete the execution of the query. Another challenge is what happens to the warehouse when the individual databases are updated? How are the updates propagated to the warehouse? How can security be maintained? These are some of the issues that are being investigated.

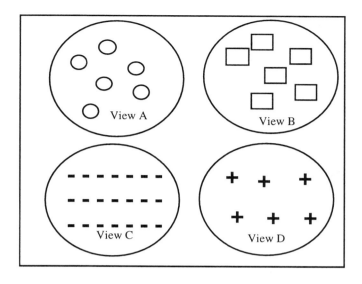

Figure 8-2. Multiple Views of the Data

This chapter is organized in the following way. Technologies for data warehousing is the subject of section 8.2. The discussion here includes the role of metadata as well as distributing the warehouse. Designing the data warehouse is discussed in section 8.3. In particular, data modeling, data distribution, integrating heterogeneous data sources, and security are discussed. Finally, in section 8.4, some preliminary ideas toward developing a framework for data warehousing are given.

8.2   TECHNOLOGIES FOR DATA WAREHOUSING

Figure 8-3 illustrates data warehousing technologies. That is, several technologies have to be integrated to develop a data warehouse. These include heterogeneous database integration, statistical databases, data modeling, metadata management, access methods and indexing, query language, database administration, database security, distributed database management, and high performance database management. In this section we briefly examine these technologies within the context of data warehousing.

Heterogeneous database integration is an essential component to data warehousing. This is because data from multiple heterogeneous data stores may have to be integrated to build the warehouse. There is, however, a major difference. Often in heterogeneous database integration there is no single repository to store the data. However, in a warehouse there is usually a single repository for the warehouse data and this repository has to be managed.

Statistical databases keep information such as sums, averages, and other aggregates. There are various issues for statistical databases. For example, how can summary data be maintained when the database gets updated? How can the individual data items be protected? For example, the average salary may be Unclassified while the individual salaries are Secret. Since warehouses keep summary information, techniques used to manage statistical databases need to be examined for warehouses.

```
* Data Modeling
* Database Security
* Heterogeneous Database Integration
* Distributed database
* Access methods and indexing
* Query language
* Database Administration
* High performance computing
* Metadata
```

Figure 8-3. Some Data Warehousing Technologies

Data modeling is an essential task for building a data warehouse. Is the data model influenced by the data models used by the heterogeneous data sources? Should a data model be developed from scratch? Inmon has outlined several steps to developing a data model [INMO93]. He says that at the higher level there are three stages: developing a corporate model, an enterprise model, and a warehouse model. Then at the middle level there may be a model possibly for each subject. Then at the physical level it includes features such as keys. Some argue that this is too lengthy a process and that one should get to the warehouse model directly. As more experiences are reported on developing data warehouses, this issue may be resolved.

Appropriate access methods and index strategies have to be developed for the warehouse. For example, the warehouse is structured so that query processing is facilitated. An example query may be: how many red cars were bought in 1995 by physicians costing more than 50K? Many relations have to be joined to process this query. Instead of joining the actual data, one could get the result by combining the bit maps for the associated data. That is, the warehouse may utilize an index strategy called a bit map index where essentially there is a 1 in the bit map if the answer is positive in the database. That is, if the color of the car is red, then in the associated bit map, there will be a 1. This is a simple example. Current research is focusing on developing more complex access methods and index strategies.

Developing an appropriate query language for the warehouse is an issue. This would depend on the data model utilized. If the model, say, is relational, then an SQL-based language may be appropriate. If the data model is object-oriented, then an ODMG-based language may be appropriate. One may also need to provide visual interfaces for the warehouse.

Database administration techniques may be utilized for administering the warehouse. Is there a warehouse administrator? What is the relationship between the warehouse administrator and the administrator of the data sources? How often should the warehouse be audited? Should the warehouse be audited? Inmon has given some reasons as to why it may not be a good idea to audit the warehouse [INMO93]. Another administration issue is propagating updates to the database. In many cases, the administrators of the data sources may not want to enforce triggers on their data. If this is the case, it may be difficult to automatically propagate the updates.

Protecting the warehouse is a major issue. Security issues for integrating heterogeneous database systems discussed in Chapter 4 need to be examined here also. Furthermore, statistical database security also will play an import role. Security controls also have to be enforced in maintaining the warehouse. This will have an impact on querying, managing the metadata, and updating the warehouse. In addition, if multilevel security is needed, then there are additional considerations. For example, what are the trusted components of the warehouse?

High performance computing including parallel database management plays a major role in data warehousing. The goal is for users to get answers to complex queries rapidly. Therefore, parallel query processing strategies are becoming popular for warehouses. Appropriate hardware and software are needed for efficient query processing.

Metadata management is another critical technology for data warehousing. The problem is defining the metadata. Metadata could come from the data sources. Metadata will include the mappings between the data sources and the warehouse. There is also metadata specific to the warehouse. Many of the issues discussed in chapter 2 for metadata management are applicable for the warehouse. Figure

8-4 illustrates the various types of metadata that must be maintained in developing and maintaining a warehouse. There are three types of metadata. One is metadata for the individual data sources. The other is the metadata needed for mappings and transformations to build the warehouse, and the third is the metadata to maintain and operate the warehouse.

Distributed database technology plays a role in data warehousing. Should the warehouse be centralized or distributed? If it is distributed, then much of the technology for distributed database management discussed in chapter 3 is applicable for data warehousing. Figures 8-5 and 8-6 illustrate architectures for nondistributed and distributed data

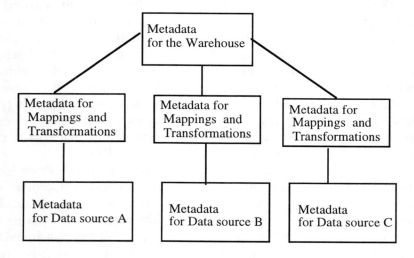

Figure 8-4. Types of Metadata

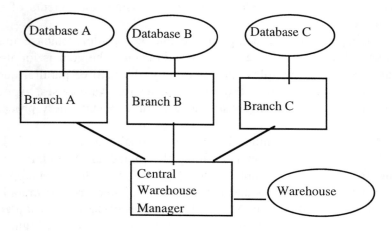

Figure 8-5. Nondistributed Data Warehouse

warehouses. In the nondistributed case, there is a central warehouse for the multiple branches, say in a bank. In the distributed warehouse case, one may assume that each bank has its local warehouse and the warehouses communicate with each other.

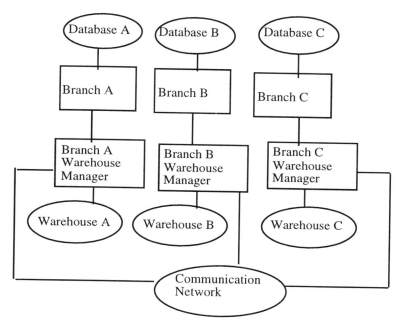

Figure 8-6. Distributed Data Warehouse

8.3 DEVELOPING THE DATA WAREHOUSE

Designing and developing the data warehouse is a complex process and in many ways depends on the application. A good reference to data warehousing is the book by Inmon [INMO93]. It describes the details of the issues involved in building a data warehouse. In this section we outline some of the steps to designing the warehouse.

There are three phases to developing a warehouse. One phase focuses on structuring the warehouse so that query processing is facilitated. That is, this phase focuses on getting the data out of the warehouse. The other phase focuses on bringing the data into the warehouse. That is, how can the heterogeneous data sources be integrated so that the data can be brought into the warehouse. The third phase is to maintain the warehouse once it is developed. That is, the process does not end when the warehouse is developed. It has to be continually maintained. We first outline the steps in each of the phases.

One of the key steps in getting the data out of the warehouse is application analysis. For example, what types of queries will the users pose? How often are the queries posed? Will the responses be straightforward? Will the users need information like summary reports? A list consisting of such questions needs to be formulated.

Another step is to determine what the user would expect from the warehouse. Would he want to deal with a relational model or an object-oriented model or both? Are multiple views needed? Once this is determined, how do you go about developing a data model? Are there intermediate models?

A third step is to determine the metadata, index strategies, and access methods. That is, once the query patterns and data models have been determined, one needs to determine what kinds of metadata have to be maintained. What are the index strategies and access methods enforced? What are the security controls?

A closely related task is developing the various schemas for the warehouse. Note that the individual databases will have their own schema. The complexity here is in integrating these schemas to develop a global schema for the warehouse. While schema integration techniques for distributed and heterogeneous databases may be used, the warehouse is developed mainly to answer specific queries for various applications. Therefore, special types of schemas such as star schemas and constellation schemas have been proposed in the literature. Products based on these schemas have also been developed. A discussion of these various types of schemas is beyond the scope of this book.

There are several technical issues in bringing the data into the warehouse from the different data sources. What information should be deleted from the individual databases when migrating the data to the warehouse? How should integrity be maintained? What is the security policy? How can inconsistencies be resolved? This requires a lot of work. Various algorithms for integrating heterogeneous databases have to be examined. At the end of this stage one would have some form of a warehouse.

Once the warehouse is designed and developed, there are also some additional considerations for maintaining the warehouse. How is the security of the warehouse maintained? Should the warehouse be audited? How often is the warehouse updated? How are the changes to the local databases to be propagated to the warehouse? What happens if a user's query cannot be answered by the warehouse? Should the warehouse go to the individual databases to get the data if needed? How can data quality and integrity be maintained?

We have outlined a number of phases and steps to developing a data warehouse. The question is, should these phases and steps be carried out one after the other or should they be done in parallel? Based on discussions with those who have actually built warehouses, it seems that many of the activities can be done in parallel. As in most software systems, there is a planning phase, a development phase, and a maintenance phase. However, there are some additional complexities. The databases themselves may be migrating to new architectures or data models. This would have some impact on the warehouse. New databases may be added to the heterogeneous environment. The additional information should be migrated to the warehouse without causing inconsistencies. These are difficult problems and there are investigations on how to resolve them. Although there is much promise, there is a long way to go before viable commercial products are developed.

In summary, a data warehouse enables different applications to view the data differently. That is, it supports multidimensional data. Data warehouse technology is an integration of multiple technologies including heterogeneous database integration, statistical databases, and parallel processing. The challenges in data warehousing include developing appropriate data models, architectures (e.g., centralized or distributed), query languages, and access methods/index strategies, as well as developing techniques for query processing, metadata management, maintaining integrity and security, and integrating heterogeneous data sources. Integrating structured and unstructured databases, such as relational and multimedia databases, is also a challenge.

While the notion of data warehousing has been around for a while, it is only recently that we are seeing the emergence of commercial products. This is because many of the related technologies such as parallel processing, heterogeneous database integration, statistical databases, and data modeling have evolved a great deal and some of them are fairly mature technologies. That is, there are now viable technologies to build a data warehouse. We expect the demand for data warehousing to grow rapidly over the next few years.

It should be noted that many of the developments in data warehousing focus on integrating data stored in structured databases such as relational databases. In the future we can expect to see multimedia data sources being integrated to form a warehouse. An overview of multimedia database management and the challenges were discussed in chapter 6.

8.5   TOWARD A FRAMEWORK FOR A DATA WAREHOUSE

As data warehousing technology matures, there will be a need to automatically generate data warehouses. At present, it appears that although there are some guidelines for building a warehouse such as those given in [INMO93], the actual developments are being carried out on a case-by-case basis. What would be desirable is an approach that would automatically generate custom-designed warehouses. For example, can one develop a framework that would generate a warehouse from user specifications? That is, the user may specify the data model, the architecture, and type of queries to be posed, and the framework would generate the modules of the warehouse. Figure 8-7 illustrates the automatic generation of a warehouse.

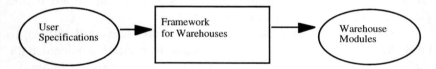

Figure 8-7. Framework for a Warehouse

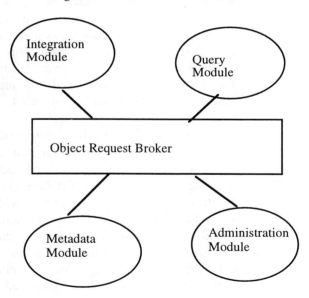

Figure 8-8. Component Integration for a Warehouse

Component integration technologies as well as framework technologies (see, for example, [TALI95]) may play a major role in the automatic generation of the warehouse. Framework technology may be used to generate the various modules of a warehouse. These

modules may include the integration module that integrates heterogeneous data sources to form the warehouse, the query module, and
the metadata module. These modules may be integrated using a
distributed object management approach as illustrated in figure 8-8.
One may also have a need to reuse some of the modules to build new
warehouses.

There is very little work on the automatic generation of
warehouses as well as on frameworks for building a warehouse. At this
stage it appears that the ideas are preliminary. We believe that this is
an area for interesting research and with the developments in
warehousing as well as component integration and framework
technologies, one can expect some results to be obtained over the
next few years.

CHAPTER 9

DATA MINING

9.1 OVERVIEW

Data warehousing was discussed in chapter 8. A data warehouse assembles the data from heterogeneous databases so that users query only a single point. The responses that a user gets to a query depends on the contents of the data warehouse. That is, the data warehouse in general does not attempt to extract information from the data in the warehouse. A closely related technology, which is used to convert the data in the warehouse into some useful information, is data mining. That is, data mining is the process of posing a series of appropriate queries to extract information, often previously unknown, from large quantities of data in the database. Figure 9-1 illustrates the relationships between data warehousing and data mining. Note that having a warehouse is not necessary to do mining. That is, data mining can be applied to databases also. However, a warehouse structures the data in such a way so as to facilitate query processing.

Essentially, for many organizations, the goals of data mining include improving marketing capabilities, detecting abnormal patterns, and predicting the future based on past experiences and current trends. There is clearly a need for this technology. There are large amounts of current and historical data being stored. Therefore, as databases become larger, it becomes increasingly difficult to support decision making. In addition, the data could be from multiple sources and multiple domains. There is a clear need to analyze the data to support planning and other functions of an enterprise.

Various terms have been used to refer to data mining. These include knowledge/data/information discovery and knowledge/data/information extraction. Note that some define data mining to be the process of extracting previously unknown information while knowledge discovery is defined to be the process of making sense out of the extracted information. In this chapter we do not differentiate between data mining and knowledge discovery. It is difficult to determine whether a particular technique is a data mining technique. For example, some argue that statistical analysis techniques are data mining techniques. Others argue that they are not and that data mining techniques should uncover relationships that are not straightforward. For example, with data mining, a medical supplies company could increase sales by targeting certain physicians in its advertising who are likely to buy the products or a credit bureau may limit its losses by selecting candidates who are not likely to default on their

payments. Such real-world experiences have been reported in
[GRUP95]. In addition, data mining could also be used to detect
abnormal behavior. For example, an Intelligence agency could
determine abnormal behavior of its employees using this technology.

Some of the data mining techniques include those based on rough
sets, inductive logic programming, machine learning, and neural
networks, among others. The data mining problems include classification (finding rules to partition data into groups), association (finding
rules to make associations between data), and sequencing (finding
rules to order data). Essentially one arrives at some hypothesis,
which is the information extracted, from examples and patterns
observed. These patterns are observed from posing a series of queries;
each query may depend on the response obtained to the previous
queries posed. There have been several developments in data mining.
These include tools such as RECON by Lockheed Martin Inc. A
discussion of data mining and the various commercial tools is given in
[GRUP95].

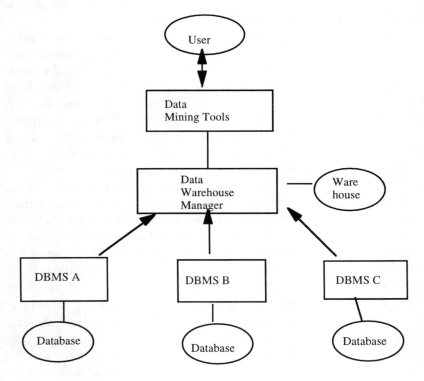

Figure 9-1. Data Mining vs. Data Warehousing

This chapter is organized as follows. Data mining technologies
are discussed in section 9.2. Approaches to data mining are discussed

in section 9.3. Challenges in data mining is the subject of section 9.4. In particular, data mining on multimedia data, visualization, security, role of metadata, mining heterogeneous data sources, and perform-ance issues are discussed.

9.2 DATA MINING TECHNOLOGIES

Data mining is an integration of multiple technologies as illustrated in figure 9-2. These include database management, ma-chine learning, visualization, statistics, and high performance com-puting. We discuss the role of each of these technologies.

Data mining research is being carried out in various disciplines. Database management researchers are taking advantage of the work on deductive and intelligent query processing for data mining. One of the areas of interest is to extend query processing techniques to facilitate data mining.

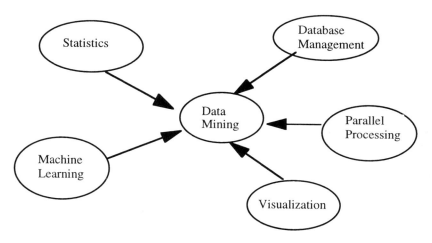

Figure 9-2. Data Mining Technologies

Machine learning has been around for a while. The idea here is for the machine to learn various rules from the patterns observed and then apply these rules to solve the problems. While the principles used in machine learning and data mining are similar, with data mining one usually considers large quantities of data to mine. There-fore integration of database management and machine learning techniques are needed for data mining.

Researchers from the computer visualization field are ap-proaching data mining from another perspective. One of their areas of focus is to use visualization techniques to aid the data mining process. In other words, interactive data mining is a goal of the visualization community. Figure 9-3 illustrates interactive data mining. Here, the database management system, visualization tool, and machine learning tool all interact with each other for data mining. Further discussion on visualization and data mining is given in section 9.4.

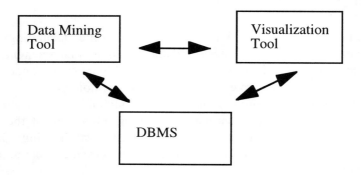

Figure 9-3. Interactive Data Mining

Researchers in statistical analysis are integrating their techniques with machine learning techniques to develop more sophisticated statistical techniques for data mining. As mentioned earlier, there is some dispute over whether statistical analysis techniques are also data mining techniques.

Finally, researchers in the high performance computing area are also working on developing appropriate techniques so that the data mining algorithms are scalable. There is also interaction with the hardware researchers so that appropriate hardware can be developed for high performance data mining.

9.3 TYPES OF DATA MINING

There are various types of data mining. By this we do not mean the actual techniques used to mine the data, but what the outcome will be. Some of these types are discussed in [AGRA93]. We describe a few here.

In one type of data mining, called "Classification", records are groups into some meaningful subclasses or clusters. So, patterns in the data are found and classes are established. An example of classification is the following. Supposing an automobile sales company has some information that all the people in its list who live in City X own cars worth more than 20K. Then they can assume that even those who are not on their list, but live in city X can afford to own cars costing more than 20K. This way the company classifies the people living in City X.

A second type of data mining is "Sequence detection". That is, by observing patterns in the data, sequences are determined. An example of sequence detection is: after John goes to the bank, he generally goes to the grocery store.

A third type of data mining is "Data dependency analysis". Here potentially interesting dependencies, relationships, or associations between the data items are detected. For example, if John, James, and William have a meeting, then Robert will also be at that meeting. It appears that it is this type of mining that is of much interest to many.

A fourth type of mining is "Deviation analysis". For example, John went to the bank on Saturday, but he did not go to the grocery store after that. Instead he went to a football game. With this type, anomalous instances and discrepancies are found.

As mentioned earlier, various techniques are used for these various types of data mining. These techniques could be based on rough sets, fuzzy logic, inductive logic programming, or neural networks, among others. Commercial products have also been developed based on these techniques and types of data mining. For a discussion we refer to [GRUP95].

9.4 CHALLENGES IN DATA MINING

9.4.1   Overview

While much progress has been made on data mining, there are several challenges. For example, due to the large volumes of data, how can the algorithms determine which technique to select and what type of data mining to do? Furthermore, the data may be incomplete and/or inaccurate. At times there may be redundant information and at times there may not be sufficient information. We have identified some areas for data mining that need further work. These include the following:

• Mining multimedia data
• Visualization and data mining
• Security aspects
• Role of metadata
• Mining heterogeneous data sources
• Performance issues

For example, current data mining tools operate on structured data. However, there are still large quantities of data that are unstructured. As stated in chapter 6, data in the multimedia databases are often semi-structured or unstructured. Data mining tools have to be developed for multimedia databases. Data mining techniques need to be integrated with visualization techniques to facilitate the mining process. Data mining could pose serious security threats. Furthermore, data mining could also be used to handle some security problems. Metadata plays an important role in data mining. There are two aspects here also. One could mine the metadata to uncover patterns. On the other hand metadata could be used to help the data mining process. Data mining on heterogeneous data sources and databases is a challenge. In this case, the results of mining the various data sources have to be integrated. Finally, a major challenge is to develop data mining approaches that are computationally feasible. Each of the above challenges will be elaborated in sections 9.4.2 to 9.4.7.

9.4.2   Mining Multimedia Data

Much of the data in the databases, especially for digital libraries as well as for many other applications, are in the form of text, maps, image, and video. Many of the current tools and techniques cannot be directly applied to such data. Some of the current directions in mining unstructured data include the following.

- Extract data and/or metadata from the unstructured databases possibly by using tagging techniques, store the extracted data in structured databases, and apply data mining tools on the structured databases. This is illustrated in figure 9-4.
- Integrate data mining techniques with information retrieval tools so that appropriate data mining tools can be developed for unstructured databases. This is illustrated in figure 9-5.
- Develop data mining tools to operate directly on unstructured databases. This is illustrated in figure 9-6.

9.4.3   Visualization

As data mining techniques mature, it will be important to integrate them with visualization techniques. There are four approaches here. One is to use visualization techniques to present the results that are obtained from mining the data in the databases. These results may be in the form of clusters or they could specify correlations between the data in the databases. The second approach applies data mining techniques to visualization. The assumption here is that it is easier to apply data mining tools to data in the visual form. Therefore, rather than applying the data mining tools to large and complex databases, one captures some of the essential semantics visually, and then applies the data mining tools. The third approach is to use visualization techniques to complement the data mining techniques. For example, one may use data mining techniques to obtain correlations between data or detect patterns. However, visualization techniques may still be needed to obtain a better understanding of the data in the database. The fourth approach uses visualization techniques to steer the mining process.

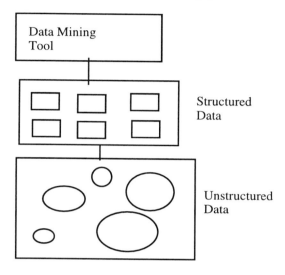

Figure 9-4. Converting Unstructured Data to Structured Data for Mining

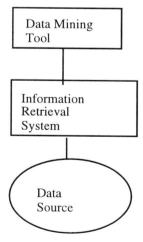

Figure 9-5. Augmenting an Information Retrieval System

In summary, visualization tools help interactive data mining and this was illustrated in figure 9-3. As illustrated in this figure, visualization tools can be used to visually display the responses from the DBMS directly so that the visual displays can be used by the data mining tool. On the other hand, the visualization tool can be used to visualize the results of the data mining tool directly. There is little work on integrating data mining and visualization tools. Some preliminary ideas were presented at the 1995 IEEE Database and Visualization Workshop (see, for example, [GRIN95]). There is much work to be done on this topic.

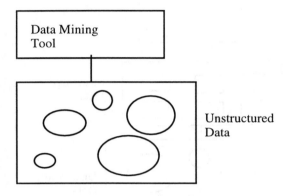

Figure 9-6. Mining Directly on Unstructured Data

9.4.4   Security

Data mining techniques have applications in intrusion detection and auditing databases. In the case of auditing, the data to be mined is the large quantity of audit data. One may apply data mining tools to detect abnormal patterns. For example, suppose an employee makes an excessive number of trips to a particular country and this fact is known by posing some queries. The next query to pose is whether the employee has associations with certain people from that country. If the answer is positive, then the employee's behavior is flagged. The use of data mining for analyzing audit databases is illustrated in figure 9-7.

While the previous example shows how data mining tools can be used to detect abnormal behavior, the next example shows how data mining tools can be applied to cause security problems. Consider a user who has the ability to apply data mining tools. This user can pose various queries and infer sensitive hypotheses. That is, the inference problem occurs via data mining. This is illustrated in figure 9-8. There are various ways to handle this problem. One approach is as follows. Given a database and a particular data mining tool, apply the tool to see if sensitive information can be deduced from the unclassified information legitimately obtained. If so, then there is an inference problem. There are some issues with this approach. One is that we are applying only one tool. In reality, the user may have several tools available to him. Furthermore, it is impossible to cover all ways that the inference problem could occur. Some of the security implications are discussed in [CLIF96].

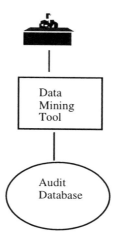

Figure 9-7. Mining an Audit Database

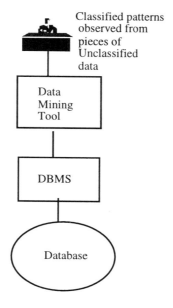

Figure 9-8. Inference Problem

Another solution to the inference problem is to build an infer- ence controller that can detect the motives of the user and prevent the inference problem from occurring. Such an inference controller lies between the data mining tool and the data source or database managed possibly by a DBMS. This is illustrated in figure 9-9. Discussions of security issues for data warehousing and mining are also given in [THUR96b, NISS96].

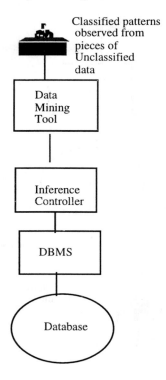

Figure 9-9. Inference Controller

9.4.5   The Role of Metadata

Metadata plays an important role in data mining. Metadata could guide the data mining process. That is, the data mining tool could consult the metadatabase and determine the types of queries to pose to the DBMS. Metadata may be updated during the mining process. For example, historical information as well as statistics may be collected during the mining process and the metadata has to reflect the changes in the environment. The role of metadata in guiding the data mining process is illustrated in figure 9-10.

There is also another aspect to the role of metadata and that is to conduct data mining on the metadata. Sometimes the data in the database may be incomplete and inaccurate and the metadata could have more meaningful information. In such a situation, it may be more feasible to mine the metadata and uncover patterns. Mining metadata is illustrated in figure 9-11.

There has been much discussion recently on the role of metadata for data mining [META96]. There are many challenges here. For example, when is it better to mine the metadata? What are the techniques for metadata mining? How does one structure the metadata to facilitate data mining? Researchers are working on addressing these questions.

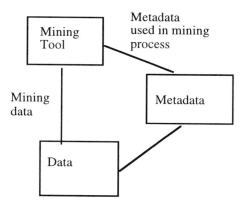

Figure 9-10. Metadata used in Data Mining

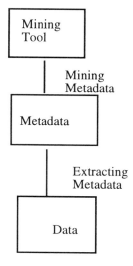

Figure 9-11. Metadata Mining

9.4.6   Mining Heterogeneous Data Sources

In this book we have placed much emphasis on heterogeneous database integration and interoperability. As discussed in chapter 4, many applications require the integration of multiple data sources and databases. These data sources may need to be mined to uncover patterns. Furthermore, interesting patterns may be found across the multiple databases. Mining heterogeneous and distributed data sources is a subject that has received little attention.

One of the challenges here is to integrate the results of the various mining tools applied to the individual data sources so that patterns may be found across data sources. This is illustrated in figure 9-12 where an integration agent integrates the results of all the mining agents. The integration agent may give feedback to the mining agents so that the mining agents may pose further queries to the data sources and obtain interesting information. That is, there is two-way communication between the integration agent and the mining agents. Another alternative is not to have an integration agent, but the various mining agents collaborate with each other and discover interesting patterns across the various data sources. This is illustrated in figure 9-13.

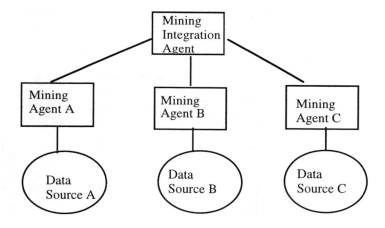

Figure 9-12. Integrating Data Mining Agents

The specific approach to mine heterogeneous data sources, that is whether to have an integration agent or whether the mining agents need to collaborate with one another, is yet to be determined. One may need both approaches or there may be yet another approach. Note also that heterogeneity may be with respect to data models, data types, and languages. This could pose additional challenges to the data mining process. There is much research to be done in this area.

9.4.7   Performance Issues
Many of the data mining techniques are computationally intensive. Appropriate hardware and software are needed to scale the data mining techniques. Database vendors are using parallel process-

ing machines to carry out data mining. That is, the data mining algorithms are parallelized using various parallel processing techniques. This is illustrated in figure 9-14.

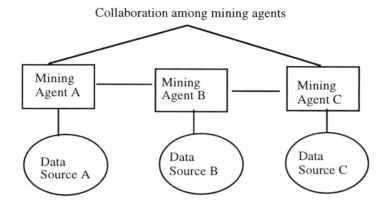

Figure 9-13. Collaboration among Mining Agents

Vendors of workstations are also interested in developing appropriate machines to facilitate data mining. This is an area of active research and development and we can expect to see a lot of progress during the next few years.

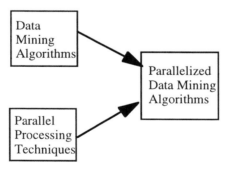

Figure 9-14. Parallel Data Mining

CHAPTER 10

DIGITAL LIBRARIES AND INTERNET DATABASE MANAGEMENT

10.1 OVERVIEW

The previous two chapters described two emerging technologies: data warehousing and data mining. Another key emerging technology is Digital libraries and Internet database management.[45] This chapter describes some of the issues with this third emerging technology. Note that data warehousing and data mining play an important role in digital libraries and Internet database management. That is, data warehouses need to be maintained on the Internet and data mining has to be carried out on the Internet to extract meaningful information from the large number of data servers.

Digital libraries are essentially digitized information distributed across several sites. The goal is for users to access this information in a transparent manner. The information could contain multimedia data such as voice, text, video, and images. The information could also be stored in structured databases such as relational and object-oriented databases.

The explosion of the users on the Internet and the increasing number of world wide web servers are rapidly advancing digital libraries. This is because digital libraries are usually hosted on networks including the Internet. That is, users could access the various digital libraries across the Internet. There is no single technology for digital libraries. It is a combination of many technologies including heterogeneous database management, mass storage management, collaborative/workflow computing, multimedia database management, intelligent agents and mediators, and data mining. For example, the heterogeneous information sources have to be integrated so that users access the servers in a transparent and timely manner. Security and privacy is becoming a major concern for digital libraries. So are other issues such as copyright protection and ownership of the data. Policies and procedures have to be set up to address these issues.

Major national initiatives are under way to develop digital library technologies. The agencies funding digital library work include the National Science Foundation, Defense Advanced Research

---

[45] Note that we have used the term digital libraries and Internet database management interchangeably. Many of the issues for digital libraries are present for Internet database management. The Internet began as a research effort funded by the U.S. Government. It is now the most widely used network in the world.

Projects Agency, and the National Aeronautical and Space Administration [NSF95]. In addition, there are numerous projects funded by
organizations such as the Library of Congress to develop digital
library technologies (see, for example, [ACM95]). Various conferences and workshops have also been established recently devoted
entirely to digital libraries (see, for example, [DIGI95]).

This chapter provides an overview of digital libraries and
Internet database management. Section 10.2 describes some of the
technology integration issues for digital libraries. Section 10.3
describes the potential uses with digital libraries. In particular, some
examples of digital libraries, locating resources, as well as Internet
access and collaboration issues are discussed. Functions of digital
libraries are described in section 10.4. These functions include query
processing, metadata management, transaction management, integrity, and security. The role of hypermedia systems in digital libraries
is elaborated in section 10.5. The importance of metadata is discussed in section 10.6. The role of Javasoft's Java for Internet
database access is discussed in section 10.7. The impact of the
Internet on client-server systems is discussed in section 10.8. Finally,
the information overload problem due to the Internet is discussed in
section 10.9.[46]

10.2 DIGITAL LIBRARY TECHNOLOGIES

Various technologies have to be integrated to develop digital
libraries. Some of the important data management technologies for
digital libraries are data mining, multimedia database management,
and heterogeneous database integration. In addition, some of the
supporting technologies such as agents, distributed object management, and mass storage are also important. Figure 10-1 illustrates the
various digital library technologies.

Integration of these technologies is a major challenge. First of
all, appropriate Internet access protocols have to be developed. In
addition, interface definition languages play a major role in the
interoperability of different systems. Due to the large amount of
data, integration of mass storage with data management will be

---

[46] Note that the terms Intranet and Internet have been used extensively during the
past year. Intranet is usually the internal network of a particular corporation.
Internet is the network that is used across corporations, individuals, and groups.
Many of the issues present for Internet database management are also present for
Intranet database management. However, there are differences between Intranet and
the Internet with respect to issues like security. In this chapter we do not distinguish between Intranets and the Internet.

critical. Data mining is needed to extract information from the databases. Multimedia technology combined with hypermedia technology is necessary for browsing multimedia data. Distributed object management will play a major role especially since the number of data sources to be integrated may be large. The remaining sections in this chapter describe the use of digital libraries, functions of digital libraries, as well as some of the key technologies.

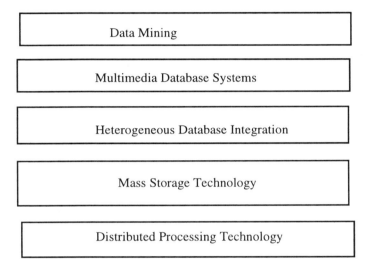

Figure 10-1. Some Technologies for Digital Libraries

10.3 USES OF DIGITAL LIBRARIES

An example of a digital library is illustrated in figure 10-2. The idea here is that there are a certain number of sites participating in this library. Note that in theory the library could also have an unlimited number of users. However, many organizations want to share the data between a certain number of groups.

The information in the form of servers, databases, and tools belongs to the library. The participating sites could place this information or someone who is designated to maintain the library. Users then query and access the information in the library.

Figure 10-3 illustrates the use of agents to maintain the library. These agents locate resources for users, maintain the resources, and even filter out information so that users only get the information they want. Agents are essentially intelligent processes. They may communicate with each other in carrying out a specific task. The role of agents in query processing for digital libraries is illustrated in figure 10-4.

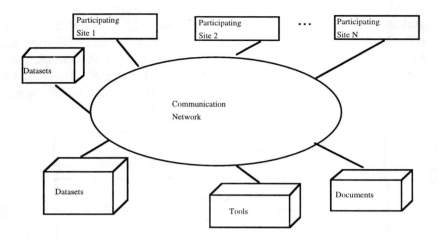

Figure 10-2. Digital Library: Example

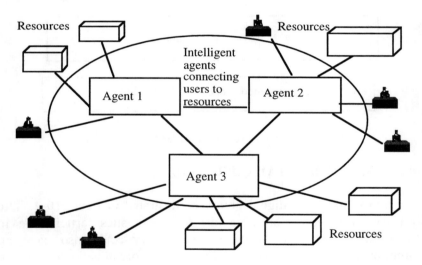

Figure 10-3. Agents for Locating Resources

Figure 10-5 illustrates the recent developments in data management technology to support digital libraries. Database management system vendors are now building interfaces to the Internet. Query languages like SQL are embedded into Internet access languages. In the example of figure 10-5, DBMS vendors A and B make their data available to applications C and D. DBMS vendors are also developing interface to the Java programming environment (to be discussed in section 10.7). Essentially what this all means is that heterogeneous databases are integrated through the Internet.

One can also take advantage of the digital library technology for collaborative work environments. As illustrated in figure 10-6, suppose organization A wants to develop some technology such as integrating heterogeneous databases. They access the WWW and find out the names of other organizations who already have developed such systems. They may like what is said about the system developed by organization B. They contact organization B and get a demonstration of the system through the Internet.

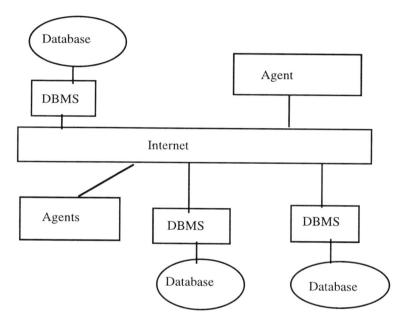

Figure 10-4. Agents for Query Processing

10.4   FUNCTIONS

10.4.1   Database Management Functions

Database management functions for digital libraries include those such as query processing, metadata management, security, and integrity. In [THUR96c] we have examined various database management system functions and discussed the impact of Internet database access on these functions. Some of the issues are discussed here.

One of the major functions is data representation. The question is, is there a need for a standard data model for digital libraries and Internet database access? Is it at all possible to develop such a standard? If so, what are the relationships between the standard

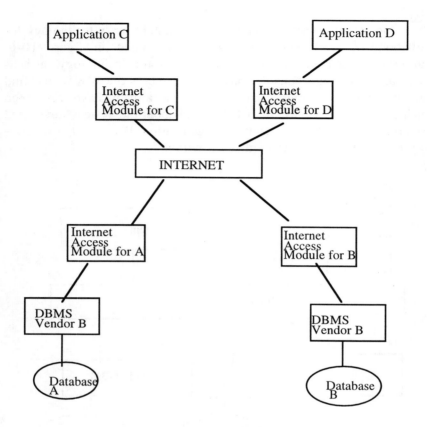

Figure 10-5. Database Access through the Internet

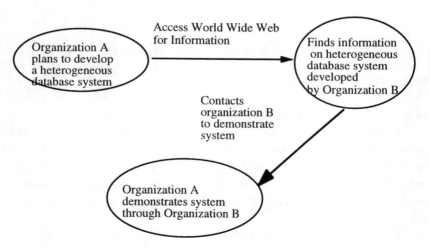

Figure 10-6. Collaboration through the Internet

model and the individual models used by the database? Note that various data representation schemes such as SGML (Generalized Markup Language), HTML (Hypertext Markup Language), and ODA (Office Document Architecture) are being examined (see, for example, [ACM96]). Are they sufficient or is another representation scheme needed?

Querying and browsing are two of the key functions. First of all, an appropriate query language is needed. Since SQL is a popular language, appropriate extensions to SQL may be desired. Query processing involves developing a cost model. Are there special cost models for Internet database management? With respect to browsing operation, the query processing techniques have to be integrated with techniques for following links. That is, hypermedia technology has to be integrated with database management technology.

Updating digital libraries could mean different things. One could create a new web site, place servers at that site, and update the data managed by the servers. The question is, can a user of the library send information to update the data at a web site? The issue here is security privileges. If the user has write privileges, then he could update the databases that he is authorized to modify. Agents and mediators could be used to locate the databases as well as to process the update.

Transaction management is essential for many applications. There may be new kinds of transactions on the Internet. For example, various items may be sold through the Internet. In this case, the item should not be locked immediately when a potential buyer makes a bid. It has to be left open until several bids are received and the item is sold. That is, special transaction models are needed. Appropriate concurrency control and recovery techniques have to be developed for the transaction models.

Metadata management is a major concern for digital libraries. The question is, what is metadata? Metadata describes all of the information pertaining to the library. This could include the various web sites, the types of users, access control issues, and policies enforced. Where should the metadata be located? Should each participating site maintain its own metadata? Should the metadata be replicated or should there be a centralized metadata repository? Metadata in such an environment could be very dynamic especially since the users and the web sites may be changing continuously. The role of metadata will be described in section 10.6.

Managing multimedia data is a concern. All of the issues described in chapter 6 apply for digital libraries. In addition, synchronization and distribution issues are more complex. Data from different web servers may have to be synchronized before being displayed to the user.

Storage management for Internet database access is a complex function. Appropriate index strategies and access methods for handling multimedia data are needed. In addition, due to the large volumes of data, techniques for integrating database management technology with mass storage technology are also needed.

Security and privacy is a major challenge. Once you put the data at a site, who owns the data? If a user copies the data from a site, can he distribute the data? Can he use the information in papers that he is writing? Who owns the copyright to the original data? What role do digital signatures play? Mechanisms for copyright protection and plagiarism detection are needed. In addition, some of the issues discussed in chapter 4 on handling heterogeneous security policies will be of concern.[47]

Maintaining the integrity of the data is critical. Since the data may originate from multiple sources around the world, it will be difficult to keep tabs on the accuracy of the data. Data quality maintenance techniques need to be developed for digital libraries and Internet database access. For example, special tagging mechanisms may be needed to determine the quality of the data.

Heterogeneous database access, data warehousing, and data mining are important functions of digital libraries. The various heterogeneous data sources have to be integrated to provide transparent access to the user, and some of the details will be given in section 10.4.3. In some cases, the data sources have to be integrated into a warehouse. Data mining helps the users to extract meaningful information from the numerous data sources. Since the data in the libraries could have different semantics and syntax, it will be difficult to extract useful information. Sophisticated data mining tools are needed for this purpose. A discussion on interactive data mining and its impact on the world wide web is given in [THUR96d]. Figure 10-7 illustrates data warehousing and data mining on the Internet.

10.4.2 Interoperability

Since all of the functions discussed in section 10.4.1 are impacted by interoperability on the Internet, we address interoperability in this section. Interoperability between heterogeneous data sources is a major issue for digital libraries. Modules for interconnecting the different data sources and handling various types of

---

[47] Also, there has been a lot of discussions on the notion of a "firewall" to protect the internal information from external users. We do not address firewall issues in this chapter. For more details we refer the reader to [FIRE].

heterogeneity are needed. Much of the discussion in chapter 4 is applicable to digital libraries. Furthermore, due to the potentially large number of data sources, one could expect distributed object management technology to play a major role for digital libraries and database access through the Internet. For example, different data sources may be encapsulated as objects and they may communicate through an ORB. A high-level illustration is shown in figure 10-8.

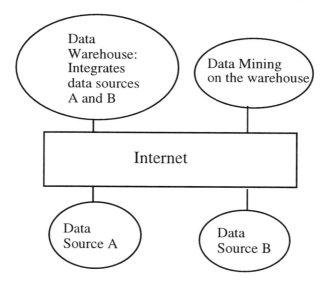

Figure 10-7. Data Warehousing and Mining on the Internet

A major challenge in ORB-based interoperability is to develop appropriate interfaces between the ORB and the Internet. That is, extensions to IDL are needed for Internet database access. Another challenge with the Internet is to connect different components of the database management system. Different vendors may provide different components. For example, a query module may be developed by vendor A and a transaction module possibly with real-time processing capability may be developed by vendor B. The two modules may need to be accessed through the Internet. ORB technology would facilitate such integration also. This is illustrated in figure 10-9. OMG's Internet SIG is focusing on ORB Interfaces to the Internet. As stated in chapter 5, alternatives to OMG's CORBA technology, such as Microsoft Corporation's Distributed OLE/COM are also viable technologies for Internet database access.

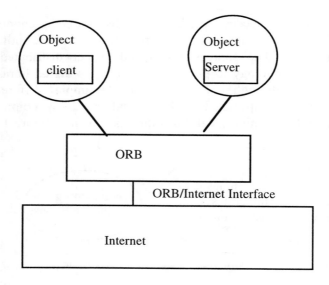

Figure 10-8. Internet-ORB-based Interoperability

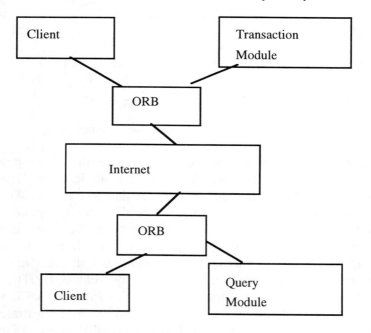

Figure 10-9. ORB-based Component Integration

10.5 HYPERMEDIA TECHNOLOGY AND BROWSING

We have briefly discussed hypermedia technology in Chapter 6. This technology has been around for quite a while. However, the developments with Internet technology have really given a new direction and momentum to hypermedia technology.

As illustrated in figure 6-2, a hypermedia database management system essentially includes both a multimedia database management system and a linker. The linker is the component of a hypermedia database system that facilitates browsing of various data sources. For example, by following links, it is possible for users to go through large amounts of information in a short space of time. An example of linking various data sources is illustrated in figure 10-10. With the emergence of the Internet, many are now familiar with the various browsers that are now available. The relationships between the user, the browser, and the Internet is illustrated in Figure 10-11.

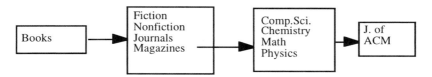

Figure 10-10. Linking various Topics

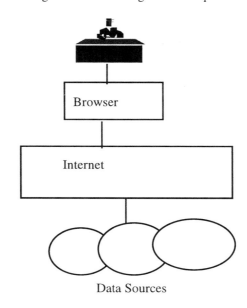

Data Sources

Figure 10-11. Browsing on the Internet

While significant developments have been made, it is still very difficult for the users to manage these large quantities of data. With current browsers one can go from one topic to another by following links. One can also get quite lost in what has been called Cyberspace.

Very quickly the whole task of browsing could become quite over-whelming. What is needed are "Intelligent Browsers" that will help the users to determine where they are, and how they can backtrack in a meaningful way. Agents will play a major role in intelligent brows-ing. In addition, appropriate metadata management techniques will also be critical. Metadata may include information about the various data sources as well as dynamic information such as the current status of various users browsing the data sources.

10.6 THE ROLE OF METADATA

We discussed some of the metadata management issues for Internet database management. Maintaining appropriate metadata is critical for intelligent browsing. As one goes through the Cyberspace, the metadata which describes the navigation patterns should get updated. This metadata is consulted periodically so that a user can have some idea as to where he is. Metadata sort of becomes like a Map. Furthermore, the Internet metadata manager should continu-ally give advice to the users.

Appropriate techniques are needed to manage the metadata. These include querying and updating the metadata. The Internet environment is very dynamic. This means that the metadata must be updated continually as users browse through the Internet as well as when data sources get updated. Furthermore, as new data sources get added, the changes have to be reflected in the metadata. Metadata may also include various security policies. The metadata must also be available to the users in a timely manner. Finally, appropriate models for the metadata are also needed. These models may be based on the various data models or may utilize the models for text and multime-dia data.

Metadata repositories may be included with the various data servers or there may be separate repositories for the metadata. A scenario having multiple data servers and metadata repositories is illustrated in figure 10-12.

There is a lot of research that is being carried out on metadata management for the Internet (see, for example, [AIPA95, AIPA96, META96]). However, much remains to be done before efficient techniques are developed for metadata representation and manage-ment. Defining the metadata is also a major issue.

10.7   THE ROLE OF JAVA

Javasoft, a subsidiary of SUN Microsystems Inc., has developed a breakthrough product called Java [JACK96].[48] Essentially Java is a programming language that was designed to overcome some of the limitations and problems with C++ such as dealing with pointers. Soon this language has become one of the breakthrough products in computer science. While systems can be coded in Java, it was soon found that Internet-based programming is simplified a great deal with Java. Essentially, various programs can be written in Java and are called Java Applets. These Java applets are incorporated into HTML (Hypertext Markup Language) programs.[49] When the HTML programs are executed in an Internet browser environment, the embedded applets are executed. One could then download various Java applets and embed them into HTML programs. These applets when executed may solve specific problems. Several such applets are now available on the Internet. Executing applets on the Internet is illustrated in figure 10-13.

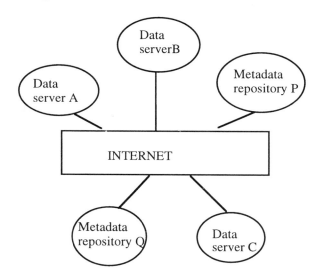

Figure 10-12. Metadata Repositories on the Internet

---

[48]   Information on Java can be found in various web pages. An example URL is: http://splash.javasoft.com/jdbc/.

[49]   Note that HTML is the language that is used for Internet programming. That is, web pages are written in HTML. These programs are executed through various browsers. Not all browsers can handle Java applets. However, we expect the number of browsers to handle Java applets to increase.

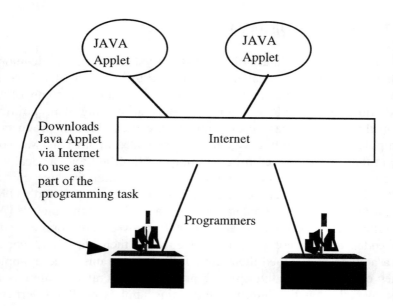

Figure 10-13. Java Programming over the Internet

Now, what is of interest to the data management community is accessing various database management systems from Java applications. Since more and more applications are now being written in Java, embedding SQL calls into Java is needed for Java programs to access relational database management systems. In the same way, to access object-oriented database management systems, embedding, say, OQL (object query language) calls into Java is needed. A standard called JDBC (Java Database Connectivity) has been developed for database access for Java programs. JDBC is in many ways similar to ODBC discussed in chapter 5. Clients as well as database servers build interfaces compliant with JDBC. An example approach to communication through JDBC is illustrated in figure 10-14. Note that in many cases JDBC code may be implemented on top of ODBC. That is, ODBC server drivers may lie between the JDBC server code and the actual servers. A high level view of such a scenario is illustrated in figure 10-15.

We have only briefly discussed the role of Java in Internet database management. Furthermore, it is only recently that standards like JDBC have been proposed, We can expect to see major advances in this area in the near future. Furthermore, while we can expect the number of Java-based application programs to increase by a significant amount, we can also expect more and more database management systems (i.e., the servers) to be programmed in Java. For a discussion of JDBC, we refer to [JDBC].

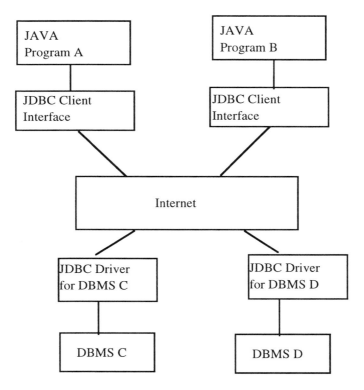

Figure 10-14. DBMS Access through JDBC

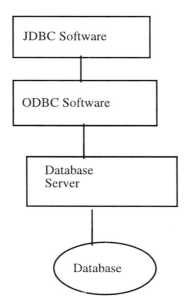

Figure 10-15. ODBC/JDBC Connection

10.8 IMPACT OF INTERNET ON CLIENT-SERVER SYSTEMS

One of the major issues faced by the data management community is the impact that the Internet will have on client-server technology. Some argue that with the Internet and languages like Java, one does not need sophisticated clients. That is, all one needs is some sort of terminal to interface to the Internet and all of the application programs and other software can be downloaded and executed.

Others argue that client-server technology will still be alive and well. While much of the software could be downloaded from remote sites and executed, there is still software that is specific to a client's need. Furthermore, there is still work on, say, integrating heterogeneous databases and other data sources that will be specific to a particular client. Especially if the systems form some sort of loose federation, which will likely be the case with so many systems and databases, then there will be a lot of client-dependent software. In summary, while general purpose software development has progressed a great deal, there is still work to do in tailoring the software to a client's need.

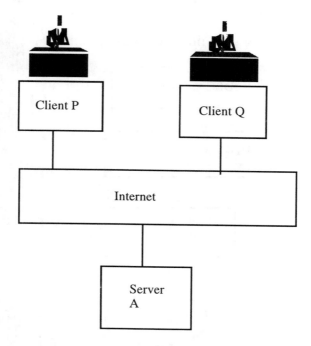

Figure 10-16. Client-Server Communication on the Internet

Figure 10-16 illustrates how the Internet can be used for communication between the client and the server. A user interfaces to the Internet through the client and accesses the various data servers. In figure 10-17 we illustrate the concept where the user interfaces to the Internet through a terminal and the client module is on the Internet and invoked by the user as needed. Through this client module, the user can access the data servers.

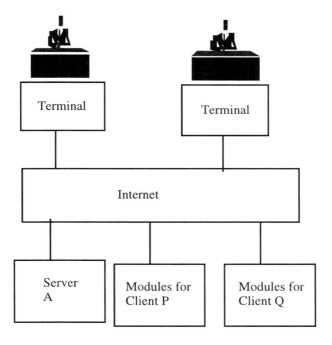

Figure 10-17. Terminal-Client-Server Communication on the Internet

We feel that it is still too early to forecast the future of client-server technology. The Internet is still not mature, and at present there is a need for client-server technology. The arguments in favor of the existence of client-server technology are rather strong. However, with the maturing of Java and the possible emergence of even newer technologies, we can expect to have major breakthroughs with Internet database access. Therefore, the future of client-server technology will be clearer within the next few years.

10.9 INFORMATION OVERLOAD PROBLEM

One of the major problems with the Internet is information overload. Because humans can now access large amounts of information very rapidly, they can quickly become overloaded with information and in some cases the information may not be useful to them. Furthermore, in certain other cases, the information may even be harmful to the humans. The technologies that we have discussed in this chapter, if implemented successfully, would prevent this information overload problem.

For example, agents may filter out information so that users get only the relevant information. Data mining technology could extract meaningful information from the data sources. Security technology could prevent users from getting information that they are not authorized to know.

In addition to computer scientists, researchers in psychology, sociology, and other disciplines are also involved in examining various aspects of Internet database management. We need people in multiple disciplines to collaboratively work together to make the Internet a useful tool to human beings.

One of the emerging goals of web technology is to provide appropriate support for data dissemination. This deals with getting the right data/information at the right time to the analyst/user (directly to the desktop if possible) to assist in carrying out various functions. The complete range of technologies for data dissemination is beyond the scope of this book.

CHAPTER 11

DATABASE SUPPORT FOR COLLABORATION

11.1 OVERVIEW

While the previous three chapters have focused on some of the emerging technologies for data management, this chapter focuses on database support for an emerging application, namely collaborative computing. In particular, we will discuss how the various data management technologies described in the previous chapters of this book will support collaborative computing.

Although the notion of computer supported cooperative work (CSCW) was first proposed in the early 1980s, it is only recently that much interest is being shown in this topic. Several research papers have now been published in collaborative computing and prototypes/products have been developed. Collaborative computing enables people, groups of individuals, and organizations to work together with one another in order to accomplish a task or a collection of tasks. These tasks could vary from participating in conferences, solving a specific problem, or working on the design of a system. Specific contributions to collaborative computing include the development of team workstations (where Groupware creates a shared workspace supporting dynamic collaboration in a work group), multimedia communication systems supporting distributed workgroups, and collaborative computing systems supporting cooperation in the design of an entity (such as an electrical or mechanical system).[50] Several technologies including multimedia, artificial intelligence, networking and distributed processing, and database systems as well as disciplines such as organizational behavior and human computer interaction have contributed significantly towards the growth of collaborative computing.

One aspect of collaborative computing of particular interest to the database community is workflow computing. Workflow is defined as the automation of a series of functions that comprise a business process such as data entry, data review, and monitoring performed by one or more people. An example of a process that is well suited for workflow automation is the purchasing process. Applications can range from simple user-defined processes such as document review to complex applications such as manufacturing processes. Original custom-made workflow systems developed over the past twenty

---

[50] See the discussions in the Communications of the ACM, Special Issue in Collaborative Computing, December 1991 [ACM91b].

years for applications such as factory automation were built using a centralized database. Many commercial workflow system products targeted for office environments are based on a messaging architecture. This architecture supports the distributed nature of current workteams. However, the messaging architecture is usually file based and lacks many of the features supported by database management systems such as data representation, consistency management, tracking, and monitoring. Although the emerging products show some promise, they do not provide the functionality of database management systems.

This chapter will identify the database systems technology issues to support collaborative computing in general and workflow computing applications in particular. Many of the ideas discussed here also apply for collaborative computing systems. However, we have limited the scope by focusing mainly on workflow applications. There are two ways to design the data management system for the workflow application. One is to take a top-down approach and design the entire application and then determine the type of data management system that is needed. The other is to focus only on the data management system. The data management system developed under the first approach would be specialized for the particular application whereas the one developed under the second approach would be a more general purpose one. We discuss both approaches here.

This chapter is organized as follows. First some examples on database support for collaboration will be given in section 11.2. Architectural issues for workflow management systems are discussed in section 11.3. General purpose database management system support for workflow applications is discussed in section 11.4. In particular, data representation and manipulation as well as the role of metadata are discussed. Designing a data management system from scratch utilizing an object-oriented design and analysis approach is described in section 11.5.

11.2 SOME EXAMPLES

As mentioned in section 11.1, a collaborative computing system should enable multiple groups and teams from different sites to collaborate on a project. Figure 11-1 illustrates an example where teams A and B are working on a geographical problem such as analyzing and predicting the weather in North America. The two teams must have a global picture of the map as well as any notes that

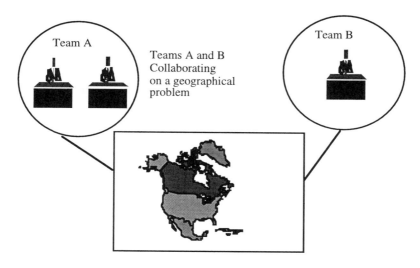

Figure 11-1. Collaboration Example

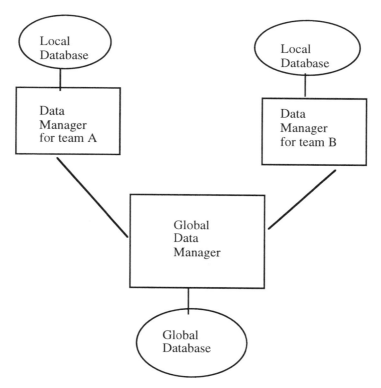

Figure 11-2. Database Support

go with it. Any changes made by one team should be instantly visible to the other team and both teams communicate as if they are in the same room.

To enable such transparent communication, data management support is needed. One could utilize a database management system to manage the data or some type of data manager that provides some of the essential features such as data integrity, concurrent access, and retrieval capabilities. In the above example, the database may consist of information describing the problem the teams are working on, the data that is involved, history data, as well as the metadata information. The data manager must provide appropriate concurrency control features so that when both teams simultaneously access the common picture and make changes, these changes are coordinated.

One possible scenario for the data manager is illustrated in figure 11-2 where each team has its own local data manager and there is a global data manager to maintain any global information, including the data and the metadata. The local data managers communicate with the global data manager. The global data manager illustrated in this figure is at the logical level. At the physical level the global data manager may also be distributed. The data managers coordinate their activities to provide features such as concurrency control, integrity, and retrieval.

11.3   ARCHITECTURAL SUPPORT FOR WORKFLOW COMPUTING

As stated in section 11.1, workflow computing is a special case of collaborative computing. This section and the next two discuss various aspects of database support for workflow computing applications.

A database management system for a workflow application manages the database that contains the data required for the application. For a workflow application, the data could be purchase orders, requisitions, and project reports, among others. Like some of the other systems discussed in this book, there are various ways to integrate workflow systems with the database management systems. We discuss two of the approaches. In one approach, there is loose integration between the workflow management system and the database management system. This is illustrated in figure 11-3. With this approach, one could use a commercial database management system for the workflow application. In the second approach, illustrated in figure 11-4, there is tight integration between the workflow management system and the database management system.

With this approach, often the database management system is a special purpose one.

The database management system could be centralized or distributed. All of the advantages and disadvantages for centralized and distributed database systems discussed in part I also apply for database management systems designed for workflow applications. In addition, the database management system should provide additional support for special transactions for workflow systems. Some of the database management system issues are discussed in section 11.3. Note that one could also utilize distributed object management systems to encapsulate the components of the workflow management system.

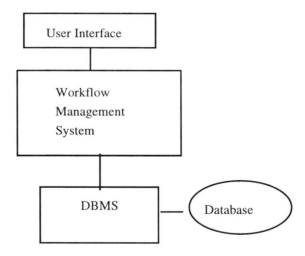

Figure 11-3. Loose Integration between Workflow System and DBMS

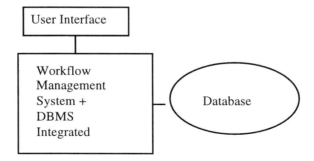

Figure 11-4. Tight Integration between Workflow System and DBMS

As mentioned earlier, workflow computing is an aspect of collaborative computing. As illustrated in figure 11-1, collaborative computing encompasses many more features such as team members collaborating on a project, designing a system, and conducting a meeting. One could build a collaborative application on top of a workflow management system. The relationship between database management system, workflow management system, and collaborative computing system is illustrated in figure 11-5.

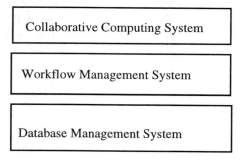

Figure 11-5. Relationship between Systems

11.4   DATABASE SUPPORT FOR WORKFLOW APPLICATIONS

11.4.1   Overview of Database Management Functions

The database management functions for workflow applications will depend on the functionality requirements. These requirements can in general be divided into various categories including data representation and data manipulation. The data representation requirements include support for complex data structures to represent (i) objects like documents, spreadsheets, and mail messages, (ii) the workflow rules which determine the electronic routing of the objects, (iii) tracking data which monitor the status of the objects, (iv) the actions by users, (v) deadlines imposed on the actions, and (vi) security constraints. Special formats for presenting the objects to the users may also be needed. Data manipulation requirements include (i) querying and browsing the database, (ii) managing the metadata, which describes the data in the database, (iii) mechanisms for concurrent access to the data, such as modifying the workflow or the objects, (iv) special view mechanisms for the users, (v) support for remote database access, and (vi) integrating with the databases of other workgroup applications such as project management and document management.

The data model for a workflow application should support the data representation requirements. Various types of data models including semantic models such as an object-oriented model as well as simple models which consist of nodes and links are being investigated for this purpose. Also, a data model which accommodates different representation schemes may be needed for the different types of data. For example, the workflow rules may be represented in rule bases and the documents, spreadsheets, and messages may be represented as complex objects. The data model should also provide the support to enforce integrity and security constraints, maintain different versions and configurations, and also represent the changes that an object goes through within a transaction. Also, if the objects are to be represented to the user in a different scheme, then mappings between the different schemes have to be stored. The data model should also be flexible to support ad hoc changes and schema evolution. The use of temporal constructs may be needed to represent historical and/or time-dependent data objects.

Since workflow applications are distributed in nature, both centralized as well as distributed architectures need to be examined for the data management systems. For example, should all of the data such as workflow rules and objects be stored in a centralized location or should the data be distributed across the different workstations? If the architecture is distributed, then should it support a heterogeneous environment? From the discussion of the functionality requirements of workflow applications described by Marshak in the March 1992 issue of the Office Computing Report [MARS92], it appears that the database should be fully integrated with the application. This means that the environment is most likely to be homogeneous. Note that if the workflow application has to be integrated with other applications such as project management, then there may be a need to integrate the heterogeneous databases. Another issue here is whether to store all of the data in the database. For example, changes that an object goes through during a transaction may be transient and need to be stored only until the duration of the transaction. In this case, the changes could be stored in temporary storage. If the changes have to be stored for historical purposes, then the database could be used.

The functions of the data management system should provide support for the data manipulation requirements. One of the main issues here is developing a suitable model of concurrency control (see, for example, [ALON96, SHET93]). Since the goal is to enable the collaborators to share as much data as possible, a fine-grained granularity locking approach seems more appropriate than a coarse-grained one. Furthermore, alternatives to locking as a concurrency control mechanism as well as variations to the locking technique are being explored by researchers. In general, the model should be flexible so that a user can lock one part of an object while his peers could work with other parts of an object. Furthermore, it is also desirable for the collaborators to be notified almost instantly if any part of an object is being modeled by a user, and if so by whom. If this feature is not provided, then it will be difficult to maintain the consistency of the objects. Concurrency control support is also needed for updating the workflow rules. In addition to developing suitable concurrency control algorithms, appropriate recovery mechanisms need to be developed to handle system failures and transaction aborts. Workflow transaction management is an active research area. This research is also being transferred into commercial products. Other functions of the system include querying and browsing, managing the metadata, enforcing appropriate access control policies, managing different versions and configurations, and monitoring the changes to an object within a transaction. In addition, the system must manage the links between the different users' shared objects. Since metadata plays an important role in collaborative computing, a discussion of this role is given in section 11.4.2.

In summary, workflow applications will require efficient support for managing the database which may possibly be distributed. This section has identified some of the issues that need to be investigated. In particular, approaches to developing a data management system as well as issues on developing a data model, architecture, and modules for such a system which satisfy the functionality requirements were discussed. While the developments in database systems technology have contributed significantly to support new generation applications, applying these developments as well as generating new developments for collaborative computing applications in general, and workflow computing applications in particular, is the next challenge. Database system vendors are integrating their products with workflow systems. We can expect significant developments to be made in workflow-based database management systems.

11.4.2 The Role of Metadata

Metadata plays a major role for collaborative computing and workflow applications. Metadata not only describes the data in the database such as the schemas, it also contains other information such as access control rules, links between different objects, policies, information about the various teams collaborating, information about the various versions, and other historical information. For workflow computing applications, metadata includes information about projects, schedules, and other activities. Metadata should be used by the various teams to support their collaboration and also help in providing a global synchronized picture of the problem being handled.

An appropriate model for the metadata is needed. Again this model could be closely linked with the models used by the data managers or it could be completely independent. Various schema transformations between different representations are also included in the metadata. The metadata manager should provide support for querying and updating the metadata as well as giving advice to the various collaborating teams and guide the decision making process.

The metadata manager could be centralized or distributed. This design may depend on the architecture selected for the environment. If the database is distributed, say each team having its own local database, then there could be a metadata manager for each database. The various metadata managers have to communicate with each other.

Metadata research for workflow computing as well as collaborative applications is just beginning. However, with the recent emphasis on metadata for various applications including digital libraries, one can expect more results on metadata issues for collaborative computing.

11.5   ON DESIGNING WORKFLOW APPLICATIONS

Many workflow applications are complex and designing them from scratch is a difficult process. The requirements have to be generated first. Then the static, dynamic, and functional aspects of the application have to be represented using an appropriate model. Object-oriented design and analysis methodologies are showing a lot of promise for designing various information systems applications. Such approaches could also be utilized for workflow applications. We have been conducting some preliminary research on using Rumbaugh et al.'s [RUMB91]. Object Modeling Technique (OMT) for designing workflow applications. We discuss some of the issues here.

OMT consists of three phases. The analytical phase, the system design phase, and the object design phase. During the analytical phase, an object model, dynamic model, and functional model are developed. The object model is used to capture the entities of the application and the relationship between the entities. The dynamic model is used to capture the timing aspects of the application and determine potential inconsistencies. The functional model is used to

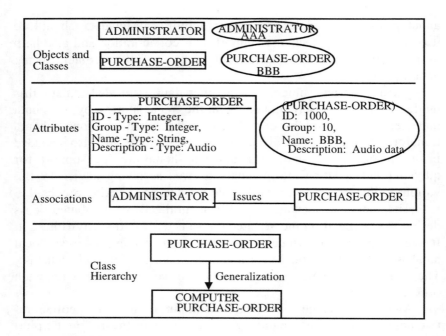

Figure 11-6. Object Model for Workflow

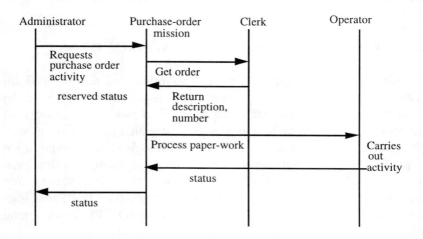

Figure 11-7. Dynamic Model for Workflow Application

generate the methods for the objects. During the system design phase, the components of the system are identified. That is, the design of the operating system, the database management system, transactions, and other features are designed. During the object design phase the actual algorithms are determined.

Figure 11-6 illustrates an object model for a workflow application. In particular, representation of the entities such as classes, objects, and attributes of objects, representing the associations between the entities, as well as inheritance hierarchy are shown in this figure.

Figure 11-7 illustrates the dynamic model for the application. In this example, an administrator requests a purchase order activity. This activity is then carried out by a clerk and an operator. Potential inconsistencies are detected. For example, there may be timing problems such as the administrator requesting the activity to be carried out in 10 minutes and it is not possible to get an order in less than 30 minutes. It is assumed that the classes Administrator, Purchase-order mission, Clerk, and Operator are identified during the object modeling phase.

The functional model generates the methods. In this example, the methods may be: Carry-out-purchase-order-activity on class purchase-order-mission; Request-purchase-order-number on class clerk; and Execute-purchase-order on class operator. During the system design phase, the components of the application are determined. For example, at this stage it is determined as to whether to use a relational database management system or an object-oriented database management system. The detailed algorithms and the specific systems are determined during the object design phase.

Note that in this section we have discussed some of the preliminary issues in designing a workflow computing application from scratch.[51] Much research is needed on utilizing such object-oriented approaches for designing workflow computing as well as collaborative computing applications.

---

[51]   Some of these issues are also discussed in [LAVE94].

CONCLUSION TO PART III

Let us examine how the technologies described in part III relate to the framework. Part III has essentially described information extraction and sharing. It builds on the technologies presented in parts I and II. Database and distributed database system technologies are needed for data warehousing, Internet database management as well as for collaborative computing. Furthermore, heterogeneous database integration issues are needed to build data warehouses. Multimedia database management is key to Internet database management. Data mining builds on data warehousing as well as some of the basic database management system functions. Some additional technologies such as artificial intelligence, machine learning, and statistics, which are not part of data management, are also needed for data mining.

While systems based on technologies in parts I and II essentially are distributed and heterogeneous database systems handling multimedia and legacy data, the systems based on technologies in part III enable the extraction and sharing of the data in the databases. These databases could be distributed, heterogeneous, containing multimedia data, and scattered throughout the world and connected by the Internet. In addition, the technologies in part III also enable useful work to be carried out jointly by people in different countries partly by accessing the data in the databases. Furthermore, previously unknown information can also be extracted from the data in the databases.

CHAPTER 12

SUMMARY AND DIRECTIONS

12.1 ABOUT THIS CHAPTER

This chapter brings us to a closure on this book: Data Management Systems Evolution and Interoperation. We have addressed various technologies for data management and have showed how they relate to each other. In particular, we have provided a framework for data management. In this chapter, we first summarize the contents of this book. The important points of each chapter will be reiterated. Then we will provide some directions for research and development in data management. We believe that the integration of data management technologies is a critical need, and research should be directed toward accomplishing this. Then some guidelines for building data management systems will be given. In particular, issues on business modeling as well as issues on proceeding from concept to implementation will be discussed. Finally, we give the reader some suggestions on where to go from here.

The organization of this chapter is as follows. Section 12.2 summarizes this book. Directions for data management research and development is the subject of section 12.3. Some guidelines for building data management systems are given in section 12.4. Finally, in section 12.5, we give some suggestions to the reader as to where to go from here.

12.2 SUMMARY OF THIS BOOK

This book has described a framework for data management systems and provided an overview of the various technologies for data management systems. The framework is a three-layer framework. The technologies belonging to each layer build on the technologies at the lower layers as well as on supporting technologies. The supporting technologies include networking, distributed processing, distributed object management, and agents, among others. The data management technologies are utilized by application technologies such as collaborative computing, expert systems, visualization, and mobile computing.

Technologies in layer I are database systems and distributed database systems. We provided an overview of various database management systems such as relational, object-oriented, and object-relational systems. Then we described architectures for database management, as well as functions of a DBMS. Distributed database

217

systems build on DBMSs. We described various architectures for a distributed database system and then selected one architecture for further examination. Then we provided an overview of the functions of a distributed database system.

Technologies in layer II enable interoperation and migration of database systems. We described various types of heterogeneity and then focused on federated database systems as well as on client-server architectures. We also described heterogeneity with respect to multimedia data types. That is, multimedia database systems are discussed at some length. Finally, issues on migrating legacy database systems as well as interoperation between legacy systems and newer systems are discussed.

Technologies in layer III enable information extraction and sharing. Note that while technologies in layers I and II focus on simple access to databases, distributed databases, and heterogeneous multimedia databases, extracting useful information from these databases is addressed by the technologies in layer III. In particular, we described the issues of data warehousing and data mining. Accessing digital libraries and Internet database management are also addressed in layer III technologies. We expect significant advances to be made in Internet database management over the next several years. Finally layer III technologies also addressed data sharing and collaboration. A particular type of collaborative computing system called workflow management system was given some consideration. The focus was on the use of databases by workflow management systems.

The book also addressed some key features such as security and integrity. With respect to security, both multilevel security and discretionary security issues were given some consideration. Transaction management, which includes concurrency control and recovery issues, as well as enforcing integrity constraints, were addressed. Other types of database systems such as deductive database systems were also discussed. The role of metadata was given some consideration in several of the chapters.

It should be noted that the data management technologies described here are not comprehensive.[52] There are several important topics that have not been included. These include performance analysis, benchmarking, modeling and simulation, and scientific database management systems, and the usage of databases by various applications. Addressing all of these topics is beyond the scope of this book. However a considerable amount of general information as

---

[52] A comprehensive view of data management technologies was given in figure 1-2.

well as references were provided should the reader want an in-depth coverage of a particular topic

12.3 DIRECTIONS FOR DATA MANAGEMENT RESEARCH AND DEVELOPMENT

Each data management technology area discussed here, especially in parts II and III, has several topics that need further research and development work. For example, in the case of heterogeneous database integration, while work has been done on query processing and transaction management, topics such as security and integrity need further research. For example, approaches to maintaining consistency have to be developed. In addition, techniques for enforcing access control rules across multiple databases are needed. In the area of client-server databases, the challenge is to determine where to place the various database management system and distributed database management system modules. The three-tiered architecture is becoming quite popular. However, achieving good performance is a challenge. We can expect to see an increase in the use of distributed object management technologies for interoperability. In the case of legacy database and application migration, issues on encapsulating entire systems and applications are becoming clearer. However, fine-grained encapsulation is a challenge. That is, one needs to go into the application module, break it into pieces, and encapsulate the pieces so that they can be reused. There are several challenges for developing multimedia database systems. Much of the work has been focusing on data modeling and architectural issues. Efficient indexing strategies for voice and video data need further work. In addition, issues such as data quality, security, and quality of service have received little attention.

The technologies described in part III are becoming very popular. Data warehousing and data mining are becoming common terms. The challenge in data warehousing is to bring the data from the heterogeneous data sources into the warehouse. Security and integrity issues also need to be examined for a data warehouse. Data mining technology is being used by various applications to detect patterns. The challenge here is to determine what data are to be mined and what technique to use. Data may often be incomplete or sometimes redundant. Getting the data in the right form poses a major challenge. We can expect the demand for digital libraries and Internet database access to explode. Efficient techniques are needed to access and maintain the Internet databases. Security and integrity play an important role here. Finally the various application technologies have to effectively use databases. We have only briefly examined database support for collaborative computing. Integrating database systems with collaborative computing systems is a challenge.

While several areas need further work on the individual technologies described in this book, integration of these different technologies to put together efficient systems is the major challenge. The message here is that for many applications, database systems are no longer going to be stand-alone systems or even distributed homogeneous systems. That is, while the technologies described in part I are important for data management systems, we may see less demands for such systems. For many applications, we believe that database systems are going to be integrated with application technologies so that efficient access to the databases can be provided. We have discussed some aspects of integration in this book. For example, we have discussed how collaborative computing and database systems can be integrated. However, developing operational systems is the next major challenge. As mentioned in this book, there will be a need for people in different parts of the world to collaborate on a project via the Internet. The data needed for the collaboration may also be located in different databases at different sites. Integrating these database systems, possibly heterogeneous and multimedia in nature, over the Internet will become a necessity.

In summary, the message that we have continued to give in this book is that system interoperability and evolution are going to be the major challenges in the next century for data management systems. Various types of data management systems have to be integrated with one another as well as integrated with applications. The ultimate goal is to put together efficient, secure, reliable, and easy-to-use systems to carry out various sophisticated functions for the humans.

12.4 SOME GUIDELINES FOR BUILDING INFORMATION SYSTEMS

In section 1.6. we described briefly how information systems could be put together from the technologies at different layers. Now that we have a better understanding of some of these technologies, let us revisit the subject of building information systems.

While general purpose information systems that meet the needs of many applications are desirable, such systems may not meet the performance and functional requirements of all applications. Therefore, information systems are driven by domain applications. Let us briefly examine the steps involved in developing these systems for specific applications.

The first step is to identify the application objects. That is, the entities of the applications, the functions, and relationships have to be identified. These objects are coming to be known as business objects. In the case of the medical domain, the business objects may be physicians, surgical procedures, and medical records.

The next step is to design infrastructures to host these objects. An infrastructure may include a data management system, transaction processing subsystem, scheduling, and distributed object management services. Depending on the needs of the application, the database system may be hosted on an infrastructure and it could be centralized or distributed.

The third step is to define the service objects. These objects could be printing services, mail services, and other such services to support the application. For example, for medical applications, patient monitoring could be a service object. Figure 12-1 illustrates the three step process while figure 12-2 illustrates the objects.

Now, implementing the objects illustrated in figure 12-2 is another issue. Although one does not have to be constrained to object technology, distributed object management-based approaches are becoming very popular. This is because with this approach one

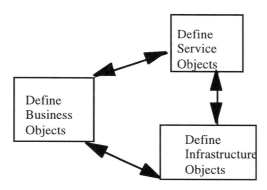

Figure 12-1. Steps to Information Systems Design

need not define all the details inside an object at once. These details may be defined progressively. However, it is important to define the interfaces to an object. Therefore, if the environment is dynamic, the details of objects can be changed to reflect the real-world. Figure 12-3 illustrates an object-based approach where an expert system service object communicates with a database system infrastructure object to carry out its task for the user.

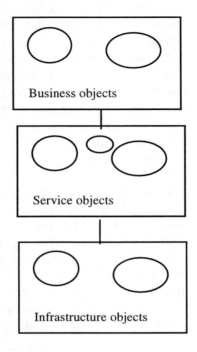

Figure 12-2. Objects for Information Systems

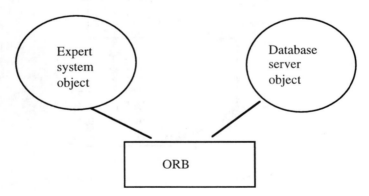

Figure 12-3. Object-based Implementation

Note that what we have discussed in this section are some guidelines to building information systems. Some of the current trends seem to be following this direction. As more and more developments are made on data management, infrastructures, services, and distributed object management technologies, one can expect significant progress to be made in information systems design and development.

12.5 WHERE DO WE GO FROM HERE?

We have provided a broad, but fairly comprehensive overview of data management systems evolution and interoperation. This is a book written for managers of information systems as well as those wanting to get a broad overview of the field. We have also listed several references throughout the book. These references are given in the reference section following this chapter. For a reader who wants more depth on a particular topic, we refer to these references. We have also listed the various topics that have not been addressed in this book, such as benchmarking and performance analysis. For a researcher or a developer who wants details on how to implement a particular technique or learn about the consequences of the various techniques discussed here, these references will be an excellent source of information. However, all the textbooks and experience reports give information about the various concepts and also what other people have experienced. Therefore, we urge the researchers and developers to start experimenting with the technologies discussed here and eventually build systems. In many cases, one learns from one's own experiences. We also encourage managers to support the researchers and developers to work in some of the emerging technology areas as well as giving support to the staff in learning new areas such as object technology.

Much of the focus in this book has been on data and information management, extraction, and sharing. Data and information are critical resources and users are now overloaded with data and information. Therefore, tools and techniques are essential to make data and information manageable for the users. As stated in chapters 1 and 10, the right data/information has to be brought to the user at the right time. Interoperability plays a major role in this process. As we have discussed in chapters 1 and 2, there is another key aspect to data and information and that is data and information survivability. While information management for the users is a critical need, it is also equally important to ensure that this information is accurate, of high quality, and that the systems can handle failures and intrusions. That is, techniques and tools are needed so that information can be brought to the users in a timely manner even in adverse situations. We have briefly touched on information survivability and discussed the database system role on this topic in chapter 2. This field is still young and we expect results to be produced over the next few years.

We believe that there are exciting opportunities in data management with the emergence of new technologies such as data warehousing, data mining, collaboration, and the Internet. As mentioned in chapter 1, there is no end to data management. As data and information become more and more important to carry out the functions of an enterprise, the need for data management and the demand for experts in data management will continue to grow. The opportunities and challenges in this field are endless.

References

REFERENCES

[ACM90] Special Issue on Heterogeneous Database Systems, ACM Computing Surveys, September 1990.

[ACM91a] Special Issue on Next Generation Database Systems, Communications of the ACM, October 1991.

[ACM91b] Special Issue on Computer Supported Cooperative Work, Communications of the ACM, December 1991.

[ACM94] Proceedings of the ACM Multimedia Database Systems Workshop, CA, November 1994 (Ed: B. Thuraisingham, B. Berra, and K. Nwosu).

[ACM95] Special Issue on Digital Libraries, Communications of the ACM, May 1995.

[ACM96] Special Issue on Electronics Commerce, Communications of the ACM, June 1996.

[ADIB96] Adiba, M., "STORM: An Object-Oriented Multimedia DBMS," in Multimedia Database Systems, Kluwer Publications, MA, 1996 (Ed: K. Nwosu, B. Thuraisingham, and B. Berra).

[AFSB83] Air Force Studies Board, Committee on Multilevel Data Management Security, "Multilevel Data Management Security," National Academy Press, NY, 1983.

[AGRA92] Agrawal, D. and El Abbadi, A., "Transaction Management in Database Systems," Database Transaction Models for Advanced Applications, Morgan Kaufmann, CA, 1992 (Ed: A. Elmagarmid).

[AGRA93] Agrawal, A., Imielinski, T., and Awami, A., "Database Mining a Performance Perspective," IEEE Transactions on Knowledge and Data Engineering, Vol. 5, December 1993.

[AIPA95] Proceedings of the Symposium on Advanced Information Processing and Analysis, Tysons Corner, VA, March 1995.

[AIPA96] Proceedings of the Symposium on Advanced Information Processing and Analysis, Tysons Corner, VA, March 1996.

[ALON96] Alonso, G. et al., "Exotica/FMDC: A Workflow Management System for Mobile and Disconnected Clients," Distributed and Parallel Databases Journal, Vol. 4, #3, 1996.

[BABA96] Babacci, M., "Information Survivability," IEEE Computer, November 1996.

[BANE87] Banerjee, J. et al., "A Data Model for Object-Oriented Applications," ACM Transactions on Office Information Systems, Vol. 5, 1987.

[BELL75] Bell D. and LaPadula, L., "Secure Computer Systems: Unified Exposition and Multics Interpretation," Technical Report No: ESD-TR-75-306, Hanscom Air Force Base, Bedford, MA, 1975.

[BELL92] Bell D. and Grimson, J., "Distributed Database Systems," Addison Wesley, MA, 1992.

[BENS95] Bensley, E. et al., "Evolvable Systems Initiative for Real-time C3 Systems," Proceedings of the 1st IEEE Complex Systems Conference, Ft. Lauderdale, FL, October 1995.

[BENY90] Benyon, D., "Information and Data Modeling, Blackwell Scientific Publication," Oxford, U.K., 1990.

[BERN87] Bernstein, P. et al., "Concurrency Control and Recovery in Database Systems," Addison Wesley, MA, 1987.

[BLAU95] Blaustein, B. et al., "Autonomy and Confidentiality: Secure Federated Data Management," Second International Conference on Next Generation Information Technologies and Systems, Naharia, Israel, June 1995.

[BROD84] Brodie, M. et al., "On Conceptual Modeling: Perspectives from Artificial Intelligence, Databases, and Programming Languages," Springer Verlag, NY, 1984.

[BROD86] Brodie, M. and Mylopoulos, J., "On Knowledge Base Management Systems," Springer Verlag, NY, 1986.

[BROD88] Brodie, M. et al., "Readings in Artificial Intelligence and Databases," Morgan Kaufmann, CA, 1988

[BROD95] Brodie M. and Stonebraker, M., "Migrating Legacy Databases," Morgan Kaufmann, CA, 1995.

[BUCH92] Buchmann, A. et al., "A Transaction Model for Active Distributed Object Systems," Database Transaction Models for Advanced Applications, Morgan Kaufmann, CA, 1992 (Ed: A. Elmagarmid)

[BUNE82] Buneman, P., "Functional Data Model," ACM Transactions on Database Systems, 1983.

[CATT91] Cattell, R., "Object Data Management Systems," Addison Wesley, MA, 1991.

[CERI84] Ceri, S. and Pelagatti, G., "Distributed Databases, Principles and Systems," McGraw Hill, NY, 1984.

[CHEN76] Chen, P., "The Entity Relationship Model - Toward a Unified View of Data," ACM Transactions on Database Systems, Vol. 1, 1976.

[CHOR94] Chorafas, D., "Intelligent Multimedia Databases," Prentice Hall, NJ, 1994.

[CIKM95] Proceedings of the Intelligent Knowledge Management Conference (CIKM) Workshop on Intelligent Agents, Baltimore, MD, December 1995.

[CLIF96] Clifton, C. and Marks, D., "Security and Privacy Issues for Data Mining," Proceedings of the ACM SIGMOD Conference Workshop on Data Mining, Montreal, Canada, June 1996.

[CODD70] Codd, E. F., "A Relational Model of Data for Large Shared Data Banks," Communications of the ACM, Vol. 13, #6, June 1970.

[DAS92] Das, S., "Deductive Databases and Logic Programming," Addison Wesley, MA, 1992.

[DATE90] Date, C. J., "An Introduction to Database Management Systems," Addison Wesley, MA, 1990 (6th edition published in 1995 by Addison Wesley).

[DCI96] Proceedings of the DCI Conference on Databases and Client Server Computing, Boston, MA, March 1996.

[DEVO82] Devor, C. et al., "Five-Schema Architecture Extends DBMS to Distributed Applications," Electronic Design, March 1982.

[DIGI95] Proceedings of the Advances in Digital Libraries Conference, McLean, VA, May 1995, (Ed: N. Adam et al.).

[DMH94] Data Management Handbook, Auerbach Publications, NY, 1994 (Ed: B. von Halle and D. Kull).

[DMH95] Data Management Handbook Supplement, Auerbach Publications, NY, 1995 (Ed: B. von Halle and D. Kull).

[DMH96] Data Management Handbook Supplement, Auerbach Publications, NY, 1996 (Ed: B. Thuraisingham).

[DOD94] Proceedings of the DOD Database Colloquium, San Diego, CA, AFCEA Publications, 1994.

[DOD95] Proceedings of the DOD Database Colloquium, San Diego, CA, AFCEA Publications, 1995.

[DOD96] Proceedings of the DOD Database Colloquium, San Diego, CA, AFCEA Publications, 1996.

[ELMA85] Elmasri, R. et al., "The Category Concept - An Extension to the Entity Relationship Model," Data and Knowledge Engineering Journal, Vol. 1, #1, North Holland, 1985.

[ELMA92] Elmagarmid, A., "Database Transaction Models for Advanced Applications," Morgan Kaufmann, CA, 1992.

[FIRE] "Fire Walls and Security," White Paper by VITAL Integrations Solutions Inc., URL: http://www.vitalsite.com/firewall.html.

[FOWL95] Fowler, M., "A Comparison on Object-Oriented Design and Analysis Techniques," White paper published by Martin Fowler's Consulting Company, 1995.

[FROS86] Frost, R., "On Knowledge Base Management Systems," Collins Publishers, U.K., 1986.

[GALL78] Gallaire, H. and Minker, J., "Logic and Databases," Plenum Press, NY, 1978.

[GASS88] Gasser, M., "Building Secure Systems," Von Nostrand, NY, 1988.

[GRAU82] Graubart, R. and Woodward, J., "A Preliminary Naval Surveillance DBMS Security Model," Proceedings of the IEEE Symposium on Security and Privacy, Oakland, CA, April 1982.

[GRIN95] Grinstein, G. and Thuraisingham, B., "Data Mining and Visualization: A Position Paper," Proceedings of the Workshop on Databases in Visualization, Atlanta GA, October 1995.

[GRUP95] Grupe F. and Owrang, M., "Database Mining Tools", in the Handbook of Data Management Supplement, Auerbach Publications, 1995 (Ed: B. von Halle and D. Kull).

[HINK75] Hinke, T. and Schaefer, M., "Secure Data Management System," Technical Report, RADC-75-266, Systems Development Corporation, November 1975.

[HJEL96] Hjelsvold, R., Midtstraum, R., and Sandsta, O., "Searching and Browsing a Shared Video Database," in Multimedia Database Systems, Kluwer Publications, MA, 1996 (Ed: K. Nwosu, B. Thuraisingham, and B. Berra).

[IEEE87] Proceedings of the IEEE, Special Issue on Heterogeneous Database Systems, May 1987.

[IEEE89] "Parallel Architectures for Databases," IEEE Tutorial, 1989 (Ed: A. Hurson, et al.).

[IEEE91] Special Issue on Multidatabase Systems, IEEE Computer, December 1991.

[IEEE93a] Special Issue on Multimedia Database Management Systems, IEEE Transactions on Knowledge and Data Engineering, August 1993.

[IEEE93b] Special Issue on Data Mining, IEEE Transactions on Knowledge and Data Engineering, December 1993.

[IEEE95] Proceedings of the 1st IEEE Multimedia Database Management System Workshop, IEEE Computer Society Press, 1995.

[IEEE96] Proceedings of the 2nd IEEE Multimedia Database Management System Workshop, IEEE Computer Society Press, 1996.

[IFIP] Proceedings of the IFIP 11.3 Database Security Working Conferences, 1987-1996.

[IMIE92] Imielinski, T. et al., "Distributed Databases for Mobile Computing," Proceedings of the 1992 Very Large Database Conference, Vancouver, BC, August 1992.

[INMO93] Inmon, W., "Building the Data Warehouse," John Wiley and Sons, NY, 1993.

[JACK96] Jackson, J. and McCellan, A., "Java by Example" Sunsoft Press, Prentice Hall Publication, 1996.

[JAJO90] Jajodia, J. and Sandhu, R., "Polyinstantiation Integrity in Multilevel Relations," Proceedings of the IEEE Symposium on Security and Privacy, Oakland, CA, 1990.

[JDBC] White Papers on JDBC
URL: http://splash.javasoft.com/jdbc/.

[KIM85] Kim, W. et al., "Query Processing in Database Systems," Springer Verlag, NY, 1985.

[KORT86] Korth, H. and Silberschatz, A., "Database System Concepts," McGraw Hill, NY, 1986.

[KOWA74] Kowalski, R. A., "Predicate Logic as a Programming Language," Information Processing 74, Stockholm, North Holland Publications, 1974.

[KUHN92] Kuhn, E. et al., "Multidatabase Transactions and Query Processing in Logic," Database Transaction Models for Advanced Applications, Morgan Kaufmann, CA, 1992 (Ed: A. Elmagarmid)

[LARS84] Larson J. and Rahimi, S., IEEE Tutorial on Distributed Database Management Systems, IEEE Computer Society Press, 1984.

[LAVE94] Lavender, B. and Thuraisingham, B., "Applying OMT for Designing Workflow Applications," Proceedings of the 1st MITRE Data Management Symposium, McLean, VA, June 1994.

[LLOY87] Lloyd, J., "Foundations of Logic Programming," Springer Verlag, Heidelberg, Germany, 1987.

[LOOM95] Loomis, M., "Object Databases," Addison Wesley, MA, 1995.

[LUNT90] Lunt, T. et al., "SeaView Security Policy and a Formal Model for a Multilevel Secure Database Management System," IEEE Transactions on Knowledge and Data Engineering, June 1990.

[MAIE83] Maier, D., "The Theory of Relational Databases," Computer Science Press, Rockville, MD, 1983.

[MARS92] Marshak, R., "Workflow Computing," Patricia Seybold's Office Computing Report, March 1992.

[MDDS94] Proceedings of the Massive Digital Data Systems Workshop, published by the Community Management Staff, Washington D.C., 1994.

[META96] Proceedings of the 1st IEEE Metadata Conference, Silver Spring, MD, April 1996.
URL: http://www.nml.org/resources/misc/metadata/proceedings/.

[MINK88] Minker, J., "Foundations of Deductive Databases and Logic Programming," Morgan Kaufmann, CA, 1988.

[MIT] Technical Reports on Data Integrity and Quality, Sloan School, Massachusetts Institute of Technology, Cambridge, MA, (URL: http://web.mit.edu/cisr/www/cisrpubs.html).

[NISS96] Proceedings of the National Information Systems Security Conference, Baltimore, MD, October 1996.

[NODI92] Nodine, M. et al., "A Cooperative Transaction Model for Design Databases," Database Transaction Models for Advanced Applications, Morgan Kaufmann, CA, 1992 (Ed: A. Elmagarmid).

[NSF90] Proceedings of the Database Systems Workshop, Report published by the National Science Foundation, 1990 (also in ACM SIGMOD Record, December 1990).

[NSF95] Proceedings of the Database Systems Workshop, Report published by the National Science Foundation, 1995 (also in ACM SIGMOD Record, March 1996).

[NWOS96] Nwosu, K., Thuraisingham, B, and Berra B., "Multimedia Database Systems, Design and Implementation Strategies." Kluwer Publications, MA, 1996.

[ODBC96] A Synergex ODBC White Paper
URL: http://www.synergex.com/odbc/wht_papr.htm (articles also in Database Programming and Design, Miller Freeman, CA, 1996).

[ODMG93] "Object Database Management Group Specifications," Morgan Kaufmann, CA, 1993.

[OMG95] "Common Object Request Broker Architecture and Specification," OMG Publications, John Wiley, NY, 1995.

[OOMO93] Oomoto, E. and Tanaka, K., "OVID: Design and Implementation of a Video-Object Database System," IEEE Transactions on Knowledge and Data Engineering, August 1993.

[OOPS94] Proceedings of the OOPSLA 1994 Conference Workshop on "Is CORBA Ready for Duty?", Portland, OR, October 1994. (Ed: W. Andersen et al.).

[ORFA94] Orfali, R., Harkey, D., and Edwards, J., "Essential, Client Server Survival Guide," John Wiley, NY, 1994.

[ORFA96] Orfali, R., Harkey, D., and Edwards, J., "The Essential, Distributed Objects Survival Guide," John Wiley, NY, 1994.

[OSZU91] Oszu, T., and Valduriez, P., "Principles of Distributed Database Systems," Prentice Hall, NY, 1991.

[OW96] Proceedings of the Object World West Conference, San Jose, CA, August 1996.

[RAM89] Ram, S., "Architectures for Distributed Database Management Systems," Journal of Systems and Software, North Holland, 1989.

[RAM93] Ram, S., "Enforcing Semantic Integrity Constraints in Multidatabase Systems," Presented at the TIMS/ORSA Conference, Phoenix, AZ, November 1993.

[RAMA93] Ramamritham, K., "Real-time Database Management Systems," Distributed and Parallel Database Systems Journal, Vol 1, 1993.

[RAMA94] Ramakrishnan, R., Applications of Deductive Databases, Kluwer Publications, MA, 1994.

[RENN95] Renner, S., Scarano, J., and Rosenthal, A., "Data Interoperability Between C3I Systems," Proceedings of the DOD Database Colloquium, San Diego, CA, AFCEA Publications, 1995.

[RUMB91] Rumbaugh, J. et al., "Object Modeling Technique," Prentice Hall, Englewood Cliffs, NJ., 1991.

[SCHE90] Scheuermann, P. et al., Report on the Workshop on Heterogeneous Database Systems, ACM SIGMOD Record, Vol. 19, #4, December 1990.

[SCHM89] Schmidt, J. and Thanos, C., "Foundations of Knowledge Base Management," Springer Verlag, NY, 1989.

[SHET90] Sheth, A. and Larson, J., " Federated Database Systems for Managing Distributed, Heterogeneous, and Autonomous Databases," ACM Computing Surveys, Vol. 22, #3, 1990.

[SHET92] Sheth, A. et al., "Using Polytransactions to Manage Independent Data," Database Transaction Models for Advanced Applications, Morgan Kaufmann, CA, 1992 (Ed: A. Elmagarmid).

[SHET93] Sheth, A. and Rusinkiewicz, M., "On Transactional Workflows," IEEE Data Engineering Bulletin, Vol. 16, 1993.

[SIGM90] Special Issue on Next Generation Database Systems, ACM SIGMOD Record, December 1990.

[SQL3] "SQL3," American National Standards Institute, Draft, 1992 (a version also presented by J. Melton at the Department of Navy's DISWG NGCR meeting, Salt Lake City, UT, November 1994).

[STAC90] Stachour, P., and Thuraisingham, B., "Design of LDV - A Multilevel Secure Relational Database Management System," IEEE Transactions on Knowledge and Data Engineering, Vol. 2, #2, 1990.

[TALI95] "The Power of Frameworks," Taligent Press, Addison Wesley Publications, 1995.

[TANG92] Tang, A. and Scoggins, S., "Open Networking with OSI," Prentice Hall, NJ, 1992.

[TANN90] Tannenbaum, A, "Computer Networks," Prentice Hall, NJ, 1990.

[TCSE85] "Trusted Computer Systems Evaluation Criteria," Department of Defense Document, 5200.28-STD, Washington D.C., 1985.

[TDI91] "Trusted Database Interpretation," Department of Defense Document, Washington D.C., 1991.

[THOM92] Thompson, C. et al., "Open OODB," IEEE Computer, Special Issue on Object Technology, October 1992 (version also presented at the Department of Navy's DISWG NGCR meeting, Monterey, CA, April 1993).

[THUR90a] Thuraisingham, B., "Security Issues for Object-Oriented Database Systems," Journal of Object-Oriented Programming," SIGS Publications, April 1990.

[THUR90b] Thuraisingham, B., "Security Issues for Multimedia Database Management Systems," Proceedings of the 4th IFIP Database Security Conference, Halifax, England, September 1990.

[THUR91] Thuraisingham, B., "Security Issues for Distributed Database Management Systems - II," Computers and Security, Elsevier Science Publishers, U.K., December 1991.

[THUR92a] Thuraisingham, B. and Venketeraman, V., "A View of Information Modeling Related to Data Modeling," Information Systems Management Journal Auerbach Publications, 1992.

[THUR92b] Thuraisingham, B., "Recent Developments in Trusted Database Management Systems," ACM SIGMOD Record, September 1992.

[THUR93a] Thuraisingham, B., Ford, W., and Collins M., "Design and Implementation of a Database Inference Controller," Data and Knowledge Engineering Journal, North Holland, December 1993.

[THUR93b] Thuraisingham, B. and Ko, H., "Concurrency Control for Trusted Database Management Systems," ACM SIGMOD Record, December 1993.

[THUR93c] Thuraisingham, B., "Distributed Database Systems: Developments and Challenges," Local Area Network Handbook Supplement, Auerbach Publications, NY, 1993.

[THUR94] Thuraisingham, B., "Security issues for Federated Database Management Systems," Computers and Security, Elsevier Science Publishers, UK, December 1994.

[THUR95a] Thuraisingham, B., "Massive Data and Information Systems Initiative at MITRE," Proceedings of the 2nd MITRE Data Management Symposium, McLean, VA, June 1995.

[THUR95b] Thuraisingham, B., "Information Demands Drive Database Interoperability," SIGNAL Magazine," AFCEA Publications, VA, December 1995.

[THUR96a] Thuraisingham, B. and Dao, S., "Multimedia Database Management Systems," in Advances in Database Management Systems, McGraw Hill, NY, 1996 (Ed: P. Fortier).

[THUR96b] Thuraisingham, B., "Data Warehousing, Data Mining, and Security," Proceedings of the 10th IFIP Database Security Conference, Como, Italty, 1996.

[THUR96c] Thuraisingham, B., "Internet Database Management," Database Management, Auerbach Publications, NY, 1996.

[THUR96d] Thuraisingham, B., "Interactive Data Mining and the World Wide Web," Proceedings of Compugraphics Conference, Paris, France, December 1996.

[TING92] Ting., T.C., Demurjian, S., and Hu., M., "A Specification Methodology for User Role-based Security in an Object-Oriented Design Model," Proceedings of the 6th IFIP Database Security Conference, Vancouver, BC, August 1992.

[TNI87] "Trusted Network Interpretation," Department of Defense Document," Washington D.C., 1987.

[TRUE89] Trueblood, R. and Potter, W., "Hyper-Semantic Data Modeling," Data and Knowledge Engineering Journal, Vol. 4, #4, North Holland, 1989.

[TSIC82] Tsichritzis, D. and Lochovsky, F., "Data Models," Prentice Hall, Englewood Cliffs, NJ, 1982.

[ULLM88] Ullman, J. D., "Principles of Database and Knowledge Base Management Systems," Volumes I and II, Computer Science Press, Rockville, MD 1988.

[VEIJ92] Veijalainen, J., "The S-Transaction Model," Database Transaction Models for Advanced Applications, Morgan Kaufmann, CA, 1992 (Ed: A. Elmagarmid).

[WIED92] Wiederhold, G., "Mediators in the Architecture of Future Information Systems," IEEE Computer, March 1992.

[WOEL86] Woelk, D. and Kim, W., "Object-Oriented Approach to Multimedia Databases," Proceedings of the ACM Conference on Office Information Systems, 1986.

[YANG88] Yang, D. and Torey, T., "A Practical Approach to Transforming Extended ER Diagrams into the Relational Model," Information Sciences, Vol. 42, 1988.

[YEAR96] Proceedings of the Year 2000 and Data Warehousing Conference, DAG Group, Orlando, FL, November 1996.

Appendix

COMMERCIAL STATUS

1. TRENDS WITH COMMERCIAL PRODUCTS

This appendix describes some example commercial data management products. We have provided an overview of the various groups of products and selected a product from each group and discussed them in more detail. The groups include relational database systems, object-oriented database systems, object relational database systems, interoperability, replication servers, data warehousing, and data mining. As stated earlier, all of the information on these products has been obtained from published materials and various web pages. Since commercial technology is advancing rapidly, the status of these products as described here may not be current. Due to this reason, we have described the products in the appendix. Again our purpose is to give an overview of what is out there at present and not the technical details of these products.

Numerous commercial data management system products are now emerging. Major DBMS vendors are developing distributed processing capabilities as well capabilities for handling data replication through the replication server technologies. These products include relational database systems developed by Oracle Corporation, Sybase Inc., Informix Inc., IBM Corporation, and Microsoft Corporation, object-oriented database system products developed by Object Design Inc., Gemstone Systems Inc., Versant Object Technology, and Ontos Inc., and object-relational system products developed by Illustra Technologies (now owned by Informix Corporation) and UniSql Inc. Furthermore, gateways are being developed for interoperability. In addition, products for data warehousing, data mining, multimedia database management, and Internet database access have also been developed.

In this chapter we have described some specific products. We have selected one product from each group: relational database systems (Oracle7, formally known as Oracle7™Server, product of Oracle Corporation), object-oriented database systems (ObjectStore, product of Object Design Inc.), object-relational database systems (Illustra, product of Illustra Technologies/Informix Corporation), replication technology (Replication Server, product of Sybase Inc.), interoperability (OmniReplicator, product of PRAXIS International Inc.), multidatabase system (UNISQL/M, product of UniSql Inc.), component integration (OLE/DB, product of Microsoft Corporation) data warehousing (Red Brick Data Warehouse, product of Red Brick Systems Inc.), and data mining (RECON, product of Lockheed Martin Inc.). For convenience, we have grouped the products

241

according to the technologies: database systems; replication and integration; and data warehousing and mining. The products in these three groups are described in sections 2, 3, and 4, respectively.

We discuss only some of the key features of these products. It should be noted that all of the information about these products has been obtained from published material either from user manuals or from web pages. We have listed all these references in section 5. As mentioned in the preface, due to the rapid developments in commercial data management technology, many of these products may not be current even when this book is published. Note that various data management magazines, books, and trade shows such as Database Programming and Design (Miller Freeman publishers), Data Management Handbook Series (Auerbach publications), and DCI's Database Client Server Computing Conferences have several articles and presentations discussing the commercial products). We urge the reader to take advantage of the information presented in these magazines, books, and conferences and keep up with the latest developments with the vendor products. Furthermore, in areas like Internet database management, we can expect the developments to be changing very rapidly. The various web pages are also a useful source of information.

It should also be noted that we are not endorsing any of these products. We have chosen a particular product only to explain specific technology. We would have liked to have included discussions of many more products. But such a discussion is beyond the scope of this book.

2 DATABASE SYSTEMS TECHNOLOGY

2.1 Relational Database System

Numerous products for database management, server technology, and applications are developed by the Oracle Corporation. A discussion of all these products is beyond the scope of this book. In this section we discuss the essential features of relational database management using Oracle's Oracle7^{TM}Server Release 7.3 as an example. The information for this discussion is obtained from [1]. (Note that from now on we will use the term Oracle7 for Oracle7^{TM}Server).

Oracle7 relational database management system is a suite of products to support various functions including query processing, on-line transaction processing, data warehousing, workgroup management, and Internet access, among others. High performance transaction processing is accomplished through a multi-server multi-threaded architecture. Several user requests are coordinated simultaneously. Sophisticated query optimization strategies are supported. B-Tree-based access methods as well as hashing techniques are used for efficient retrieval. Concurrency control is provided by row-level locking for both data and indexes.

Special query processing and indexing techniques for data warehousing applications are also supported. The index techniques include bit-mapped indexes, hash joins, and partitioned data. The query optimizer for data warehousing is cost-based and supports queries such as start queries and snow-flake queries. The query optimizer takes syntax as well as dynamic database environment into consideration. In addition, parallel database processing techniques are utilized for efficiency. A parallel query architecture supports parallel execution of various operations including sorts, aggregation, and table creation.

Other features supported include appropriate backup strategies and recovery methods to handle transaction and site failures. Replicated databases are made consistent with suitable replication handling mechanisms. Both synchronous and asynchronous replication capabilities are provided. Oracle7 also supports distributed database capabilities including distributed query processing and transaction management. Interoperability with non-Oracle systems are provided through gateways. Oracle7 is fully integrated with web technology so that the Oracle database can be accessed through the web. Finally, SQL-based query languages, natural language support, application development, security, and auditing features are also supported. Note that a multilevel secure version of the Oracle7 product is also available.

In addition to the above, Oracle7 also provides reliability, scalability, and availability. Being reliable, it provides any type of data, whether it be relational, video, text, images, spatial, messaging, web, or secured data. Being scalable, it provides all of this data from the workgroup environment all the way up to the enterprise-wide environment using data warehousing. Being available, it provides near 24x7x365 performance using Oracle's backup and recovery ability.

In summary, Oracle7 offers several products to support essential database management system functions such as query processing and transaction management as well as additional features such as distributed database management, data warehousing, and Internet database access.

2.2 Object-Oriented Database System

Object-oriented database management systems integrate object-oriented programming languages with database management techniques. ObjectStore, a product of Object Design Inc., is one of the few OODBMSs that are available in the marketplace. It provides the following capabilities:

- high performance in managing non-record oriented complex data structure
- migration from existing applications
- C and/or C++ development
- distributed data management services
- support for cooperative work.

We discuss various features of ObjectStore in the following paragraphs. The information on ObjectStore has been obtained from [2].

ObjectStore has a virtual memory mapping architecture (VMMA) and uses memory mapping, caching, and clustering to optimize data access. VMMA enables uniform treatment of persistent as well as non-persistent (i.e., either C or C++) data.

There are two kinds of databases; one is a file database which is a regular operating system file and the other is the RAWFS databases and is managed by the server. There are two auxiliary processes required for the execution of ObjectStore applications: ObjectStore Server and Cache Manager. The Server handles all the access to ObjectStore databases. There is a Cache Manager for all the applications on a machine. In Release 4.1, there is ObjectStore/Single which is an integration of the Server and the Client into a single process. It has database level locking granularity.

Schema: Schema information about a database is also stored in the database. Schema is stored as C++ objects. Classes are not runtime objects and therefore the representations are generated before link-time for each application which stores information in a database. So, these representations are available at run-time. Schema information for an application is stored in an object file as well as in an ObjectStore database. Schema is generated by ObjectStore's schema generator.

To store persistent data in ObjectStore, memory must be allocated. Overloaded "operator new" functions are used to allocate persistent memory. Before this memory is accessed, certain actions must be carried out. They are: (i) creating and opening a database, (ii) starting a transaction, and (iii) retrieving and creating a database root.

In ObjectStore, persistent memory is accessed only within a transaction. Since ObjectStore is a multi-user system, concurrency control techniques are to ensure that the consistency of the database is maintained. As of Release 4.0, ObjectStore provides Multi Version Concurrency Control (where read-only transactions get an older but consistent version of the data and update transactions do not block against read-only transactions) and archive logging (point-in-time roll forward or media recovery). As of Release 3.0, it provides on line backup. As of Release 4.1, it provides asynchronous replication facilities on the server.

While C++ is useful for navigational data access, in certain cases support for associative queries is preferred. ObjectStore supports query processing. The query optimizer module is part of the query processor. Query facilities are used from within C++ programs. That is, no special query language is provided. Query types include single-element queries, existential queries, and nested queries. A single element query retrieves one element of a collection. An existential query questions whether there is an element satisfying the selection criterion. A nested query is one where a query string itself contains queries.

Query evaluation consists of first analyzing the query expression, binding the free variables and function references in the query, and interpreting the bound query. Queries may be pre-analyzed so that certain steps are not repeated each time the query is posed. Indexing techniques are used for efficiently evaluating a query. Operations for indexing include adding and dropping an index.

Other features supported by ObjectStore include collections, data integrity, security, metaobject protocol, schema evolution, and compaction.

2.3   Object-Relational Database System

An object-relational database system combines the useful features of both relational and object-oriented database systems. Relational database systems are popular due to their simple structure and efficient query language such as SQL. Object-oriented database systems have the ability to support complex objects. Object-relational systems support both features, and Illustra object-relational database system, a product of Illustra Technologies (now owned by Informix Corporation), is one of the first object-relational database systems.

Features: The Illustra server is both a relational database management system as well as an object-oriented database management system. Some of the relational data management features include support for data access via the query language SQL, access control capabilities, support for data integrity, transaction management and recovery, and query optimization facility. Its object-oriented data management features include the ability to create new data types, support to access various data types, support for encapsulation, inheritance, and polymorphism, and data access through object IDs.

In addition to these features, Illustra also supports active database management features such as rules, alerts, and triggers. The rule mechanism provides the facility for taking certain actions when certain events occur under certain conditions.

One of the special features of Illustra is the support for Data Blades. Data blade modules support extensibility. One could use a specific data blade module for a specific need. Management of new data types is also achieved through special data blades. For example, data blade modules would support some special access methods that cannot be supported under B-Trees. Illustra supports D-Tree for Text and R-Tree for spatial data. Another example of a data blade module is one that supports time-series data used for various applications that deal with time and sequencing. The next few paragraphs provide a more detailed description of time series data blade modules and spatial database modules of Illustra.

Time Series Data: Time series data are used for various applications such as those in the financial domain. These include computing averages, maintaining portfolio summaries, and calculating risk factors. Through the time series data blade module, the Illustra database management system understands the time series data and treats them as first class types. Various operations are then performed on these time series data types.

Two kinds of time series data have been identified. One is regular time series where the data arrival is predictable and the other is irregular time series. It is stated in the Illustra white papers that the system currently supports regular time series, and work on supporting irregular time series is under way (see, for example, [3]). The time series operations supported by the data blade module include entering or updating data, accumulating running sums and averages of time series entries, and performing joins of multiple time series based on time stamps.

Another key feature for supporting time series data is data feed. Usually data is sent to the database through queries. However, for time series data, especially for irregular time series, data needs to flow to the server as it arrives. The data feed mechanism of Illustra supports the flow of data to the server with proper authorization controls.

Spatial Data: Support for multimedia data is needed for various applications in multiple domains. Illustra provides support for multimedia data types again through the data blade facility. It is stated in [3] that relational database management systems deal with multimedia data through BLOBs (Binary Large Objects). One cannot query BLOBs say based on content which is a disadvantage. In the case of spatial data such as maps and other kinds of geographic data, relational database management systems now use multi-dimensional tables. Since relational database engines were developed mainly for single dimensional tables, they lack efficient access to multi-dimensional tables. Illustra handles multimedia as well as spatial data again through data blades.

The 2D and 3D spatial data blades of Illustra are user-installable extensions to the Illustra server that provide support for data in 2-dimensional and 3-dimensional spaces respectively. For example, as stated in the Illustra white papers [3], the 2D spatial data blade module addresses 10 data types that describe common planar geometric shapes and polygons of arbitrary complexities. In addition, over 200 functions for creating and maintaining these objects are supported. An access method called R-Tree access method is also supplied with these spatial database modules for efficient access to spatial data. Special indexing strategies are also supported by R-Trees.

3. REPLICATION AND INTEGRATION

3.1   Replication

One of the early products for replication technology is Sybase Inc.'s Replication Server, part of Sybase's System 10 product family [4]. Replication technology overcomes the limitation with two-phase commit, transaction snapshot, and trigger mechanisms. As stated in the Sybase white papers, with two-phase commit protocol, all of the sites have to wait until the transaction commits (see, for example, [4]). This depends on many messages sent between the coordinator and recipient. With snapshot mechanisms, replicated copies are updated according to a pre-defined schedule and no integrity is maintained. With transaction triggers, there is integrity, but executing triggers has a performance impact. Replication technology can be used to handle many situations such as one primary copy and multiple secondary copies or multiple primary copies and one secondary copy.

The essential features of Sybase's Replication Server are the following. Modification to a database are detected by a process called the Log Transfer Manager. This process also runs on the same node as the source database. It then sends the changes to a Replication Server process. Multiple Replication Servers coordinate with each other and send the changes to the target databases. The target databases then get updated. All this is carried out maintaining transaction integrity and data protection. Data is queued temporarily in stable queues in case of system failures.

Sybase's Replication Server product provides support for distributed updates. That is, users may make changes to the replicated copies of the source data. Furthermore, it provides support for the same data to be modified by users in replicated sites. These updates can be supported both in the asynchronous or synchronous mode.

3.2   Interoperability

Praxis International Inc. has developed a product to integrate heterogeneous database systems. However, this product also handles replication. It is called the OmniReplicator [5]. OmniReplicator can be regarded to be a third-party product to integrate multiple DBMS vendor products. It is stated in [6] that many of the replication server products from DBMS vendors are geared toward handling replication of their own products making use of gateways, whereas the OmniReplicator is vendor neutral.

Some of the features of OmniReplicator, as given in [6], are the following. This tool supports various types of replication including snapshots, multiple copy simultaneous updates, uni-directional updates, and bidirectional updates. It carries out the replication task in four stages. First it detects all the changes to the source database. Then it stores these changes so that they can be transmitted to the target databases. The third step is to customize changes appropriate to the target platforms, and the last step is to carry out the changes according to schedules. Various modules communicate with each other to carry out the replication task. The director process is the interface to the OmniReplicator architecture. It enables a DBA to specify various aspects of replication. The coordinator process controls the replication task. The change selector process detects the changes to the source databases. The dispatcher processes determine the target databases and how the changes are to be propagated. The distributor process delivers the changes to the target databases. The network distribution manager process connects the source and target databases.

3.3   Multidatabase System

UniSQL/M is a product of UniSql Inc. and provides a solution to interoperability through the federated database systems approach. Note that UniSQL is an object-relational database. However, in this section we only discuss the multidatabase capabilities of UniSQL as stated in [7]. UniSQL/M integrates not only UniSQL databases, but also relational databases. UniSQL/M maintains global schema and is responsible for global query and transaction processing. It sends appropriate queries and transactions to the local database systems. There is a gateway/driver for each relational database system used.

As stated in [7], the features of UniSQL/M include the following. It supports a global query language called SQL/M. Each local database system operates in its native mode and no changes have to be made to the local systems. It supports distributed transactions with both queries and updates. It provides a global schema and data model having the full capability of object models.

Construction of the global schema by UniSQL/M follows the approach discussed in chapter 4 of this book, which is essentially that of Sheth and Larson. The local database systems export the schemas to the federation. UniSQL/M integrates the export schemas and resolves conflicts. Global queries and transactions are based on the global schema. The data model supported by UniSQL/M is essentially an object-oriented model with support to represent relationships as in the case of a relational model. This way UniSQL/M can integrate both relational as well as object-oriented schemas.

UniSQL/M is a full-fledged database management system. Each UniSQL/M integrates multiple local. Also, each UniSQL/M is based on the client-server approach with multiple UniSQL/M clients communicating with a single UniSQL/M server. Interactive SQL/M queries as well as other interfaces such as C, C++, Smalltalk, ODBC, and graphical user interfaces are supported. The major functions supported by UniSQL/M include global database schema management, distributed query processing, and distributed transaction management.

3.4   Component Integration

A product based on component integration is Microsoft Corporation's OLE DB. As stated in [8], OLE DB is a specification for a set of data access interfaces so that various data stores containing all types of data could be accessed. In a way, OLE DB specifications form an industry standard for accessing multiple heterogeneous databases in a uniform and seamless manner.

Through OLE DB, data from legacy databases are displayed in a tabular form. Furthermore, one could build various components such as query processor, transaction manager, and integrity manager separately and integrate them through OLE DB. OLE DB supports data providers, data consumers, data service providers, as well as business component developers.

It should be noted that OLE DB does not replace ODBC. While ODBC technology enables access to SQL-based databases, OLE DB takes advantage of ODBC for accessing these SQL databases.

We have stressed in this book that Internet data management and component-based integration will be the way of the future. OLE DB and similar products are the first step to accomplish this.

4. DATA WAREHOUSING AND MINING

4.1   Data Warehouse

Various database management system vendors including Oracle Corporation, Sybase Inc., and Informix Corporation have now developed data warehousing products. In this section we describe a data warehousing product from Red Brick Systems Inc. It is called Red Brick™ Warehouse 5.0 which is the latest version of Red Brick's product series. Some information on this product can be found in [9].

As quoted by Red Brick (private communication), Red Brick Warehouse is an open, relational, but specialized database designed from the ground up to address the data warehousing marketplace. The product's key advantages stem from the integration of very sophisticated join, indexing, and parallel processing technologies all focused on addressing the performance, functionality and scalability needs of data warehousing environments. Integration is a key aspect as the Red Brick Warehouse architecture provides fast, consistent response times to complex queries against large datasets. Other features include subquery analysis in nested queries as well as returning initial rows to a query so that analysts can work with them while the remaining rows are being returned. In addition, parallel query processing as well as schema changes are also supported.

Red Brick Intelligent SQL has been a feature since the first version of Red Brick (version 1.5) in 1991. These business analysis extensions were incorporated to help answer the questions analysts ask about their corporate data that are difficult or impossible to ask in standard SQL. Providing this functionality is in keeping with Red Brick's philosophy that one needs a specialized database engine for data warehousing.

Data Mining is part of the 5.0 release and is integrated as a simple extension of SQL. To utilize the data mining technology requires learning some new, simple SQL syntax. It is stated in [9] that integrating the data mining process with warehousing is a better approach than applying stand-alone data mining tools.

4.2   Data Mining

As discussed in chapter 9, several data mining tools are now commercially available. In this section we briefly discuss the product by Lockheed Martin Inc. It is called RECON™. The information is obtained from [10]. It should be noted that several research papers have also been published on RECON (information on this product is also given in some of the references listed in chapter 9).

RECON works on relational database systems such as those developed by Oracle Corporation, Sybase Inc., and Informix Corporation. It supports both data exploration through bottom-up data mining as well as pattern validation through top-down data mining. For example, an analyst can hypothesize patterns such as all those who live in Manhattan own cars worth more than 20K. RECON helps the analyst to validate the hypothesized pattern against the database. In the case of data exploration, RECON finds patterns previously unknown. Various deduction techniques are used for data exploration.

As stated in [10], the application domains for RECON include stock portfolio creation and analysis, portfolio trading, loan risk analysis, credit analysis, marketing data analysis, and retail data analysis.

5. REFERENCES

[1]White paper on Oracle7™Server Release 7.3, Oracle Corporation, 1996 (see also Oracle Magazine by Oracle Corporation).

[2] User Guide on ObjectStore, Object Design Inc., 1993 (date information obtained: initial version: July 1993, updated information obtained in August 1996).

[3] White papers on Ilustra, Illustra Technologies (Informix Corporation), URL: http://www.hiway.co.nz/illustra3.html
(date information obtained: July 1996).

[4] White papers on Replication Server, Sybase Inc.,
URL: http://www.sybase.com/products/system11/repsrvr.html
(date information obtained: October 1996).

[5] White Papers on Omni Replicator,
URL: http://www.praxisint.com/omnirepx.html
(date information obtained: August 1996).

[6] Data Warehousing and Replication, Praxis International Inc.'s OmniReplicator, Hurwitz Group, Inc.
(date information obtained: August 1996).

[7] White Papers on UNISQL/M, Unisql Inc.,
URL: http://www.unisql.com/product_info/unisqlm.html
(date information obtained: August 1996).

[8] White Paper on OLE/DB, Microsoft Corporation,
URL: http://microsoft.com/oledb/prodinfo/prodinfo.html
(date information obtained: October 1996).

[9] White papers on Red Brick, Red Brick Systems Inc.,
URL: http://www.redbrick.com/rbs/whouse50.html
(date information obtained: October 1996).

[10] White papers on RECON, Lockheed Martin Inc.
Artificial Intelligence Center, Palo Alto, CA.
URL: http://godard.oec.uniosnabrueck.de/fachgeb/winf2/fachinfo/
datam01.html (date information obtained: October 1996).

Index

Index

A

agents, 14, 86, 106, 108, 109, 111, 184, 187-189, 204
architecture, 3, 23, 25, 35-38, 57, 58, 60-62, 72, 78-80, 86, 88, 91, 95, 103, 105, 108, 113-117, 120, 127, 128, 145, 148, 149, 170, 206, 211-213, 218, 219, 239, 240, 244
autonomy, 18, 60, 85, 86, 90, 91, 95, 100, 106

B

browsing, 70, 124-127, 134, 141, 189, 197, 198, 205, 212

C

client-server, 1, 6, 10, 16, 18, 19, 83, 113-117, 119, 123, 124, 128, 145, 156, 188, 202, 203, 218, 219, 245
collaborative computing, 11, 12, 14, 15, 205, 206, 208, 210, 212, 213, 216-218, 220
component integration, 25, 53, 110, 171, 245
concurrency control, 3, 9, 40, 41, 50, 52, 67, 71, 75, 100, 111, 112, 116, 135, 140, 149, 193, 208, 211, 218, 240
CORBA, 18, 83, 114, 120-122, 128, 195

D

data administration, 5, 46
data management, 1, 2, 5-15, 17-20, 23, 25, 42, 56, 80, 83, 102, 109, 115, 141, 142, 160, 161, 188, 190, 200, 202, 205, 206, 208, 211, 212, 216-224, 237, 238, 240, 241
data mining, 1, 2, 5, 6, 7, 9, 11, 14, 19, 39, 51, 53, 125, 142, 159, 173-180, 182-185, 187, 188, 194, 216, 218, 219, 224, 237, 246
data model, 2, 5, 6, 17, 23, 25, 26, 28, 30- 35, 38, 42, 43, 46, 50, 55, 65, 83, 86, 88, 93, 96, 99, 100, 102, 105, 109, 112, 124, 126, 131-133, 139, 141, 142, 163, 164, 165, 168- 170, 184, 191, 198, 211, 212, 219, 245
data quality, 43, 140, 219

data warehouse, 1, 18, 19, 143, 159, 161-164, 167, 169, 170, 173, 187, 216, 219
database administration, 46, 57, 74, 163
database management, 1, 3, 5, 10, 11, 13, 19, 20, 23, 25, 29, 31, 42, 45, 46, 50, 52, 53, 55, 57, 70, 72, 74-78, 83, 85, 88, 91, 93, 96, 99, 102, 109, 111, 112, 114, 115, 119, 120, 121, 125, 126, 130, 140, 142, 148, 149, 159, 163, 165, 166, 175, 176, 187, 188, 191, 193- 195, 197, 198, 200, 204, 206, 208- 210, 212, 214-216, 218, 237-239, 241, 242, 245, 246
database system, 1-11, 14, 15, 17-19, 23, 25, 29, 33-36, 39, 42, 43, 46-50, 53-56, 57, 58, 61, 65, 66, 68-70, 72-75, 77-80, 83, 85, 86, 88, 90, 91, 93-95, 97, 99, 100, 102, 103, 105, 107, 108, 111-113, 116, 118, 120, 121, 125, 129, 141, 142, 145, 151, 156, 159, 165, 197, 205, 206, 209, 212, 216-220, 237, 241, 244-246
deductive database, 5, 7, 20, 23, 25, 48, 51, 74, 75, 218
digital library, 126, 188, 189, 191
distributed database, 3, 6, 11, 14, 15, 17, 19, 23, 57, 58, 61, 62, 64, 65, 67-69, 71-80, 85, 88, 90, 95, 106, 112, 113, 137, 156, 159, 163, 166, 209, 216, 217-219, 239
distributed processing, 11, 14, 15, 72, 80, 112, 205, 217, 237

E

entity-relationship, 25-27, 30, 38, 46
evolvable system, 83, 146, 147, 149

F

fault tolerance, 12, 20, 25, 38, 39, 45, 47, 56
federated database, 5, 10, 18, 61, 83, 85, 86, 88, 91, 102, 103, 111, 113, 116, 145, 218, 244
framework, 2, 6, 10, 11, 12, 13, 14, 17, 19, 23, 47, 80, 83, 94, 156, 163, 170, 171, 216, 217

R

S

T

V

W

Y